Mastering SVG

Ace web animations, visualizations, and vector graphics with HTML, CSS, and JavaScript

Rob Larsen

BIRMINGHAM - MUMBAI

Mastering SVG

Commissioning Editor: Kunal Chaudhari
Acquisition Editor: Karan Gupta
Content Development Editor: Arun Nadar
Technical Editor: Surabhi Kulkarni
Copy Editor: Safis Editing
Project Coordinator: Sheejal Shah
Proofreader: Safis Editing
Indexer: Mariammal Chettiyar
Graphics: Alishon Mendonsa
Production Coordinator: Deepika Naik

First published: September 2018

Production reference: 1190918

Published by Packt Publishing Ltd.
Livery Place
35 Livery Street
Birmingham
B3 2PB, UK.

ISBN 978-1-78862-674-3

www.packtpub.com

`mapt.io`

Mapt is an online digital library that gives you full access to over 5,000 books and videos, as well as industry leading tools to help you plan your personal development and advance your career. For more information, please visit our website.

Why subscribe?

- Spend less time learning and more time coding with practical eBooks and Videos from over 4,000 industry professionals

- Improve your learning with Skill Plans built especially for you

- Get a free eBook or video every month

- Mapt is fully searchable

- Copy and paste, print, and bookmark content

PacktPub.com

Did you know that Packt offers eBook versions of every book published, with PDF and ePub files available? You can upgrade to the eBook version at `www.PacktPub.com` and as a print book customer, you are entitled to a discount on the eBook copy. Get in touch with us at `service@packtpub.com` for more details.

At `www.PacktPub.com`, you can also read a collection of free technical articles, sign up for a range of free newsletters, and receive exclusive discounts and offers on Packt books and eBooks.

Contributors

About the author

Rob Larsen is an experienced frontend engineer, team lead, and manager. He is an active writer and speaker on web technology with a special focus on the continuing evolution of HTML, CSS, and JavaScript. He is a co-author of *Professional jQuery*, the author of *Beginning HTML and CSS*, and the author of *The Uncertain Web*. He's also an active member of the open source community as a maintainer of several popular projects.

About the reviewer

Danny Allen is a full-stack web developer who focuses on user experience design and implementation as founder of the international consultancy Wonderscore Ltd (wonderscore[dot]co[dot]uk).

He is passionate about building high-quality, accessible, and usable experiences on the web.

Danny currently lives and works in the United Kingdom.

His portfolio and contact details can be found at dannya[dot]com.

Packt is searching for authors like you

If you're interested in becoming an author for Packt, please visit authors.packtpub.com and apply today. We have worked with thousands of developers and tech professionals, just like you, to help them share their insight with the global tech community. You can make a general application, apply for a specific hot topic that we are recruiting an author for, or submit your own idea.

Table of Contents

Preface

This book is for web developers and designers looking to add scalable, device-independent animation, images, and visualizations to their projects. Scalable Vector Graphics is an image file format introduced in 1998 by the World Wide Web Consortium (W3C). For many years, it languished behind poor browser compatibility and an unfriendly API. Over the past few years, it has become a vital part of the modern web development toolkit. SVG offers many important features for the modern web. For example, in a world of multiple device resolutions, it offers a simple path to high-quality image scaling without having to produce multiple resolutions for your image and without having to jump through complicated markup patterns. Also, being built in XML-based markup, it also allows easy access to common JavaScript patterns for creating highly interactive interfaces.

This book will teach you the fundamentals of working with SVG as static images, in CSS, inline as elements in an HTML document, and as a scripted part of animations or visualizations.

Who this book is for

This book is for web developers interested in exploring Scalable Vector Graphics. It is written from the perspective of a frontend web developer, but anyone with experience with JavaScript, CSS, and XML-based grammars should find this book accessible.

Prior experience with SVG is not required.

What this book covers

`Chapter 1`, *Introducing Scalable Vector Graphics*, introduces the basics of SVG and will show you some fundamental examples of working with the format.

`Chapter 2`, *Getting Started with Authoring SVG*, introduces the fundamental concepts for authoring SVG in detail.

`Chapter 3`, *Digging Deeper with SVG Authoring*, introduces more advanced concepts for authoring SVG, including transformations, clipping and masking, and importing SVG elements into a document.

`Chapter 4`, *Using SVG in HTML*, adds further details about using SVG elements and SVG images in HTML documents.

Chapter 5, *Working with SVG and CSS*, introduces the reader to using SVG images in CSS, replacing PNGs and Gifs in the modern web development toolkit. This chapter also introduces the many ways you can use CSS to modify SVG elements.

Chapter 6, *JavaScript and SVG*, teaches the reader the basic JavaScript SVG Application Programming Interface by introducing the common Document Object Model methods that allow a developer to access and manipulate SVG properties.

Chapter 7, *Common JavaScript Libraries and SVG*, teaches the basics of interfacing with SVG from common libraries and frameworks includding jQuery, AngularJS, Angular, and ReactJS.

Chapter 8, *SVG Animation and Visualizations*, looks at examples of doing visualizations and animations with SVG.

Chapter 9, *Helper Libraries Snap.svg and SVG.js*, looks at two current libraries that help with common SVG tasks: Snap.svg and SVG.js.

Chapter 10, *Working with D3.js*, introduces basic uses of D3 and walks through some simple examples in order to whet your appetite for this powerful library.

Chapter 11, *Tools to Optimize Your SVG*, focuses on the different tools available to optimize SVGs.

To get the most out of this book.

This book assumes that you have knowledge of HTML, XML, CSS, and JavaScript. Knowledge of Node.js and npm-based development is also helpful.

Before you get started, it will help to ensure you have Node.js installed. You will also need a text editor. The samples in the book were written with Visual Studio Code, but any text editor will suffice.

Download the example code files

You can download the example code files for this book from your account at www.packt.com. If you purchased this book elsewhere, you can visit www.packt.com/support and register to have the files emailed directly to you.

You can download the code files by following these steps:

1. Log in or register at `www.packt.com`.
2. Select the **SUPPORT** tab.
3. Click on **Code Downloads & Errata**.
4. Enter the name of the book in the **Search** box and follow the onscreen instructions.

Once the file is downloaded, please make sure that you unzip or extract the folder using the latest version of:

- WinRAR/7-Zip for Windows
- Zipeg/iZip/UnRarX for Mac
- 7-Zip/PeaZip for Linux

The code bundle for the book is also hosted on GitHub at `https://github.com/PacktPublishing/Mastering-SVG`. In case there's an update to the code, it will be updated on the existing GitHub repository.

We also have other code bundles from our rich catalog of books and videos available at `https://github.com/PacktPublishing/`. Check them out!

Download the color images

We also provide a PDF file that has color images of the screenshots/diagrams used in this book. You can download it here: `https://www.packtpub.com/sites/default/files/downloads/9781788626743_ColorImages.pdf`.

Conventions used

There are a number of text conventions used throughout this book.

`CodeInText`: Indicates code words in text, database table names, folder names, filenames, file extensions, pathnames, dummy URLs, user input, and Twitter handles. Here is an example: "Mount the downloaded `WebStorm-10*.dmg` disk image file as another disk in your system."

A block of code is set as follows:

```
<svg xmlns="http://www.w3.org/2000/svg" width="350" height="150" viewBox="0
0 350 150" version="1.1">
    <circle cx="100" cy="75" r="50" fill="rgba(255,0,0,.5)"/>
    <circle cx="100" cy="75" r="50" fill="rgba(255,0,0,.5)"
     transform="translate(10)" />
    <circle cx="100" cy="75" r="50" fill="rgba(255,0,0,.5)"
     transform="translate(75,0)" />
</svg>
```

When we wish to draw your attention to a particular part of a code block, the relevant lines or items are set in bold:

```
types {
    image/svg+xml svg svgz;
}
```

Any command-line input or output is written as follows:

```
$ npx create-react-app react-svg
```

Bold: Indicates a new term, an important word, or words that you see onscreen. For example, words in menus or dialog boxes appear in the text like this. Here is an example: "In this document, we've created a stylized letter **R**."

 Warnings or important notes appear like this.

 Tips and tricks appear like this.

Get in touch

Feedback from our readers is always welcome.

General feedback: If you have questions about any aspect of this book, mention the book title in the subject of your message and email us at customercare@packtpub.com.

Errata: Although we have taken every care to ensure the accuracy of our content, mistakes do happen. If you have found a mistake in this book, we would be grateful if you would report this to us. Please visit www.packt.com/submit-errata, selecting your book, clicking on the Errata Submission Form link, and entering the details.

Piracy: If you come across any illegal copies of our works in any form on the Internet, we would be grateful if you would provide us with the location address or website name. Please contact us at copyright@packt.com with a link to the material.

If you are interested in becoming an author: If there is a topic that you have expertise in and you are interested in either writing or contributing to a book, please visit authors.packtpub.com.

Reviews

Please leave a review. Once you have read and used this book, why not leave a review on the site that you purchased it from? Potential readers can then see and use your unbiased opinion to make purchase decisions, we at Packt can understand what you think about our products, and our authors can see your feedback on their book. Thank you!

For more information about Packt, please visit packt.com.

1
Introducing Scalable Vector Graphics

Scalable Vector Graphics (SVG) is one of the most powerful components of modern web development. If used properly, it can solve common problems relating to the design, development, and delivery of imagery and user interfaces

SVG is an XML-based markup language used to define images. What HTML is to text, SVG is to images.

SVG is very flexible. It can be implemented as a standalone image and used as the `src` of an image or as a background image in CSS such as a PNG, GIF, or JPG. It can also be embedded directly into an HTML page and manipulated with CSS or JavaScript to create animations, visualizations, and interactive charts.

So, if SVG is that important and can do so much, why isn't it even more widely used? Why does it feel like we're only scratching the surface of what's possible with it? Why does it still feel like a *new* thing?

The problem is, not everyone knows everything that SVG is capable of and not everyone who knows what it's capable of is able to implement SVG solutions in an optimal manner. This book aims to help everyone interested in using SVG to get over those hurdles and master this vital technology.

SVG has had a circuitous route to its place in the pantheon of modern web development technologies. Released in 1999 (it's older than XHTML), SVG languished for a decade because of lack of support in the then dominant Internet Explorer browsers. The technology started to gain favor several years ago with JavaScript libraries, such as Raphaël, which added programmatic fallback support for older versions of IE and the trend has only grown stronger since. Thankfully, the tide has fully turned. All modern versions of Internet Explorer and Edge have support for SVG and there's strong support for the technology from all browser manufacturers, including, of course, Chrome and Firefox.

By the end of this chapter, you will understand the basics of SVG in its many guises. You will be able to take existing SVG images and use them in web pages and CSS with confidence and you'll be well on your way to the promised land of SVG mastery.

This chapter will cover the following topics:

- An introduction to fundamental SVG grammar and vector graphics in general
- The whys and hows of using SVG as the `src` file of an image
- Basic usage of SVG as a CSS background image
- The benefits and differences of using SVG embedded directly in a document
- A brief introduction to Modernizr and feature detection

Creating a simple SVG image

If you're at all familiar with HTML, then the basics of an SVG document are going to be familiar to you. So let's get the mystery out of the way early and take a look at a simple SVG document.

The following code sample shows the basic structure of SVG. The first element is the standard `xml` declaration, indicating that the following should be parsed as an XML document. The second element is where the fun begins. It defines the root SVG element (in the same way that there's a root HTML element in an HTML document). `height` and `width` define the intrinsic dimensions of the document. The **XML NameSpace (xmlns)** is a reference to the schema that defines the current XML element. You'll learn about `viewBox` in more detail in the next chapter. There are many other attributes possible on an SVG element. You will learn more about them throughout this book.

In this first example, following the SVG element, there's a single SVG `text` element. The `text` element, like the SVG element, has many possible attributes that you'll learn about as you make your way through the book. In this case, there are four attributes related to the display of the element. The `x` and `y` attributes represent the position of the top-left corner of the text element as points on a coordinate plane. `font-family` maps to the familiar CSS property of the same name and defines the specific font that should be used to display the text. `font-size` also maps to the common CSS property of the same name.

The attributes that accept *length values* (in this example `width`, `height`, and `font-size`) are provided without a unit (for example, `px`, `em`, and `%`.) When these values are presented as attributes, the unit is optional. If no unit is provided, the values are specified as being user units in the user space. You'll learn more about the way that values are calculated in SVG throughout the book. For now, just remember that, in practice, user units will be equivalent to pixels.

Finally, there is the content of the `text` element, the simple message **Hello SVG**:

```
<?xml version="1.0" encoding="UTF-8"?>
<svg width="250" height="100" viewBox="0 0 250 100" version="1.1"
xmlns="http://www.w3.org/2000/svg">
<text x="0" y="50" font-family="Verdana" font-size="50">
    Hello SVG
  </text>
</svg>
```

Saved as `1-1-hello-world.svg` and opened in a browser, the previous markup renders as in the following screenshot:

Hello SVG

Now that you've seen the most basic example of an SVG document, let's take a look at the basic usage of SVG images and elements in a variety of ways.

Using SVG as a content image

In this section, you'll learn about the single most basic usage of an SVG image, using it the same way you would use a JPG, PNG, or GIF, as the `src` of an `img` element. If you've done any work with HTML at all then you will know how to do this since it's just an image element, but you should start to think about *all* the different ways you can use SVG, and this is a big one.

Looking at the following code sample, there's nothing special at all about the `img` element. There's an `src` pointing to the SVG image, `height` and `width` to define the image's dimensions, and an `alt` attribute to provide a textual representation of the image for screen readers and other cases where the image may not display:

```
<!doctype html>
<html lang="en">
```

```
    <head>
        <meta charset="utf-8">
        <title>Mastering SVG - Inserting an SVG Image into an HTML
         Document</title>
    </head>
    <body>
      <img src="1-2-circles.svg" width="250" height="250" alt="an image
        showing four circles lined up diagonally across the screen">
    </body>
</html>
```

Running the preceding code in a browser renders the following:

One thing that might be a slight problem is that not all web servers, by default, set the correct MIME type for SVG. If the MIME type is set incorrectly, some browsers will not display the SVG image correctly. As one common example, Microsoft's IIS may need a specific configuration setting changed (`https://docs.microsoft.com/en-us/iis/manage/managing-your-configuration-settings/adding-ie-9-mime-types-to-iis`) to properly serve SVG images. The correct MIME type is `image/svg+xml`.

Drawing with code

Before you learn about other basic implementations, it's worth taking a look at the previous screenshot in a little more depth. Instead of just being text like the first example (which, after all, you could have just done in HTML), it shows four circles diagonally arranged across the canvas. Let's take a look at the source of that image and learn our first visual element in SVG, the `circle` element.

The following code sample shows the `circle` in action. It also shows how simple changes in markup attribute values can create visually interesting patterns. In it there are five `circle` elements. These all take advantage of four new attributes. `cx` and `cy` represent the center *x* and center *y* coordinates of the element on a coordinate plane. `r` represents the radius of the circle. `fill` defines the color that will fill the `circle`. `fill` accepts any valid CSS color value (`https://developer.mozilla.org/en-US/docs/Web/CSS/color_value`). In this case, we're using a **red**, **green**, **blue**, **alpha** (**RGBA**) value to fill this with variations on pure red. The first few values remain the same while the fourth value, the alpha, doubles every time from `.125` to `1` (fully opaque). Similarly, `cx`, `cy`, and `r` double each time. This produces the pattern you saw earlier. This isn't the most elaborate SVG image, but it does show you how easy basic SVG elements are to use and understand:

```
<?xml version="1.0" encoding="UTF-8"?>
<svg width="250" height="250" viewBox="0 0 250 250" version="1.1"
xmlns="http://www.w3.org/2000/svg">
        <circle cx="12.5" cy="12.5" r="6.25" fill="rgba(255,0,0,.125)">
        </circle>
        <circle cx="25" cy="25" r="12.5" fill="rgba(255,0,0,.25)">
        </circle>
        <circle cx="50" cy="50" r="25" fill="rgba(255,0,0,.5)"></circle>
        <circle cx="100" cy="100" r="50" fill="rgba(255,0,0,.75)">
        </circle>
        <circle cx="200" cy="200" r="100" fill="rgba(255,0,0,1)">
        </circle>
</svg>
```

Scalable + vector graphics

Now that you've seen an example of a drawing created with SVG, it might be useful to take a second to explain the *VG* in SVG and why that makes the file format *scalable*.

With raster (bitmap) file formats, you're probably familiar with formats such as JPG, PNG, or GIF. You can think of the image data as being stored pixel by pixel, so each point in an image is stored in the file and read out by the browser or graphics program pixel by pixel and row by row. The size and quality of the image is constrained by the size and quality at the time of creation.

There are optimizations for all the bitmapped file formats that limit the actual amount of data stored. For example, GIFs use the LZ77 algorithm to collapse redundant pixels down to a backpointer and reference pixel. Imagine if your image has 100 pixels of pure black in a row. The algorithm will search through the image for a sequence of same-bytes and when a sequence is encountered, the algorithm will search backwards through the document to find the first instance of that pattern. It will then replace all those pixels with instructions (a backpointer) on how many characters back to search and how many pixels to copy to fill in the number of same-bytes. In this case, it would be 100 (pixels to search) and 1 (pixels to copy).

Vector graphics, on the other hand, are defined by vectors and control points. To simplify significantly, you can think of vector graphics as being a set of numbers that describe the shape of a line. They may be a set of specific points or they may be, as in the case of the circle earlier, a set of instructions on how to create a specific type of object. The `circle` element doesn't store every pixel that makes up the circle. It stores the *arguments* used to create the circle.

Why is this cool? One reason is that because it's just a set of instructions defining the shape, which you can scale in or out, and the rendering engine will just calculate new values accordingly. For that reason, vector graphics can scale infinitely without loss of fidelity.

If that's all confusing to you, don't worry about it. The more you work with them, the more familiar you'll be with the way vector graphics work. In the meantime, the following set of examples and figures will help to illustrate the difference. First, look at the following markup. It represents four images, using the exact same SVG image as the source. The image represents the SVG logo. The dimensions are set at the image's natural size and then 2x, 4x, and 8x, the image's natural size:

```
<img src="svg-logo-h.svg" width="195" height="82" alt="The SVG
  logo at natural dimensions">
<img src="svg-logo-h.svg" width="390" height="164" alt="The SVG
  logo 2x">
<img src="svg-logo-h.svg" width="780" height="328" alt="The SVG
  logo 4x">
<img src="svg-logo-h.svg" width="1560" height="656" alt="The SVG
  logo 8x">
```

Rendered in the browser, that markup produces the following. Notice that it's completely crisp all the way up to 8x, the original size:

Now, look at the same markup, this time with PNGs. It follows the same pattern:

```
<img src="svg-logo-h.png" width="195" height="82" alt="The SVG
  logo at 'natural' dimensions">
<img src="svg-logo-h.png" width="390" height="164" alt="The SVG
  logo 2x">
<img src="svg-logo-h.png" width="780" height="328" alt="The SVG
  logo 4x">
<img src="svg-logo-h.png" width="1560" height="656" alt="The SVG
  logo 8x">
```

But now, see the result. Notice that, at the natural level, there is no difference between the SVG and PNG. The pixels in the PNG are enough to match the vector-defined lines in the SVG Version. Also, notice how the image gets progressively worse as the image gets larger. There is no way for the browser to get more information (more pixels) out of the bitmapped format to fill in the details at the larger size. It simply scales up the pixels that it has, with terrible results (especially at the 8x level):

Using SVG in CSS

A common usage of SVG is as a background image in CSS. There are benefits to this approach in terms of file size and scalability in **responsive web design** (**RWD**). In today's multi-device, multi-form factor world, the ability to offer high-quality images at a range of device sizes and resolutions (including high pixel density devices) is an important one. While there are optimized solutions for raster display images (in the form of the `picture` element and the `srcset` and `sizes` attributes) and you can use media queries to present different images or image sizes in CSS, the ability to do one image for all devices is huge. SVG in CSS allows us to do that easily

While you'll learn about the intersection of SVG and CSS in Chapter 5, *Working with SVG and CSS*, let's take a look at a basic example now to whet your appetite.

The following page has a `div` tag with a class of header. The only thing to really note here is a reference to an SVG file in the `url` value of the `background` property:

```
<!doctype html>
<html lang="en">
    <head>
        <meta charset="utf-8">
        <title>Mastering SVG- Using SVG images in CSS</title>
        <style type="text/css">
            .header {
                color: #ffffff;
                background: url(1-3-gradient.svg) repeat-x;
                width: 500px;
                height: 40px;
                text-align: center;
            }
        </style>
    </head>
    <body>
      <div class="header"><h1>CSS!</h1></div>
    </body>
</html>
```

This code produces the following when run in a browser. This simple example, which is no different than any other CSS implementation, will scale to the highest points-per-inch display without any loss of smoothness in the gradient. This is achieved simply by using SVG:

Gradients in SVG

As you continue to learn about basic SVG usage, I'm going to continue to tease new concepts in authoring SVG itself. The next features I'm going to introduce you to will be the definitions (defs) section, the gradient element, and the rect element.

The following example shows the source of the SVG element in the previous example. Everything beyond the root svg element itself is different to the previous example.

First up, there's the defs element. defs is an organizational element designed to hold definitions of graphical objects to be used later in the document. We immediately meet the linearGradient element, which defines (you guessed it!) a linear gradient. x1, x2, y1, and y2 define the *gradient vector* of the gradient. You'll learn more about that in Chapter 2, *Working with SVG and CSS*, but for now, just know that it defines the direction of the gradients. The default is 0 at the left and 1 to the right. Setting x2 to 0 and y2 to 1 changes the angle from a horizontal left-to-right gradient to a vertical top-to-bottom gradient.

The look of the gradient is actually defined as child stop elements. Each has two attributes, offset and stop-color. The offset accepts either a percentage or a number between 0 and 1, representing the placement of the gradient stop on the totality of the gradient vector. This example is the simplest: one color at 0% and another at 100%. stop-color accepts any valid color value:

```
<svg width="10" height="40" viewBox="0 0 10 40" version="1.1"
xmlns="http://www.w3.org/2000/svg">
 <defs>
 <linearGradient id="gradient" x1="0" x2="0" y1="0" y2="1">
 <stop offset="0%" stop-color="#999999"/>
 <stop offset="100%" stop-color="#000000"/>
 </linearGradient>
 </defs>
 <rect x="0" y="0" width="10" height="40" fill="url(#gradient)"/>
</svg>
```

As these are just instructions on how to render the gradient, it's possible to stretch and shift the background image in this case with zero loss of fidelity. The browser will just calculate new values and render a new, perfect gradient.

The following example shows a tweak to the CSS that stretches the header to be half of the height of the browser (using the vh unit) and forces the header background image to fill the available space (background: size: contain):

```
<!doctype html>
<html lang="en">
 <head>
   <meta charset="utf-8">
   <title>Mastering SVG- Using SVG images in CSS</title>
   <style type="text/css">
  .header {
   color: #ffffff;
   background: url(1-3-gradient.svg) repeat-x;
   width: 500px;
   height: 50vh;
   text-align: center;
   background-size: contain;
  }
  </style>
 </head>
 <body>
   <div class="header"><h1>CSS!</h1></div>
 </body>
</html>
```

As you can see in the following screenshot, the same background image handles the resizing with flying colors. This is true (as you'll learn) for anything else you can do with SVG.

Directly embedding SVG in an HTML document

In my opinion, the most exciting usage of SVG is as an inline element in an HTML document. While you will learn about SVG images as a separate file format and all the ways that SVG images can be used to develop modern web apps, the largest portion of this book will show you ways to interact with SVG elements embedded directly into the document. This is important because it is not possible to animate or otherwise manipulate the individual elements of an externally-referenced SVG file; this is only possible if the SVG elements are available directly (via the **Document Object Model (DOM)**) on the page.

The following example shows a simple inline SVG image with three circles and teases one of the most powerful tools you have when working with inline SVG: CSS! CSS can be used to style SVG elements in the same way that you can style regular HTML elements. This opens up a world of possibilities. The properties used here are probably new to you since they are SVG-specific, but just like the background-color or border properties you're used to, you can adjust the basic look and feel of SVG elements with CSS. In this next example, the CSS defines a default fill color for all circles, adds a border to the second circle, and then changes the fill color for the third circle. If you're not already scheming of ways to use CSS to manipulate SVG elements, rest assured you'll have plenty of ideas after reading Chapter 5, *Working with SVG and CSS*:

```
<!doctype html>
<html lang="en">
    <head>
        <meta charset="utf-8">
        <title>Mastering SVG - Using SVG images in CSS</title>
        <style type="text/css">
            circle {
              fill: rgba(255,0,0,1);
            }
            .first {
              opacity: .5;
            }
            .second {
              stroke-width: 3px;
              stroke: #000000;
            }
            .third {
              fill: rgba(0,255,0,.75);
            }
        </style>
    </head>
    <body>
```

```
            <svg width="400" height="250" viewBox="0 0 400 250" version="1.1"
            xmlns="http://www.w3.org/2000/svg">
              <circle cx="100" cy="100" r="25" class="first"></circle>
              <circle cx="200" cy="100" r="25" class="second"></circle>
              <circle cx="300" cy="100" r="25" class="third"></circle>
              </svg>
          </body>
        </html>
```

Opening a browser will show the results of all that CSS:

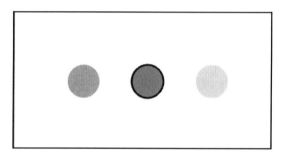

Feature detection and Modernizr

While overall support for SVG on the global web (`https://caniuse.com/#search=svg`) is now very high, it's not uniform and there are still non-supporting browsers out there. This is where Modernizr, the feature detection library, can be useful. If your user base is broad or you're using newer (even experimental) features, you can use Modernizr to detect browser compatibility with your important features and adjust your code accordingly.

There are two ways this works. One is the classes that Modernizr can place on the HTML element. The other is the global Modernizr object that contains results for all the tests as *Booleans*. Before we move on, I'll show you examples of both tools in action.

The Modernizr project provides hundreds of tests. Since some of the tests are quite expensive (in terms of resources needed to compute, when working with Modernizr, you want to use just the tests you need for your application. In this case, I've created a specific build of Modernizr that tests for multiple SVG features and nothing else. When added to an HTML page, this file will add classes to the HTML element indicating support for various SVG features

Here's the output of the HTML element in Microsoft Edge. The `no-smil` class indicates that Edge doesn't support **Synchronized Multimedia Integration Language** (**SMIL**), but does support everything else we're testing for:

```
<html class=" svg svgclippaths svgforeignobject svgfilters
  no-smil inlinesvg svgasimg" lang="en">
```

Output from the latest Chrome Version indicates support for all tested features:

```
<htmlclass=" svg svgclippaths svgforeignobject svgfilters smil
  inlinesvg svgasimg" lang="en" >
```

And finally, Internet Explorer 8 (IE8), which has no SVG support at all:

```
<HTML class=" no-svg no-svgclippaths no-svgforeignobject no-svgfilters
  no-smil no-inlinesvg no-svgasimg" lang="en">
```

Using these classes would allow you to, as a simple example, provide a PNG `fallback` function for CSS background images in IE8:

```
<!doctype html>
<html lang="en">
    <head>
        <meta charset="utf-8">
        <title>Mastering SVG- Modernizr</title>
        <style type="text/css">
            .header {
                color: #ffffff;
                background: url(1-3-gradient.svg) repeat-x;
                width: 500px;
                height: 40px;
                text-align: center;
            }
            .no-svg .header {
                background: url(1-3-gradient.png) repeat-x;
              }
        </style>
    </head>
    <body>
      <div class="header"><h1>CSS!</h1></div>
    </body>
</html>
```

As was mentioned, Modernizr also exposes a global Modernizr JavaScript object with each of the tests available as a Boolean. The following example shows how to access that Boolean and using an `if` statement for the code approximately, depending on whether or not SVG is supported:

```
<!doctype html>
<html lang="en">
    <head>
        <meta charset="utf-8">
        <title>Mastering SVG- Monderizr JavaScript Object</title>
        <script src="modernizr-custom.js"></script>
    </head>
    <body>
      <script>
        if (Modernizr.svg){
          // do things with SVG
        } else {
          //create a non-SVG fallback
        }
      </script>
    </body>
</html>
```

In general, the rest of this book will not focus on `fallbacks` for older browsers, but it is useful to know that they're available if you're working in an environment where you need to support a broad range of browsers and devices.

Summary

In this chapter, we learned about the basics of SVG including several SVG-specific elements, such as `circle`, `text`, and the elements used to make SVG gradients. We also learned about several ways to use SVG in HTML documents and as a background image in CSS.

We also learned about the Modernizr feature detection library and how to use it to create `fallbacks` for browsers that don't support SVG or specific SVG features.

In `Chapter 2`, *Getting Started with Authoring SVG*, you'll learn about many more SVG features as you will expand your knowledge of authoring SVG documents.

Getting Started with Authoring SVG

2

Now that you've dipped your toes in the water of SVG, it is time to take a deeper look at common SVG elements and their usage. This chapter will focus on the most common SVG elements and their usage, covering some that you've already learned about in more depth, and then introducing many other elements that you'll use in creating SVG images.

This chapter will cover the following topics:

- Basic SVG shapes
- The SVG positioning system
- Gradients and patterns
- Using SVG images generated from software programs, such as Adobe Illustrator, Inkscape, and Sketch

Positioning in SVG

As you saw in `Chapter 1`, *Introducing Scalable Vector Graphics*, SVG elements use a coordinate plane positioning system. Elements in an SVG document are located using *x* and *y* coordinates. This should be familiar to you from your geometry class or, more specifically to the web, if you're used to working with CSS, absolutely positioned elements. The following code shows two variations on the positioning scheme that you've already seen with both a circle element, which uses (`cx`, *center x*), and (`cy`, *center y*), attributes to place the `circle` element based on the center of the circle and the `rect` element, which will use the `x` and `y` attributes to place the upper left-hand corner of the square on the coordinate plane:

```
<svg xmlns="http://www.w3.org/2000/svg" width="350" height="150"
  viewBox="0 0 350 150" version="1.1">
  <circle cx="100" cy="75" r="50" fill="rgba(255,0,0,1)"/>
  <rect x="200" y="25" width="100" height="100"
```

```
        fill="rga(0,0,255,1)"/>
    </svg>
```

Rendered in the browser, it looks like this:

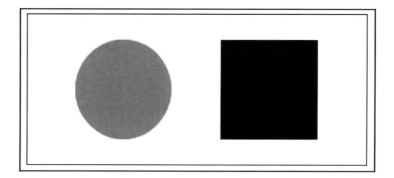

With the exception of using the two center properties to place an element based on its center, *x* and *y*, this should look just like positioning an element in CSS. Where it gets interesting is in the intersection of height and width and the value of the viewBox attribute on the SVG element itself.

viewBox and viewport in SVG

The height and width attributes define the *viewport* of the SVG element. The viewport can be thought of in the same way as the viewport in your browser. It defines the visible dimensions of the SVG document. The dimensions of the underlying SVG document can be larger than the viewport and, as with HTML, elements can be offscreen entirely. Everything that is visible is within the dimensions of the viewport.

If you just set the height and width attributes of an SVG element and don't use the viewBox attribute, it will behave in a manner equivalent to what you would expect if you've worked with CSS. In the case of the previous example, the viewport coordinate system will start with the coordinates (0,0) and will end at (350, 150).

 Throughout this book, coordinates will be rendered as (x value, y value).

In this case, each user unit will default to one pixel on the screen.

The `viewBox` attribute lets you change that initial viewport coordinate system. By redefining that coordinate system, you can shift and scale the underlying SVG document in interesting ways. Instead of trying to *describe* what's possible, let's look at some examples.

In every example we've shown so far, we've used the `viewBox` attribute and it's been set to match the dimensions of the `height` and `width` attributes of the viewport. What happens if we change the `height` and `width` attributes of the SVG element and don't change `viewBox` to match? Adding a second SVG element with new `height` attributes and `width` equal to double the original values creates a second version of the image at twice the size:

```
<svg xmlns="http://www.w3.org/2000/svg" width="700" height="300"
  viewBox="0 0 350 150" version="1.1">
  <circle cx="100" cy="75" r="50" fill="rgba(255,0,0,1)"/>
  <rect x="200" y="25" width="100" height="100"
  fill="rga(0,0,255,1)"/>
</svg>
```

This is what it looks like in a browser. As you can see, the viewport has been doubled, but since `viewBox` has the same dimensions, the exact same coordinates on the `circle` and `rect` elements create a scaled-up version of the image. In this case, the user units are no longer equivalent to one pixel, but the calculations inside the SVG element remain the same:

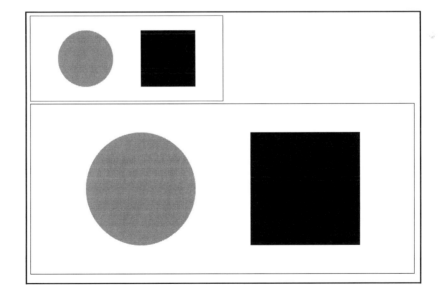

You could scale this up as large as you like and it would render perfectly.

What happens if we adjust the `viewBox` attribute itself? What does the value of the `viewBox` attribute represent?

The `viewBox` attribute takes four parameters: `min-x`, `min-y`, `width`, and `height`. `min-x` and `min-y` define the upper-left corner of `viewBox`. Now, `width` and `height` determine the width and height of that `viewBox`. Playing with these values shows how they interact with the height and width of the viewport. The first two examples change the *x* and *y* positions of the viewport's coordinate system. The first example offsets it by 20% (70 and 30 are 20% of the SVG width and height) in the positive direction. The second example offsets it by 20% in the negative direction. The third example changes the width and height of the `viewBox` attribute, shrinking it by half:

```
<svg xmlns="http://www.w3.org/2000/svg" width="350" height="150"
viewBox="70 30 350 150" version="1.1"> <circle cx="100" cy="75" r="50"
   fill="rgba(255,0,0,1)"/> <rect x="200" y="25" width="100"
   height="100" fill="rga(0,0,255,1)"/> </svg>
<svg xmlns="http://www.w3.org/2000/svg" width="350" height="150"
 viewBox="-70 -30 350 150" version="1.1"> <circle cx="100" cy="75"
   r="50" fill="rgba(255,0,0,1)"/> <rect x="200" y="25" width="100"
height="100" fill="rga(0,0,255,1)"/> </svg>
<svg xmlns="http://www.w3.org/2000/svg" width="350" height="150"
   viewBox="0 0 175 75" version="1.1"> <circle cx="100" cy="75" r="50"
   fill="rgba(255,0,0,1)"/> <rect x="200" y="25" width="100" height="100"
   fill="rga(0,0,255,1)"/> </svg>
```

Rendered in the browser, you can see the effect of those changes to the `viewBox` attribute. The offsets move the circle and square closer relative to the upper left-hand corner of the viewport. Shrinking the size of the `viewBox` attribute by half and keeping the size of `rect` and `circle` the same, effectively doubles the size of the rendered elements. The viewport stays the same size so the `viewBox` attribute and associated user units scales up by a factor of 2 to fit. All the elements inside it are scaled up as necessary:

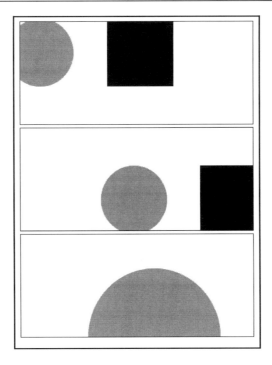

The following diagram shows what's at work in a little more depth (the black outline overlay represents the viewBox viewport):

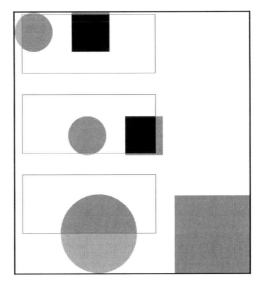

There is still more to learn about positioning in SVG, but we're going to tackle those topics as they arise throughout this rest of the book.

Now let's take a deeper look at some of the other elements that make up the SVG experience.

Introducing paths

By far the most important element in the SVG specification is the `path` element. `path` allows you to draw lines and shapes using vectors defined by a series of commands passed in as values to the `d` attribute. Remember when I mentioned that one of the biggest roadblocks to SVG adoption was the lack of a friendly API? This `path` element is likely to be the biggest sore spot in the entire specification. The values you might see in a `d` attribute can be incredibly dense and difficult to read. How difficult to read? Feast your eyes on the *S* element from the SVG logo:

```
<path id="S" d="M 5.482,31.319 C2.163,28.001 0.109,23.419 0.109,18.358
C0.109,8.232 8.322,0.024 18.443,0.024 C28.569,0.024 36.782,8.232
36.782,18.358 L26.042,18.358 C26.042,14.164 22.638,10.765 18.443,10.765
C14.249,10.765 10.850,14.164 10.850,18.358 C10.850,20.453 11.701,22.351
13.070,23.721 L13.075,23.721 C14.450,25.101 15.595,25.500 18.443,25.952
L18.443,25.952 C23.509,26.479 28.091,28.006 31.409,31.324 L31.409,31.324
C34.728,34.643 36.782,39.225 36.782,44.286 C36.782,54.412 28.569,62.625
18.443,62.625 C8.322,62.625 0.109,54.412 0.109,44.286 L10.850,44.286
C10.850,48.480 14.249,51.884 18.443,51.884 C22.638,51.884 26.042,48.480
26.042,44.286 C26.042,42.191 25.191,40.298 23.821,38.923 L23.816,38.923
C22.441,37.548 20.468,37.074 18.443,36.697 L18.443,36.692 C13.533,35.939
8.800,34.638 5.482,31.319 L5.482,31.319 L5.482,31.319 Z"/>
```

Without knowing what's going on, that's impossible to parse and even knowing the rules for the `d` attribute, it's difficult to keep track of.

Let's look at a simpler example so that you can get your head around the syntax. In this document, we've created a stylized letter **R**. Here's how to read the instructions of the `d` attribute:

1. (M)ove to point `(100,100)`.
2. Draw a (L)ine to `(100,300)`.
3. Draw a (L)ine to `(150,300)`.
4. Draw a (L)ine to `(150,150)`.

5. Draw a (S)mooth cubic Bézier curve from the current point to the point (150,175) with (250,150) as the second control point. Control points provide directional information used to draw the curve. This version of the cubic Bézier curveto instruction is actually shorthand indicating that the control points are reflected. It's possible in other formats to define multiple control points in pointing in different directions. This will create a more complex curve.

6. Draw a (L)ine to (200,300).

7. Draw a (L)ine to (250,300).

8. Draw a (L)ine to (225,225).

9. Draw a (S)mooth cubic Bézier curve from the current starting point to the point (100,100) with (350,100) as the second control point:

```
<svg xmlns="http://www.w3.org/2000/svg" width="500" height="500"
viewBox="0 0 500 500" version="1.1">
       <path d="M100,100 L100,300 L150,300 L150,150
S250,150,175,200 L200,300 L250,300 L225,225 S350,100,100,100"
stroke-width="1" stroke="#003366" fill="#cccccc"></path>
</svg>
```

Rendered in a browser, these commands produce the following:

This set of instructions is still complicated and it doesn't even touch on all of the possible options for a `path` element. The good news is that most of the time when you work with SVG these complex `paths` will be generated — either for you (using a graphical SVG editor) or by you through JavaScript. So, in reality, you just need to be able to understand the instructions and their usage. You don't need to sit there and parse through this data instruction by instruction.

More on basic shapes

Now that you've learned about `path`, let's take a look at some more straightforward parts of the SVG universe and let's examine some more basic shapes. You've already learned about `circle` and `rect`. Let's take a look at a few more basic shapes.

The line element

The `path` element allows you to draw anything you can imagine using a long series of instructions. Thankfully, there are many convenient elements that define common shapes that are a lot easier to work with than the `path` element. The first of these that you'll learn about is the `line` element.

The following example draws a grid on a 500 by 500 square. The `line` elements in use here take five arguments: x1, y1, x2, y2, and a `stroke`. The *x* and *y* coordinates indicate the beginning (x1, y1) and ending points (x2, y2) of the line. This SVG document draws a grid 100 pixels on each side in a 500 pixel square:

```
<svg version="1.1" xmlns="http://www.w3.org/2000/svg"
    width="500" height="500" viewBox="500 500 0 0">
    <line stroke="#000000" x1="0" y1="0" x2="0" y2="500" />
    <line stroke="#000000" x1="100" y1="0" x2="100" y2="500" />
    <line stroke="#000000" x1="200" y1="0" x2="200" y2="500" />
    <line stroke="#000000" x1="300" y1="0" x2="300" y2="500" />
    <line stroke="#000000" x1="400" y1="0" x2="400" y2="500" />
    <line stroke="#000000" x1="500" y1="0" x2="500" y2="500" />
    <line stroke="#000000" x1="0" y1="0" x2="500" y2="0" />
    <line stroke="#000000" x1="0" y1="100" x2="500" y2="100" />
    <line stroke="#000000" x1="0" y1="200" x2="500" y2="200" />
    <line stroke="#000000" x1="0" y1="300" x2="500" y2="300" />
    <line stroke="#000000" x1="0" y1="400" x2="500" y2="400" />
    <line stroke="#000000" x1="0" y1="500" x2="500" y2="500" />
</svg>
```

Rendered in the browser, the previous markup produces the following grid:

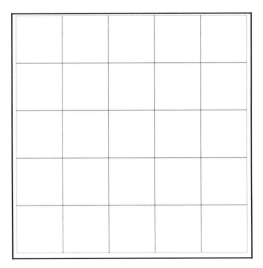

As an aside, generating a grid like this can be helpful with generating and debugging SVG documents. With a finer grained mesh on the grid, you can more easily pinpoint where calculated or manually generated positions are on the screen.

The ellipse element

ellipse is just like circle, except it takes *two radius* arguments, rx and ry for the *x* and *y* radius, respectively. This additional radius argument is needed as, otherwise, we would just be drawing a standard circle:

```
<svg width="250" height="100" viewBox="0 0 250 100"
   xmlns="http://www.w3.org/2000/svg">
   <ellipse cx="125" cy="50" rx="75" ry="25"
   fill="rgba(255,127,0,1)"/>
</svg>
```

Here's the output of that straightforward markup:

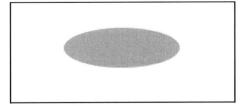

The polygon element

The `polygon` element creates close-ended shapes consisting of multiple straight lines starting from an initial `x`, `y` coordinate and ending with a final point on the coordinate plan. The `points` attribute takes a list of points on the coordinate plan to define the `polygon` element. The final point of a `polygon` element automatically connects to the first point. The following code sample draws a star:

```
<svg width="240" height="240" viewBox="0 0 240 240"
  xmlns="http://www.w3.org/2000/svg">
        <polygon points="95,95 120,5 150,95 235,95 165,150 195,235
        120,180 50,235 75,150 5,95" fill="rgba(0,0,255,1)"></polygon>
</svg>
```

The following shows the output of the preceding SVG element:

With `polygon` and `polyline`, it's just a suggestion, but not a requirement to separate the `x`, `y` pairs with commas.

The following code is programmatically equivalent to the previous example (although much harder to read). It renders the exact same shape:

```
<svg width="240" height="240" viewBox="0 0 240 240"
  xmlns="http://www.w3.org/2000/svg">
    <polygon points="95 95 120 5 150 95 235 95 165 150 195 235 120
      180 50 235 75 150 5 95" fill="rgba(0,0,255,1)"></polygon>
  </svg>
```

The polyline element

The `polyline` element creates *open-ended* shapes consisting of multiple straight lines. The `points` attribute takes a list of x, y points on the coordinate plan to define `polyline`. The following code sample traces the pattern of the constellation Draco (the dragon) in the night sky:

```
<svg width="800" height="600" viewBox="0 0 400 300"
    xmlns="http://www.w3.org/2000/svg">
    <polyline points="360,60 330,90 295,160 230,220 190,217
    175,180 155,130 155,60 135,30 100,25 90,55 65,170 80,195
    65,220 35,210 65,170" fill="none" stroke="white" stroke-width="3">
    </polyline>
</svg>
```

Run in the browser, the previous example looks like this:

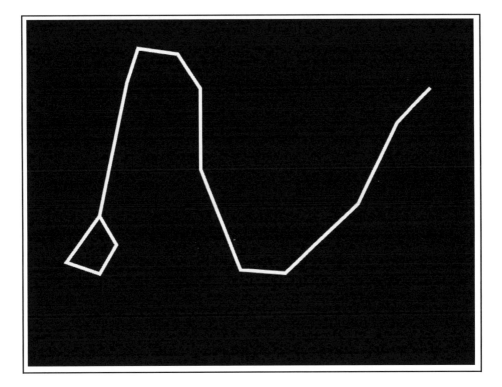

More on fills and strokes

You've seen them in use in most of the examples, now let's take a little bit of a more complete look at fills and strokes. These presentation attributes are important to SVG, especially when working with them dynamically, as it's much easier to manipulate elements directly as compared to writing dynamic CSS.

fill and stroke are collectively referred to as paint properties. fill sets the inside color of the object and stroke sets the color of the line drawn around the object. As you've already seen, they can accept any valid CSS color value. They can also accept a reference to a *paint server element* (these are hatch, linearGradient, meshgradient, pattern, radialGradient, and solidcolor), which are elements that define a paint style for the element. You've already seen one of these (linearGradient) and will learn about the more commonly supported ones shortly. Before you do, however, it's time to take a look at some stroke-specific attributes that control the way the lines appear and fit together.

stroke-dasharray

The stroke-dasharray attribute defines a list of comma-and/or whitespace-separated lengths or percentages that specify an alternating pattern of dashes and gaps that are used to stroke the line. The following example shows several different examples. The first is a series of 10 pixels on and 5 pixels off. The second example turns the pixels on and off based on the Fibonacci sequence. The third series turns the pixels on and off based on a series of prime numbers:

```
<svg width="400" height="300" viewBox="0 0 400 300"
  xmlns="http://www.w3.org/2000/svg">
  <rect x="50" y="20" width="300" height="50" fill="none"
    stroke="#000000" stroke-width="4"  stroke-dasharray="10 5"></rect>
  <rect x="50" y="80" width="300" height="50" fill="none"
   stroke="#000000" stroke-width="4"  stroke-dasharray="1, 2, 3, 5, 8,
   13"></rect>
  <rect x="50" y="140" width="300" height="50" fill="none"
    stroke="#000000" stroke-width="4"  stroke-dasharray="2, 3, 5, 7,
    11, 13, 17, 19"></rect>
</svg>
```

Rendered in the browser, the preceding code produces the following example:

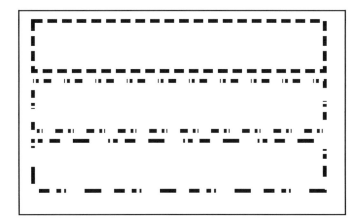

 If an odd number of values are provided as the value of the attribute then the list is repeated in order to yield an even number of values. This may not result in a pattern you expect as values might shift from dashes to spaces and create an unexpected result. In the following example the single value of 10 produces 10 on and 10 off, which is probably what you envisioned. The "15,10,5" pattern, on the other hand, produces 15 on, 10 off, 5 on, 15 off, 10 on, and 5 off. If you expect the pattern to *always* have 15 as an "on" then this might come as a surprise.

```
<svg width="400" height="300" viewBox="0 0 400 300"
   xmlns="http://www.w3.org/2000/svg">
   <rect x="50" y="20" width="300" height="50" fill="none"
    stroke="#000000" stroke-width="4"  stroke-dasharray="10">
   </rect>
   <rect x="50" y="80" width="300" height="50" fill="none"
     stroke="#000000" stroke-width="4"  stroke-dasharray="15,10,5">
   </rect>
</svg>
```

You can see this in the browser. This may be the look you're after, but if it's not, now you know why:

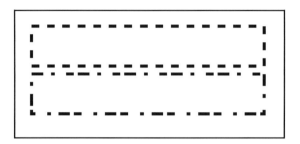

stroke-dashoffset

The `stroke-dashoffset` attribute accepts positive or negative length or percentage values and specifies the distance into the dash pattern to start rendering the dash. This offset can be seen in the following code example:

```
<svg width="400" height="300" viewBox="0 0 400 300"
xmlns="http://www.w3.org/2000/svg">
<rect x="50" y="20" width="300" height="50" fill="none"
 stroke="#000000" stroke-width="4" stroke-dasharray="10 10"></rect>
<rect x="50" y="80" width="300" height="50" fill="none"
 stroke="#000000" stroke-width="4" stroke-dasharray="10 10" stroke-
 dashoffset="25"></rect>
<rect x="50" y="140" width="300" height="50" fill="none"
 stroke="#000000" stroke-width="4" stroke-dasharray="10 10" stroke-
 dashoffset="-25"></rect>
</svg>
```

The effect of this attribute can be seen in the following screenshot:

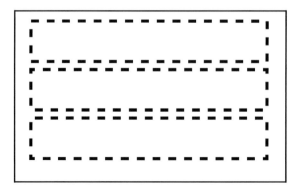

stroke-linecap

The `stroke-linecap` attribute indicates the shape to be rendered at the end of an open line. The options are `butt`, `round`, `square`, and `inherit`. The following code sample shows the different rendering options in action. The two red lines are there to show the difference between `butt` and `square`. `butt` ends the `stroke` flush with the ends of the line. The `square` cap extends beyond the end of the line to include the thickness of the `stroke`'s:

```
<svg xmlns="http://www.w3.org/2000/svg" width="500" height="400"
    viewBox="0 0 500 400" version="1.1">
  <line fill="none" stroke-width="20" stroke="#000000" x1="20" y1="100"
    x2="450" y2="100" stroke-linecap="butt" />
  <line fill="none" stroke-width="20" stroke="#000000" x1="20" y1="200"
    x2="450" y2="200" stroke-linecap="round" />
  <line fill="none" stroke-width="20" stroke="#000000" x1="20" y1="300"
    x2="450" y2="300" stroke-linecap="square" />
  <line fill="none" stroke-width="2" stroke="rgba(255,0,0,1)" x1="20"
    y1="0" x2="20" y2="400" />
  <line fill="none" stroke-width="2" stroke="rgba(255,0,0,1)" x1="450"
    y1="0" x2="450" y2="400" />
</svg>
```

The result of this can be seen in the following screenshot:

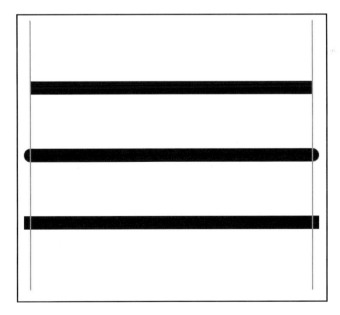

stroke-linejoin

The `stroke-linejoin` attribute defines the way that the corners of `paths` and basic shapes are rendered. The possible values are `miter`, `round`, `bevel`, and `inherit`. Round renders smoothly curved corners, `miter` produces sharp edges with only one angle for the corner, and `bevel` adds a new angle to the corner to create a compound corner:

```
<svg width="400" height="300" viewBox="0 0 400 300"
  xmlns="http://www.w3.org/2000/svg">
<rect x="50" y="20" width="300" height="50" fill="none"
  stroke="#000000" stroke-width="20"  stroke-linejoin="miter"></rect>
<rect x="50" y="100" width="300" height="50" fill="none"
   stroke="#000000" stroke-width="20"  stroke-linejoin="bevel">
</rect>
<rect x="50" y="180" width="300" height="50" fill="none"
   stroke="#000000" stroke-width="20"  stroke-linejoin="round">
 </rect>
</svg>
```

These options can be seen in the following screenshot:

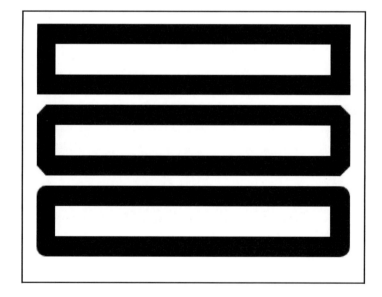

stroke-opacity

The `stroke-opacity` attribute does what you might expect. It sets the opacity of a stroked object. The following sample sets three different opacities on three separate rectangles. You can see `stroke` interact not just with the background of the page, but with the fill of the rectangle as well, as `stroke` is centered on the edge of the rectangle and part of it covers the filled-in area:

 There is no easy way to change the positioning of the `stroke` attribute on an SVG element. In graphics programs, it's possible to set the `stroke` attribute to be on the inside of the box, centered on the edge of the box (which is how SVG does it) and outside the box. There is a proposal in the new SVG strokes (`https://www.w3.org/TR/svg-strokes/`) specification to change the alignment of `stroke` (called stroke-alignment) but there isn't anything in the browser at the present time.

```
<svg width="400" height="300" viewBox="0 0 400 300"
  xmlns="http://www.w3.org/2000/svg">
 <rect x="50" y="20" width="300" height="50" fill="none"
  stroke="#000000" stroke-width="20" stroke-opacity=".25"></rect>
 <rect x="50" y="100" width="300" height="50" fill="none"
  stroke="#000000" stroke-width="20" stroke-opacity=".5"></rect>
 <rect x="50" y="180" width="300" height="50" fill="none"
  stroke="#000000" stroke-width="20" stroke-opacity="1"></rect>
</svg>
```

The output of the preceding code can be seen in the following screenshot:

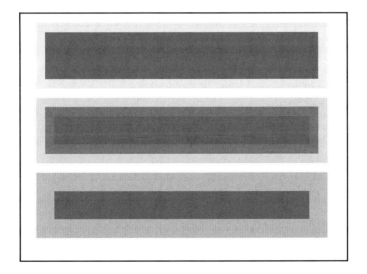

Now that we've looked at the different options for strokes, it's time to look at some of the other options for fills. These are the paint server elements that we mentioned before. You've already encountered one of them, linearGradient. You'll also learn about two others that are commonly used, radialGradient and pattern.

linearGradient and radialGradient

You've already seen the linearGradient element in Chapter 1, *Introducing Scalable Vector Graphics*. There's also radialGradient that works in much the same way, except it renders gradients that radiate around a center point. Both elements are added to the defs section and each has a series of stops with offsets and stop-colors defining the gradient.

They are then referenced by their id attribute as the argument to the fill attribute of rect:

```
<svg width="400" height="300" viewBox="0 0 400 300"
 xmlns="http://www.w3.org/2000/svg">
    <defs>
        <linearGradient id="linear">
            <stop offset="5%" stop-color="green"/>
            <stop offset="95%" stop-color="gold"/>
        </linearGradient>
        <radialGradient id="radial">
            <stop offset="10%" stop-color="gold"/>
            <stop offset="95%" stop-color="green"/>
        </radialGradient>
    </defs>
    <rect x="50" y="20" width="100" height="100" fill="url(#radial)">
    </rect>
    <rect x="200" y="20" width="100" height="100" fill="url(#linear)">
    </rect>
</svg>
```

This produces the following output:

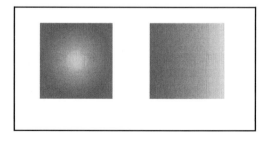

The pattern element

The final paint server we'll look at is the `pattern` element. `pattern` allows you to define a small graphic element that you can reference as `fill` or `stroke` and tile over an element in a repeating pattern. In this example, we're using a `pattern` element with a single child `polygon` element that defines two diagonal lines that combine to create a long pattern:

```
<svg width="400" height="400" viewBox="0 0 400 400"
 xmlns="http://www.w3.org/2000/svg">
    <pattern id="pattern-example" width="100" height="100"
      patternUnits="userSpaceOnUse">
    <polygon points="0,50 0,100 50,50 100,100 100,75 50,25 0,75"
      fill="#000000"></polygon>
    </pattern>
    <rect x="0" y="0" width="400" height="400" fill="url(#pattern-
      example)"></rect>
</svg>
```

Rendered out in the browser, this creates the following jagged pattern:

Authoring programs

All of the examples so far in the book have been generated by hand. In practice, as you'll learn throughout this book, SVG is often generated by software. Most of this book will look at creating and manipulating SVG using web-based tools and libraries, but SVG images can also be generated by desktop drawing applications. While working on the web, you will often work with SVG images that have been created by designers in applications, such as Inkscape (`https://inkscape.org/en/`), Adobe Illustrator (`https://www.adobe.com/products/illustrator.html`), or Sketch (`https://www.sketchapp.com/`). These applications are wonderful because they allow non-technical designers to work with SVG to create images using advanced drawing tools.

While it's not a requirement for the rest of this book, I would suggest getting your hands on something you can use to author SVG in this way. While you want to learn how to work with SVG in a dynamic, web-based environment, it's great to have the option to use advanced drawing tools to update and manipulate SVG elements. I have used both Adobe Illustrator and Inkscape over the years and many people swear by Sketch, so those are three options to start with. For just starting out, I would suggest looking first at Inkscape. Inkscape is a free, open source software released under the GNU license and it's pretty solid from a feature perspective, so it's a good default choice.

Whatever application you choose (and even if you don't choose one and simply inherit SVG images authored in one), it's good to know that there are some downsides to these applications. These applications are designed for the authoring experience and aren't producing SVG images optimized for the web so it's important to keep that in mind when pulling SVG images created by graphics program into a web project. You'll learn more about optimizing SVG images later on in the book, but you should be aware of what you're up against from the start.

Look at the following screenshot. It shows a difference between two files that both render the exact same image. The one on the left is the SVG source file output by Inkscape. The file on the right is an optimized version. As you can see, there's a lot of extra data sloshing around in the Inkscape file. That data is required by the application, but wouldn't be required on the web, so removing it allowed us to cut the file down significantly:

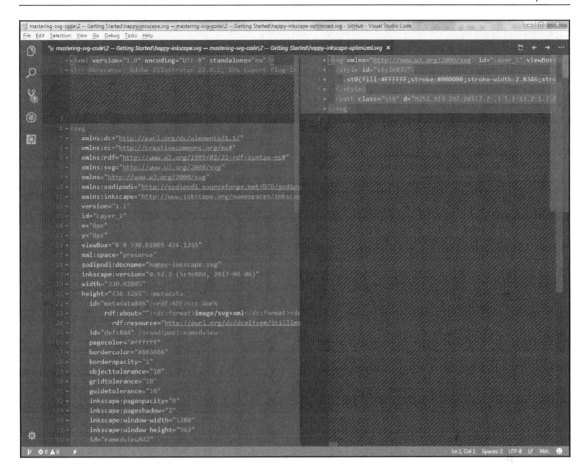

You'll learn about tools to clean up SVG files like this in `Chapter 11`, *Tools to Optimize Your SVG*.

Summary

In this chapter, you learned about multiple SVG features. You learned about `path`, which allows you to draw complex shapes using lines and curves. You also learned about a number of basic drawing tools that allow you to draw lines, ellipses, polygons, and polylines. In addition, you learned about a number of stroke and fill options.

Finally, you learned a little bit about the options for using software to draw static SVG and learned a little bit about the potential drawbacks of doing so.

In `Chapter 3`, *Digging Deeper with SVG Authoring*, you'll continue to learn about SVG authoring, adding on to the growing list of tools you've experienced, and allowing you to create even more complex SVG images.

Digging Deeper with SVG Authoring

3

So far, in this book, you've been exposed to most of the basic SVG features and elements. With just the tools you've experienced so far, you could start to do some real tasks with SVG. That said, SVG has a lot more to offer. This chapter will start to look at more advanced SVG tools. Some of these techniques will play an important role in doing dynamic SVG animations and visualizations.

The following topics will be covered in this chapter:

- Transformations
- Clipping and masking
- Importing content into SVG
- Filter effects
- Serving SVG on the web

All of these, along with the tools you've already learned about, will give you a strong SVG foundation.

Transformations

Transformations in SVG allow you to manipulate an SVG element in a variety of ways, including scaling, rotating, skewing, and translating (which looks like moving the element, but isn't exactly that). Using transformations allows you to manipulate the SVG without changing its intrinsic values (for example, height, width, x, and y) which is important when you're manipulating elements in a dynamic way.

This section will introduce you to the common transformation functions one by one, with examples of each.

translate

The `translate` transform moves the SVG element by the specified x and y coordinates. A translation changes the *origin* of the element's coordinate system.

The y coordinate is an optional argument and is assumed to be equivalent to the x argument if it's not provided.

The following sample shows three equivalent circles. The first circle is not transformed in any way. The second is transformed with a single argument (10), which moves it by 10 on the x axis and 10 on the y axis. The third is translated by "75" pixels on the x plane and 0 pixels on the y plane. The underlying element has equivalent metrics in each case but they display differently.

Why not just move the elements, you might ask. For one thing, this is useful in dynamic SVG as you don't have to track the original position of the element if you move the element around. You can simply reset the element to its original state by removing the transformation:

```
<svg xmlns="http://www.w3.org/2000/svg" width="350" height="150"
  viewBox="0 0 350 150" version="1.1">
    <circle cx="100" cy="75" r="50" fill="rgba(255,0,0,.5)"/>
    <circle cx="100" cy="75" r="50" fill="rgba(255,0,0,.5)"
    transform="translate(10)" />
    <circle cx="100" cy="75" r="50" fill="rgba(255,0,0,.5)"
    transform="translate(75,0)" />
</svg>
```

You can see the output in the following screenshot:

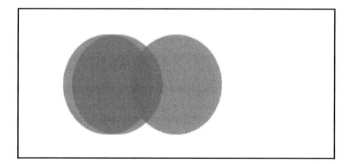

scale

The `scale` transform scales the SVG element by the specified x and y coordinates. The unit is a **factor**, so passing in two would *double* the size of the element.

As with `translate`, the y coordinate is optional and is assumed to be equivalent to the x argument if it's not provided.

If you've done CSS transforms and scaled an element, you might be surprised by the way `scale` works. Even if you haven't done CSS you might be surprised.

Scaling in SVG is from the *origin point* of the coordinate system. See the following example, showing three separate boxes. One is not scaled at all. The next two rectangles are scaled by `1.25` on both axes and then by `2` on the *x* axis and then not scaled on the *y* axis:

```
<svg xmlns="http://www.w3.org/2000/svg" width="500" height="500"
viewBox="0 0 500 500" version="1.1">
    <rect x="100" y="100" width="100" height="100" stroke="blue"
    fill="none"></rect>
    <rect x="100" y="100" width="100" height="100" stroke="red"
    fill="rgba(255,0,0,.5)" transform="scale(1.25)"></rect>
    <rect x="100" y="100" width="100" height="100" stroke="red"
    fill="rgba(255,0,0,.5)" transform="scale(2,1)"></rect>
</svg>
```

As you can see in the following screenshot, the result is that not only are the dimensions of the element scaled, the distance from the origin of the coordinate system is also scaled. The first element is adjusted in both directions along with both the x and y planes. The second element is shifted along the x axis to the right:

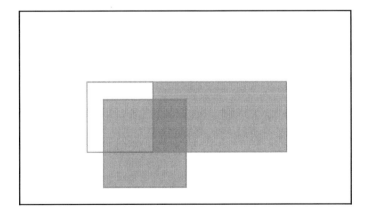

Compare that to the following code, which shows the way that CSS scaling works. Using the same scaling factors in CSS produces a totally different result. Instead of scaling from the origin of the SVG document, CSS scales out from the center point of the element itself. The syntax might look similar but the results are different:

```
<head>
<style type="text/css">
    div {
        position: absolute;
        left: 100px;
        top: 100px;
        width: 100px;
        height: 100px;
        border: 1px solid blue;
    }
    .scale-1-25 {
        transform: scale(1.25);
        border: 1px solid red;
        background: rgba(255,0,0,.5);
    }
    .scale-2-by-1 {
        transform: scale(2,1);
        border: 1px solid red;
        background: rgba(255,0,0,.5);
    }
</style>
</head>
<body>
    <div></div>
    <div class="scale-1-25"></div>
    <div class="scale-2-by-1"></div>
</body>
```

The result can be seen in the following screenshot:

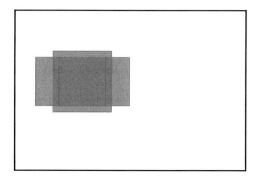

If you want to produce a similar effect with SVG, there's an interesting trick you can use. This trick is also useful to illustrate the way that the `transform` attribute can accept multiple transform functions. You're not limited to just the one.

So, how does it work? As I mentioned, the point of origin for the CSS transformation is the *center of the box being transformed*. This technique replicates that same point of origin in SVG.

To do this, you need to do a trick where you shift the point of origin for the element to a new point of origin that matches the CSS point of origin. Here's how this works. In this case, our rectangles are at (100, 100) in the coordinate system and are 100 pixels on a side. The center of the box is therefore at (150, 150). Translating the element by (150,150) sets the point of origin for these elements to the equivalent of the CSS point of origin. Remember that the CSS point of origin is the center of the box (which was (150,150) before the transformation) and that translating an element actually *changes* its point of origin.

Following the translation, we apply the scale. This happens at the new point of origin at (150, 150) (again, equivalent to what would be the CSS point of origin) and expands the squares by 1.25 and 2, respectively. Finally, we transform the element *back* to its *original* point of origin (0,0) and, because they were manipulated at the CSS equivalent point of origin (150, 150), the scaled elements are now centered appropriately:

```
<svg xmlns="http://www.w3.org/2000/svg" width="500" height="500"
  viewBox="0 0 500 500" version="1.1">
    <rect x="100" y="100" width="100" height="100" stroke="red"
    fill="rgba(255,0,0,.5)"></rect>
    <rect x="100" y="100" width="100" height="100" stroke="red"
    fill="rgba(255,0,0,.5)" transform="translate(150 150) scale(1.25)
      translate(-150 -150)"></rect>
    <rect x="100" y="100" width="100" height="100" stroke="red"
    fill="rgba(255,0,0,.5)" transform="translate(150 150) scale(2,1)
      translate(-150 -150)"></rect>
</svg>
```

The following illustration shows how this works step by step:

1. The first frame shows the starting position. The 100 pixel rectangles are placed at (100,100) and their point of origin is (0,0).
2. They are then translated by (150,150).
3. They are then transformed, from the new point of origin, (150,150), by 1.25 and (2,1), respectively.

4. They're translated back to (0,0) while still maintaining the new scale. Their actual point of origin at this point is (0,0) but it renders as if it had the CSS point of origin, (150,150):

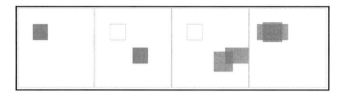

rotate

The rotate transform rotates the element by a number of degrees. This transform takes three arguments. The first is the number of degrees. The second and third arguments are x and y coordinates that define the point of origin for the rotation. If there is no point of origin for the element, the origin point of the viewport is used. This can be seen in the following two code samples, where nine rectangles are drawn on the SVG element. The first is not transformed. The next eight are rotated incrementally by ten degrees each:

```
<svg xmlns="http://www.w3.org/2000/svg" width="700" height="700"
  viewBox="0 0 700 700" version="1.1">
  <rect x="600" y="0" width="100" height="100"
   fill="rgba(255,0,0,.5)"/>
  <rect x="600" y="0" width="100" height="100"
    fill="rgba(255,0,0,.5)" transform="rotate(10)"/>
  <rect x="600" y="0" width="100" height="100"
   fill="rgba(255,0,0,.5)" transform="rotate(20)"/>
  <rect x="600" y="0" width="100" height="100"
   fill="rgba(255,0,0,.5)" transform="rotate(30)"/>
  <rect x="600" y="0" width="100" height="100"
   fill="rgba(255,0,0,.5)" transform="rotate(40)"/>
  <rect x="600" y="0" width="100" height="100"
   fill="rgba(255,0,0,.5)" transform="rotate(50)"/>
  <rect x="600" y="0" width="100" height="100"
   fill="rgba(255,0,0,.5)" transform="rotate(60)"/>
  <rect x="600" y="0" width="100" height="100"
    fill="rgba(255,0,0,.5)" transform="rotate(70)"/>
  <rect x="600" y="0" width="100" height="100"
    fill="rgba(255,0,0,.5)" transform="rotate(80)"/>
</svg>
```

As you can see in the following screenshot of the rendered code, they `arc` across the entire canvas with the `(0,0)` point of the viewport at the origin of the rotation:

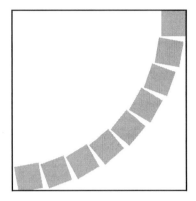

Compare that to the following, which changes the rotation point to the middle of the viewport along with the x axis and the top of the viewport on the y axis:

```
<svg xmlns="http://www.w3.org/2000/svg" width="700" height="700" viewBox="0
0 700 700" version="1.1">
    <rect x="600" y="0" width="100" height="100"
      fill="rgba(255,0,0,.5)"/>
    <rect x="600" y="0" width="100" height="100"
      fill="rgba(255,0,0,.5)" transform="rotate(10 350 0)"/>
    <rect x="600" y="0" width="100" height="100"
      fill="rgba(255,0,0,.5)" transform="rotate(20 350 0)"/>
    <rect x="600" y="0" width="100" height="100"
      fill="rgba(255,0,0,.5)" transform="rotate(30 350 0)"/>
    <rect x="600" y="0" width="100" height="100"
      fill="rgba(255,0,0,.5)" transform="rotate(40 350 0)"/>
    <rect x="600" y="0" width="100" height="100"
      fill="rgba(255,0,0,.5)" transform="rotate(50 350 0)"/>
    <rect x="600" y="0" width="100" height="100"
      fill="rgba(255,0,0,.5)" transform="rotate(60 350 0)"/>
    <rect x="600" y="0" width="100" height="100"
      fill="rgba(255,0,0,.5)" transform="rotate(70 350 0)"/>
    <rect x="600" y="0" width="100" height="100"
      fill="rgba(255,0,0,.5)" transform="rotate(80 350 0)"/>
</svg>
```

As you can see, when this code is rendered in a browser, the same elements with the same angle of rotation `arc` across the top right-hand quarter of the viewport. *The squares radiate out from the new point of origin*:

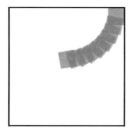

As with scaling, if you want to rotate around the center point of the element, you can use the same translation trick you learned about in that section. In the following code sample, the rectangles are translated by the equivalent of their center point (100,100), rotated by 10 degrees, and then translated back to their original point of origin:

```
<svg xmlns="http://www.w3.org/2000/svg" width="400" height="400" viewBox="0
0 200 200" version="1.1">
    <rect x="50" y="50" width="100" height="100"
    fill="rgba(255,0,0,.2)" transform="translate(100,100) rotate(10)
translate(-100,-100)"/>
    <rect x="50" y="50" width="100" height="100"
    fill="rgba(255,0,0,.2)" transform="translate(100,100) rotate(20)
    translate(-100,-100)"/>
    <rect x="50" y="50" width="100" height="100"
    fill="rgba(255,0,0,.2)" transform="translate(100,100) rotate(30)
     translate(-100,-100)"/>
    <rect x="50" y="50" width="100" height="100"
    fill="rgba(255,0,0,.2)" transform="translate(100,100) rotate(40)
    translate(-100,-100)"/>
    <rect x="50" y="50" width="100" height="100"
     fill="rgba(255,0,0,.2)" transform="translate(100,100) rotate(50)
     translate(-100,-100)"/>
    <rect x="50" y="50" width="100" height="100"
     fill="rgba(255,0,0,.2)" transform="translate(100,100) rotate(60)
     translate(-100,-100)"/>
    <rect x="50" y="50" width="100" height="100"
     fill="rgba(255,0,0,.2)" transform="translate(100,100) rotate(70)
      translate(-100,-100)"/>
    <rect x="50" y="50" width="100" height="100"
    fill="rgba(255,0,0,.2)" transform="translate(100,100) rotate(80)
     translate(-100,-100)"/>
    <rect x="50" y="50" width="100" height="100"
    fill="rgba(255,0,0,.2)" transform="translate(100,100) rotate(90)
```

```
    translate(-100,-100)"/>
  </svg>
```

This produces the following output:

skew

The `skew` transforms skew the element by an angle along the specified axis. Like `rotate` and `scale`, `skew` is based on the current origin point. The following code sample shows two sets of elements. One is skewed along the x axis. The other is skewed along the y axis. For each set of elements, there is a transform that just focuses on the `skew` and then there is another `skew` transform by the same amount that also includes the translation technique:

```
<svg xmlns="http://www.w3.org/2000/svg" width="500" height="500" viewBox="0
0 500 500" version="1.1">
   <rect x="100" y="100" width="100" height="100"
    fill="rgba(255,0,0,.1)" transform="skewX(10)"/>
   <rect x="100" y="100" width="100" height="100" stroke="blue"
    fill="none"/>
   <rect x="100" y="100" width="100" height="100"
   fill="rgba(0,255,0,.1)" transform="translate(150,150) skewX(10)
   translate(-150,-150)"/>
   <rect x="300" y="300" width="100" height="100" stroke="blue"
   fill="none"/>
   <rect x="300" y="300" width="100" height="100"
    fill="rgba(255,0,0,.1)" transform="skewY(10)"/>
   <rect x="300" y="300" width="100" height="100"
   fill="rgba(0,255,0,.1)" transform="translate(300,300) skewY(10)
    translate(-300,-300)"/>
</svg>
```

You can see the output of this code in the following screenshot. The blue square shows the original position and then the two skewed elements are arrayed on top of it to show the difference between skewing based on the original origin point and using the translation technique to change the point of origin to the center of the element:

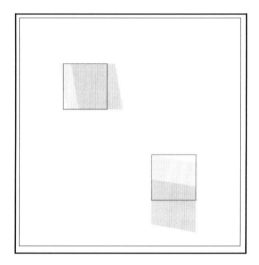

 There is another option to transform elements. You can use what's called a *transformation matrix*. Matrix transformations are powerful (they can represent any of the other transformation functions) but also complicated and they rely heavily on math. Since not everyone thinks math is fun, matrix transformations aren't as common as the other transformation functions. For that reason, I'm not going to cover them here. Realistically, you can do anything you need to do with the ones you've already learned.

Clipping and masking

Clipping and masking allow you to subtract portions of elements in an SVG document.

Clipping paths, implemented with the clipPath element, use any combination of paths, text elements, and basic shapes to serve as the outline of a simple mask. This means that everything on the inside of the clipPath element's outline is visible and everything on the outside is cropped out. Every pixel in clipPath is either on or off.

Masks, implemented with the mask element, can contain graphics, text, and basic shapes to serve as a semi-transparent mask. With a mask, each pixel value indicates the degree of opacity and can range from being fully transparent to fully opaque.

Clipping

The `clipPath` element in SVG allows you to cut a shape out of another shape. Clipping uses the geometry of the shape to define the area that's cut out. It doesn't take into account anything other than the shape, so attributes such as `stroke` and `fill` don't change the area being cut out.

The following code sample shows a very simple, but very useful, pattern for using the `clipPath` element. The basic effect is to cut out one half of a complicated element (the star we drew in Chapter 2, *Getting Started with Authoring SVG*) in order to lay it on top of another instance of that same star creating a bisected star design in red and black. While you could create two halves of the star and place them next to each other, mixing and matching instances of the same element is much more flexible.

Let's take a look at how this works.

First, in the `defs` section, we create `clipPath` element itself. Any children of the `clipPath` will be bundled together to create the clipping pattern that we'll use later. In this case, it's a simple rectangle that covers half of the canvas. It has an ID of `"box"`. Following that, we create a reusable instance of the star we created in Chapter 2, *Getting Started with Authoring SVG*. We give that an ID of `"star"`. Outside of the `defs` section, we put it all together. With two instances of the `use` element, which allows you to swap in elements defined elsewhere, we link to the star's `polygon` and insert it twice into the document, once with a red fill and once with a black fill. Note that the user element uses a fragment identifier to reference the polygon. `"#star"` is a valid, relative URL pointing to a specific `id` on this page. The second variation has a `clip-path` attribute that links to our box, `clipPath`:

```
<svg xmlns="http://www.w3.org/2000/svg" width="240" height="240" viewBox="0
0 240 240" version="1.1">
    <defs>
        <clipPath id="box" maskUnits="userSpaceOnUse" x="0" y="0"
         width="240" height="240">
            <rect x="120" y="0" width="240" height="240" fill="red" >
            </rect>
        </clipPath>
        <polygon id="star" points="95,95 120,5 150,95 235,95 165,150
            195,235 120,180 50,235 75,150 5,95"></polygon>
    </defs>
    <use href="#star" fill="red"></use>
    <use href="#star" fill="black" clip-path="url(#box)"></use>
</svg>
```

The output of that code can be seen in the following screenshot. The red instance of the star is exposed as the left half of the black star, which is clipped out by the square defined in the `clipPath` element:

Masking

Masking, in contrast to clipping, takes account of attributes beyond the simple shape of the element being cut out. As was mentioned, you leverage the full range of transparent, semi-transparent, or fully opaque pixels. This allows for interesting effects.

The following example shows how multiple masks can be used together. In this example, we make heavy use of the `defs` section and then compose an image using different reusable elements.

For starters, we create two gradients. One is a linear gradient that has five steps, mostly black, which creates a very intense band of white in the middle of the gradient. The second is a radial gradient, which has a central area of black surrounded by a very large circle of white. Using these for a mask means that each of the pixels in these gradients lands on a continuum from fully opaque (black pixels) to fully transparent (white pixels) and variable transparency in the middle.

Take a look at these gradients by themselves:

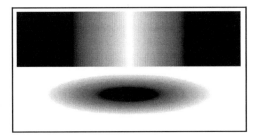

We then create a `text` element that says **Mastering SVG** and bring in a `pattern` element, which you'll recognize from `Chapter 2`, *Getting Started with Authoring SVG*.

In the body of the SVG element, we link to the text elements, using fragment identifiers (`#mastering-SVG`) pointing to the IDs of the `text` elements in the `defs` section, and apply the two masks to them with the `mask` attribute with a `url` value pointing to the fragment identifier of the `mask` attribute. Take a look at how the masks affect the text elements by themselves:

Putting it all together, we stack the two text elements on top of each other, and add a patterned box behind the text boxes:

```
<svg xmlns="http://www.w3.org/2000/svg" width="500" height="120" viewBox="0
0 500 120" version="1.1">
    <defs>
        <linearGradient id="gradient">
            <stop offset="0" stop-color="black" stop-opacity="1" />
            <stop offset=".25" stop-color="black" stop-opacity="1" />
            <stop offset=".5" stop-color="white" stop-opacity="1" />
            <stop offset=".75" stop-color="black" stop-opacity="1" />
            <stop offset="1" stop-color="black" stop-opacity="1" />
        </linearGradient>
        <radialGradient id="highlight-gradient">
            <stop offset=".25" stop-color="black" stop-opacity="1" />
            <stop offset=".75" stop-color="white" stop-opacity="1" />
```

```
        </radialGradient>
        <mask id="gradient-mask" maskUnits="userSpaceOnUse" x="0" y="0"
         width="500" height="240">
            <rect y="0" x="0" width="500" height="120"
             fill="url(#gradient)"></rect>
        </mask>
        <mask id="highlight-mask" maskUnits="userSpaceOnUse" x="0"
         y="0" width="500" height="240">
            <rect y="0" x="0" width="500" height="120"
             fill="url(#highlight-gradient)"></rect>
        </mask>
        <text id="mastering-SVG" x="10" y="75" font-size="72" text-
         anchor="left" font-weight="bold">
            Mastering SVG
        </text>
        <pattern id="pattern-example" width="100" height="100"
         patternUnits="userSpaceOnUse">
            <rect width="100" height="100" fill="darkred" x="0" y="0">
            </rect>
            <polygon points="0,50 0,100 50,50 100,100 100,75 50,25
             0,75" fill="rgb(83,1,1)">
            </polygon>
        </pattern>
    </defs>
    <rect x="0" y="0" width="500" height="120" fill="url(#pattern-
      example)"></rect>
    <use href="#mastering-SVG" fill="gold" mask="url(#gradient-mask)"
     x="120"></use>
    <use href="#mastering-SVG" fill="red" mask="url(#highlight-
mask)"></use>
</svg>
```

Running it in a browser produces the following output. As you can see, the areas of yellow and the areas of red that are visible in the two text elements blend together. There are areas of fully opaque color in the center and edges blended with areas of semi-transparent color, where the background pattern shows through, in between:

This section just touches on the possibilities of masking and clipping. You'll continue to see examples of these powerful techniques throughout this rest of the book.

Importing images into SVG

In addition to creating images wholesale in SVG, it's also possible to pull other images into an SVG document.

There are a couple of ways to do this. One way is to use the SVG image element and import the image in a way that will be familiar to you if you've used the HTML img element. In this example, we use the image element. It takes a href attribute, which acts like an img src (as seen in HTML) and it has height and width attributes. Unlike the HTML img element, it also accepts an x and y position:

> In the context of an HTML document, the HTML spec actually defines IMAGE as a synonym of img. It only exists in the context of inline SVG.

```
<svg xmlns="http://www.w3.org/2000/svg" width="1000" height="485"
viewBox="0 0 1000 485" version="1.1">
    <image href="take-2-central-2017.jpg" width="1000" height="485"
     x="0" y="0" ></image>
    <text x="300" y="400" fill="white" font-family="verdana, helvetica"
     font-size="36" text-anchor="left">
        REACT @ Central Square 2017
    </text>
</svg>
```

Rendered in the browser, we get the full photographic image with an SVG text element serving as a caption:

You can also use the image element to import in other SVG images. There are certain restrictions with that technique that limit the usefulness of the imported SVG element. They are basically treated like static images so things such as further importing images won't work; you can't import other images inside the imported SVG image. Only the *first* referenced image will be imported. To use the full power of an imported SVG image, you should use the use element and point to an external URL. With this technique, you can also target specific fragments of the imported document. This technique would allow you to create a symbol library and import the symbols into your SVG document by reference.

In this simple example, we show how using the use element and referencing a fragment of an included document imports the image properly. #image points to the id element of a specific element in the imported file, svg-with-import.svg:

```
<svg xmlns="http://www.w3.org/2000/svg" width="1000" height="970"
viewBox="0 0 1000 970" version="1.1">
<image href="svg-with-import.svg" width="1000" height="485" x="0"
y="0"></image>
<use xlink:href="svg-with-import.svg#image" width="1000" height="485" x="0"
y="485"></use>
</svg>
```

The blank space at the top of this document shows where the image is failing to load:

To get this example to work in Versions of Internet Explorer less than 8, you need to use a polyfill script called svg4everybody (`https://github.com/jonathantneal/svg4everybody`). Insert it into your document, call it when you need to use some SVG, and it just works. svg4everybody also polyfills the experience in Safari 6 and Edge 12. How to fix your page is shown in the following code sample. You include the file and then call the svg4everybody() script:

```
<script src="svg4everybody.min.js"></script>
<script>svg4everybody();</script>
```

Filters

Filters allow you to apply a variety of effects to elements or groups of elements. Filters allow you to blur images, apply lighting effects, and many other advanced image manipulation techniques. If you've ever used Adobe Photoshop or other graphics manipulation programs, these filters are just like the filters you've seen in that environment.

Filters are implemented in the defs section of the SVG document and are grouped as part of a filter element. They are referenced the same way that mask and clipPath elements are, via a fragment URL. The following example shows the common Gaussian blur filter applied to a circle:

```
<svg
xmlns="http://www.w3.org/2000/svg" width="300" height="150" viewBox="0 0
300 150">
    <filter id="blurIsm">
        <feGaussianBlur in="SourceGraphic" stdDeviation="5"/>
    </filter>
    <circle cx="75" cy="75" r="50" fill="red"/>
    <circle cx="200" cy="75" r="50" fill="red" filter="url(#blurIsm)"/>
</svg>
```

Rendered in a browser, you can see the blurred circle on the right:

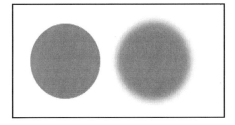

I'm not going to go through filters in detail in this book. There are a lot of them out there; there are varying (sometimes confusing) levels of browser support and they can be very complicated to explain. I did want to show you one so that you can see the basic pattern and this one is as straightforward as they come. *All* of the other filters follow the same general pattern. A `filter` or series of filters are grouped in the `defs` section and referenced with an `id` element. Just know that simple pattern and you're ready to experiment with them or to incorporate them into your projects.

Serving SVG on the web

One final note about SVG before we move into more details in the following chapters about the way that SVG interacts with the wider universe of web technology: if you're going to serve SVG on the web, you need to ensure that it's served with the correct content type. Browsers expect SVG to be served with the `"image/svg+xml"` media type. If you run into problems with SVG images not displaying and you can verify that they exist on the server, it's a good bet to check the headers (using the **Network** tab of your browser debugger of choice) to see if they're being served correctly. If they're not (for example, if they're `text/xml`), then you need to set the media type properly. This section outlines how to set the proper media type in common web servers.

Apache

Adding the correct media type in Apache is as simple as adding the following line to your `.htaccess` file:

```
AddType image/svg+xml svg svgz
```

nginx

Adding the correct media type in nginx requires you to have the following entry in your `mime.types` file:

```
types {
    image/svg+xml svg svgz;
}
```

IIS

Adding the correct media type in IIS can happen in two ways. You can add the media type using the IIS manager (`https://docs.microsoft.com/en-us/previous-versions/windows/it-pro/windows-server-2008-R2-and-2008/cc753281(v=ws.10)`) or you can add the following entries to `web.config`:

```
<configuration>
    <system.webServer>
        <staticContent>
            <remove fileExtension=".svg"/>
            <mimeMap fileExtension=".svg" mimeType="image/svg+xml"/>
            <remove fileExtension=".svgz"/>
            <mimeMap fileExtension=".svgz" mimeType="image/svg+xml"/>
        </staticContent>
    </system.webServer>
</configuration>
```

Summary

In this chapter, you learned about a large number of more advanced SVG features. You learned about multiple transformations, which allow you to manipulate SVG elements without changing their underlying structure. This opens up a number of possibilities that we'll continue to examine throughout this book.

You also learned about clipping and masking, which allow you to manipulate images by subtracting portions of them using complicated drawings. This includes the ability to use variable opacity to manipulate images.

Additionally, you learned about implementing a basic SVG filter and about serving SVG files on the web in common web servers.

In Chapter 4, *Using SVG in HTML*, you'll learn some details about using SVG within the context of an HTML document, which is where the real power of SVG is exposed for the entire world to see.

Using SVG in HTML 4

So far in this book, you've been exposed to the fundamental building blocks of SVG: the features and functionality that are defined in the SVG specification itself. While SVG can, and does, live on its own, it really shines when it's unleashed on the modern web. The web now is a multiple-device, multiple form-factor, and multiple connection speed environment, and SVG helps to solve many thorny problems facing the modern web developer. To that end, the next few chapters will focus on integrating SVG with other core technologies: HTML, CSS, and JavaScript. This chapter is very much straightforward and focuses on working with SVG inside the context of an HTML document. Everything on the web starts with HTML, so making sure your SVG is happy inside your HTML is the way to go.

You have already learned about the basics of inserting SVG into your HTML documents as images or inline SVG elements in `Chapter 1`, *Introducing Scalable Vector Graphics*. This chapter adds some details on top of that foundation.

In this chapter, you'll learn about the following:

- SVG and accessibility
- The benefits of using SVG images for responsive web design and as part of a responsive images solution
- Details about working with inline SVG in the context of an HTML document

So, let's get started!

SVG, HTML, and accessibility

Accessibility on the web strives to ensure that people with disabilities can access sites and applications. The general goal is to provide content that is served and structured in such a way that users with disabilities can access it directly or, if direct access isn't possible because of their disability (for example, audio content is needed for a hearing-impaired user), to provide properly structured alternative content that conveys the same information. This structured alternative content can then be accessed through **Assistive Technology (AT)**. The most common example of AT is the *screen reader.*

Screen readers exist for all platforms. Some free applications you can test with include the following:

- NVDA (Windows)
- Apple VoiceOver (OS X)
- Orca (Linux)

In the case of SVG, a visual format, the focus is on providing, *when it's appropriate*, textual content that describes the image.

As you're hopefully aware, HTML itself has tools and best practices for accessibility. In addition to those in HTML, there is also a set of technologies called **Accessible Rich Internet Applications (ARIA)**, which defines ways to make the web and web applications more accessible to people with disabilities. ARIA provides a set of special accessibility attributes that, when added to HTML, provide accessibility information about the page or application. For example, the `role` attribute defines the *type* of object the element is (article, menu, or image).

As you saw in `Chapter 1`, *Introducing Scalable Vector Graphics*, there are two common ways to get your SVG into your HTML document: as the `src` of an image and as an inline SVG element (or elements). This section will add some notes about working with SVG, HTML, and ARIA attributes to ensure that your content is still accessible using both techniques.

SVG as an image src

The easiest way to get SVG into a document is as the `src` of an `img` element. Doing so, as we saw in `Chapter 1`, *Introducing Scalable Vector Graphics*, is as simple as referencing the `*.svg` element the same way you would reference any image as the `src` attribute on an `img` element.

As for accessibility, if you follow best practices with regards to accessibility and images, you can continue to do the same with SVG images. The `alt` attribute should be there and, if it's needed for AT, it should properly describe the content (`https://webaim.org/techniques/alttext/`). You might wonder why you would have to do this, especially with an SVG image that already has descriptive text as part of its source. Note that any textual content in the SVG file is, in effect, locked away from a screen reader, so even if you're using SVG, a descriptive, markup-based image format, it behaves, in this case at least, just like a common bitmapped file format.

Other than the alternative text, there's just one wrinkle with older versions of Safari (older than Safari Desktop 9.1.1 or version 9.3.2 on iOS) that you should take into account. In those older versions, the `alt` text won't be being read by VoiceOver, the Apple screen reader, unless the `role="img"` ARIA role was set on the `img` element:

```
<img src="apple.svg" width="300" height="300" alt="an apple"
role="img">
```

Inline SVG

Inline SVG offers a broader palette for accessibility. For example, unlike the SVG as an `img` `src` scenario, that we just discussed, if there are one or more `<text>` elements in your SVG, then that text is available to be read directly by a screen reader. If the text is properly descriptive of the image, then you have already provided an accessible image. You don't need to do anything else.

If the text in your SVG is not descriptive of the image or if your image has no text, then you can take advantage of two SVG elements, `title`, and `desc`, to provide accessible text. These elements, coupled with the `aria-labelledby` attribute, provide a two-leveled approach to accessibility. The following code example shows the basics of how this works. The image itself is an illustration of an apple. Rendered in a browser, it looks like this:

The markup is as follows.

The SVG element itself has two important attributes. It has a `role` of `img`, which indicates that the element is identified as a graphic. It also leverages the `aria-labelledby` attribute, which references two separate IDs, `"apple-title"` and `"apple-desc"`. The `aria-labelledby` attribute creates a relationship between the element it's a property of and other elements that label it.

We meet the first of those two elements as the first child of the SVG element, the `title` element. The `title` element is available for SVG elements to provide a textual description of the element. It is not rendered directly by the browser, but should be read by a screen reader and can be rendered in a tooltip, much like how text in an `alt` attribute shows up in some browsers. It has an `id` of `"apple-title"`. Following that is the optional `desc` element. `desc` allows you to provide a longer text description of the image. It has an `id` of `"apple-desc"`. It too can be read by a screen reader and doesn't get rendered directly into the browser.

The final piece of interesting markup is `role="presentation"`, which is applied to each of the child `path` elements. Doing that pulls those elements out of the accessibility tree (https://www.w3.org/TR/svg-aam-1.0/#exclude_elements) so, from an accessibility perspective, the SVG element is treated as one graphic:

```
<!doctype html>
<html lang="en">
<head>
 <meta charset="utf-8">
 <title>Mastering SVG- Accessible Inline SVG </title>
</head>
<body>
 <svg xmlns="http://www.w3.org/2000/svg" width="300" height="300"
  viewBox="0 0 300 300" version="1.1" role="img" aria-
  labelledby="apple-title apple-desc">
 <title id="apple-title">An Apple</title>
 <desc id="apple-desc">An apple, the sweet, pomaceous fruit, of the
  apple tree.</desc>
 <path role="presentation" style="fill:#784421;stroke:none;stroke-
  width:0.26458332px;stroke-linecap:butt;stroke-linejoin:miter;stroke-
  opacity:1"
  d="m 105.75769,18.053573 c 0,0 46.1131,23.434525 34.01786,50.64881
  -12.09524,27.214284 15.875,-6.803573 15.875,-6.803573 0,0
   9.07143,-23.434524 -1.5119,-38.55357 -10.58334,-15.1190474
  -48.38096,-5.291667 -48.38096,-5.291667 z"
 />
 <path role="presentation" style="fill:#ff0000;stroke:none;stroke-
  width:0.26458332px;stroke-linecap:butt;stroke-linejoin:miter;stroke-
```

```
    opacity:1"
  d="m 146.65476,61.898812 c 0,0 -139.0952362,-66.5238097
-127.755951,73.327378 11.339285,139.85118 92.218641,132.57921
  123.220231,124.73214 23.47822,-5.94277 108.10119,52.16071
  127.00001,-111.125 C 286.06755,2.3982366 146.65476,61.898812
  146.65476,61.898812 Z"
/>

<path role="presentation" style="fill:#ffffff;stroke:none;stroke-
  width:0.26458332px;stroke-linecap:butt;stroke-linejoin:miter;stroke-
  opacity:1"
  d="m 183.69643,64.92262 c 0,0 50.21311,5.546816 41.57738,74.83928
  -2.32319,18.64109 31.75,-34.7738 21.92261,-54.428565 C
  237.36905,65.678572 219.22619,55.851191 183.69643,64.92262 Z"
/>
</svg>
</body>
</html>
```

This section describes accessibility with static SVG images. There are additional accessibility techniques possible with dynamic SVG, including other ARIA attributes, such as ARIA-live regions (https://developer.mozilla.org/en-US/docs/Web/Accessibility/ARIA/ARIA_Live_Regions). Where applicable, you'll learn about those in the following chapters. That said, getting the basics right for static SVG is a great start and learning to test your SVG with a screen reader will put you on the right path.

SVG and responsive web design

Responsive web design (**RWD**) is a technique for developing sites and applications that leverage fluid layout grids and CSS3 media queries (https://www.w3.org/TR/css3-mediaqueries/) to create layouts that can adapt and respond to the characteristics of the device or user agent, stretching and shrinking to present layouts that work on a variety of screen sizes without prior knowledge of the device characteristics.

When RWD started to take off, one of the issues that quickly bubbled up to the surface as a pain point was the difficulty of serving correctly sized images (for both file weight and dimensions), depending on any of the multitudes of variables that would impact the end user's experience. Screen resolution, pixel depth, and available bandwidth all combine to make the question of what size image to serve to a user a complex one.

What followed was a years-long quest for a markup pattern that would create responsive content images. *Content images* are images served with an `img` tag that are meant to be presented as content. This is compared to images used solely for design, which can and should already be handled with CSS. With media queries strongly supported, CSS already provides a number of tools to present the correct image depending on a number of factors.

Some of the requirements for responsive images were as follows:

- **Smallest possible file size**: This is really the core issue. It just manifests itself in many ways. In a perfect world, we would only ever send the smallest possible number of bytes needed to render the image at an acceptable quality level.

- **Take advantage of the browser preloader**: All modern web browsers use a technique where the browser skips ahead, while simultaneously reading through the document and building out the DOM, and reads through the document, looking for additional assets that it can go ahead and start to download.

- **Serve correctly sized images to multiple resolutions**: If you're serving a big image to a `2048` pixel monitor, then you want it to be a big image of `1600` pixels or more. A big image on a tablet or phone, on the other hand, might only need to be `320` or `480` pixels wide. Sending the correct amount of data, in this case, can significantly improve performance.

- **Serve the correct image for multiple pixel-ratio devices**: To produce clean images on devices with a high device pixel ratio, you need to send down proportionally larger files that are displayed for a given set of CSS pixels. Images that are crisp on a standard desktop display would show artifacts on a high pixel density display. Obviously, you can just send higher resolution images to all browsers, but those pixels come at a bandwidth price, so it's much better to just send the correct images to the correct devices.

- **Choose different sizes of images or entirely different images at different breakpoints**: There is a desire to be able to show different images for different orientations and screen resolutions. On a large screen, in an article describing flora in Tuscon, Arizona, you might use a wide image that shows a variety of the hardy plant life you can find there. On a small screen in portrait orientation, where the impact of the variety would be lost as it would display only an inch high with little detail, an image of a Saguaro cactus with a strongly vertical aspect ratio might be a better choice.

- **Use design breakpoints**: There has been plenty of development based around the concept of media query breakpoints. They're one of the primary technologies at the heart of RWD. Images need to be controlled alongside all the other design changes that occur in a responsive site.

The multiple solutions (the `picture` element and the `srcset` and `sizes` attributes) that came out of that quest are incredibly powerful. It took a while (a couple of years and lots of internet angst) but eventually, everything we needed to serve the *correct* image with the *correct* file size and the *correct* dimensions was available for us in browsers.

It's not *easy*. It's a complicated problem, as it has got a complicated solution. The coding is complicated and it is complicated to understand and it requires multiple versions generated of every image you want to present on the web.

Let's see how the new solutions work and then we'll see how SVG (where it's available to you because of image requirements) can make it a lot less complicated.

The srcset attribute

The `srcset` attribute is a new attribute added to the `img` element. You can use it alongside the new `picture` element, and we will do so in a little bit. For now, let's look at it by itself. Like I said, this stuff is complicated, so it's worth taking the time to build up slowly.

Like the standard `src` attribute, the `srcset` attribute tells the browser where to get the file to use for the contents of the `img` element. Unlike the single image that is referenced by `src`, however, the `srcset` attribute presents a comma delineated list of URLs. The `srcset` attribute also provides *hints* regarding the image size or pixel density.

Let's look at an example to understand how those hints work.

The `srcset` attribute in the following sample hints about the device pixel ratio. In this case, there are two options. The first option is `more-colors-small.jpg`, which is `600*350` (600 by 350) pixels wide and is meant to display at a standard resolution. The second image, `more-colors-large.jpg`, is `1200*700` pixels and is meant for higher resolution displays. It will still display at `600*350` *CSS* pixels but it's got enough additional image information to look clean in higher pixel density displays as well.

The `src` attribute acts as a fallback for browsers that don't support `srcset`:

```
<!DOCTYPE html>
  <html lang="en">
    <head>
      <meta charset="utf-8">
    </head>
    <body>
      <img
        srcset="more-colors-small.jpg 1x,
                more-colors-large.jpg 2x"
```

```
        src="more-colors-small.jpg"
        alt="Many colors!"
        width="600" height="350">
    </body>
</html>
```

This is the solution for the device pixel ratio use case.

With `src` as a fallback for every browser that supports images and an `alt` attribute for those that don't, this is a good, backward-compatible solution.

The srcset and sizes attributes

To solve more complicated use cases, the `srcset` attribute can work in tandem with the new `sizes` attribute to use media queries to serve separate image sources, displayed with different relative dimensions based on the browser window. The code sample illustrates how this works.

In this example, the element starts with an `src` attribute for non-supporting browsers. In this case, I've chosen a smallish image to ensure that it loads speedily, no matter what device or browser. Following that there's the new `sizes` attribute. `sizes` accepts a media query/image size pair (or list of pairs).

The following diagram breaks down the components. The first part is the media query. This media query should be familiar if you've used them in your CSS. If the query is `true`, then the image size is set to **60vw** (60% of **viewport width** (**vw**)). If the media query fails, the size falls back to the default size of **100vw**:

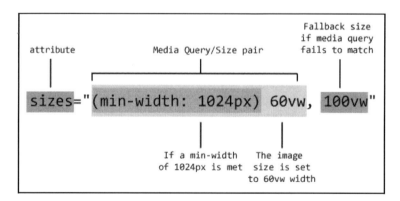

There can be any number of **media query/size pairs**. The first one to match wins and, if none match, then the fallback value is used.

The `srcset` attribute here is more expansive. The list has a series of images between `200` pixels wide and `1600` pixels wide. The second part of the value pair in the source set, instead of indicating the preferred pixel density, hints to the browser the pixel width of the image (200w, 400w, and so on). It's the up to browser to mix and match the best pixel width with the appropriate size at different dimensions and pixel densities:

```
<!doctype html>
<html lang="en">
<head>
  <meta charset="utf-8">
  <title>Mastering SVG - the srcset and sizes attributes </title>
</head>
<body>
    <img src="more-colors-400.jpg"
      alt="Many colors!"
      sizes="(min-width: 1024px) 60vw, 100vw"
      srcset="more-colors-200.jpg 200w,
              more-colors-400.jpg 400w,
              more-colors-600.jpg 600w,
              more-colors-1200.jpg 1200w,
              more-colors-1600.jpg 1600w">
  </body>
</html>
```

 The length part of `size` can be specified in any valid CSS length, which adds to the possibilities and complexity of this attribute. This chapter will stick with `vw` measurements.

The picture element

In its original concept, `picture` was designed as a parallel `img` element, modeled on the syntax of the HTML5 `video` and `audio` elements. The idea was to have a `picture` element wrapping a series of `source` elements, which would represent the options for the image source. It would wrap a default `img` element for non-supporting browsers. A `media` attribute on each source would hint to the browser the correct source to use:

```
<picture alt="original proposal">
 <source src="high-resolution.png" media="min-width:1024px">
 <source src="low-resolution.png">
 <img src="low-resolution.png" alt="fallback image">
 </picture>
```

For a variety of implementation-related reasons, this initial proposal was shot down. `srcset` filled in some of the void, but since it didn't solve all the responsive image use cases, there was always a hole in the specification landscape.

Years passed and *eventually*, after many false starts, `picture` was resurrected and reworked to fill that hole.

Now, however, instead of being a replacement for `img`, `picture` is now an *enhancement* to the `img` element to help browsers sort out the best possible solution for the source of an image.

Let's take a look at an example. While the `srcset` examples worked with different resolution versions of the same image, this `picture` example aims to provide different images for different resolutions. Here, in larger browser windows, an image that is wider than it is tall will be shown:

In browser windows smaller than 1,024 pixels, a square image will be used:

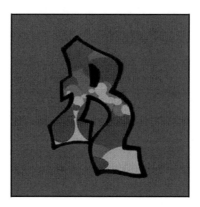

The markup for this is relatively complicated and needs some explaining.

In the `head`, notice the presence of the `picturefill.min.js` file. Picturefill (`https://github.com/scottjehl/picturefill`) is a Polyfill (`https://remysharp.com/2010/10/08/what-is-a-polyfill`) for the `picture` element, which supplies JavaScript driven picture element support to non-supporting browsers.

In the body of the HTML document, the `picture` element wraps the entire solution. It lets the browser know that it should use this `picture` element to sort out the proper source for the child `img` element. We don't get to the `img` element immediately, however. The first child element we encounter is the `source` element.

From a developer perspective, `source` works the way the original proposal intended. If the media query matches, that `source` is used. If it doesn't match, you move onto the next media query in the stack.

Here, you have a media query looking for pages with a minimum width of 1024 pixels. If the media query matches, the `srcset` attribute is used to let the browser choose between three separate source images, ranging from 600 pixels to 1600 pixels wide. Since this image is intended to be displayed at 50vw, that will give good coverage for the majority of displays. Following that, there's the fallback `img` element that also contains a `srcset`. If the browser doesn't support `picture` and `source` or if the previous media queries don't match, you use `srcset` attribute here to get the source for this image. The `sizes` attribute allows you to further adjust the display for the range of sizes smaller than 1024 pixels:

```
<!doctype html>
<html lang="en">
<head>
  <meta charset="utf-8">
  <title>Mastering SVG- picture element </title>
  <script src="picturefill.min.js"></script>
</head>
<body>
    <picture>
     <source
      media="(min-width: 1024px)"
      sizes="50vw"
      srcset="more-colors-600.jpg 600w,
        more-colors-1200.jpg 1200w,
        more-colors-1600.jpg 1600w">
      <img src="more-colors-square-400.jpg"
        alt="Many colors!"
        sizes="(min-width: 768px) 60vw, 100vw"
        srcset="more-colors-square-200.jpg 200w,
         more-colors-square-400.jpg 400w,
```

```
        more-colors-square-600.jpg 800w,
        more-colors-square-800.jpg 1200w">
    </picture>
  </body>
</html>
```

While it's complicated, this `picture` pattern solves the question of both different image sizes and different formats for separate art direction choices. Now that (lengthy) explanation is out of the way, let's take a look at how SVG can solve some of those same problems with a lot less markup. You've already seen in Chapter 1, *Introducing Scalable Vector Graphics*, an example of an SVG image as the `src` of an `img` element scaling up and down at will. In fact, with SVG, responsive images are as simple as the following code:

```
<!doctype html>
<html lang="en">
<head>
  <meta charset="utf-8">
  <title>Mastering SVG- 100% image element </title>
</head>
<body>
    <img src="more-colors.svg" width="100%">
  </body>
</html>
```

It allows you to infinitely scale up and down with no loss of fidelity or extra bytes and there's no `srcset` needed! There are ways to improve that simple solution with CSS, which we'll see in the next chapter, but for now, just know that this pattern will work. From a 3,000+ pixel behemoth monitor to a tiny feature phone (assuming it supports SVG), the preceding markup will scale nicely.

What about the art direction use case? That's also much simpler with SVG. Because we don't have to provide multiple versions of the image (every SVG image can scale as much as needed), the markup for the art direction use case is as follows.

We have the same `picture` element we saw before. There's one child `source` element that has a media query pointing to browsers larger than `1024` pixels. If that's `true`, then the landscape image will be used. Then, there's a child `img` element with a `srcset` pointing to a square image and `width` of 100%. If the media query on the first `source` element fails, we get to this image.

It's not as simple as a plain old `img` but it's a lot simpler than the version with multiple bitmapped images in each `srcset`. Output two images and you're ready to go with even the most complicated case, art direction, and scaling across multiple screen resolutions:

```
<!doctype html>
<html lang="en">
<head>
  <meta charset="utf-8">
  <title>Mastering SVG- picture element with SVG </title>
  <script src="picturefill.min.js"></script>
</head>
<body>
  <picture>
    <source
      media="(min-width: 1024px)"
      srcset="more-colors.svg">
    <img
      src="more-colors-square.svg"
      srcset="more-colors-square.svg"
      width="100%">
  </picture>
  </body>
</html>
```

While SVG isn't available for every use case, it's by far the most flexible image format for RWD. From the simple `width="100%"` technique for scaling images based on one image source to the simpler implementation of the art direction use case utilizing the `picture` element, SVG offers enormous benefits in these multiple resolutions, multiple device world.

Additional details on inline SVG in an HTML document

As you've already learned, using inline SVG is just about as straightforward as HTML markup and is often going to be the best (or only, in the case of interactive SVG) option for you to embed SVG into your documents. That said, as with anything on the web, there are always some edge cases, notes, and gotchas that you need to keep in mind when working with inline SVG. This section outlines two such concerns. The first is about trying to leverage the browser's cache and the other is to be aware of the potentially large increase in DOM complexity when working with SVG.

Caching

Unlike an SVG image linked to as the `src` of an `img` element or referenced with CSS, inline SVG can't be cached and referenced on another page or different view of a single-page application. While there remains a performance benefit to minimizing the number of HTTP requests (which inline SVG does by dropping the need for a request to a separate SVG document), that's not always the most optimal pattern. If you're using the same SVG image multiple times across multiple pages, or multiple site visits, there's going to be a benefit in having a file that can be cached and read again later. This is especially true of larger, more complicated SVG images, which can have a large download footprint.

If you really need to use inline SVG (all interactive examples, for example), you can still try to leverage the browser cache in different ways by linking to external library SVG elements using the `use` element. You might be adding some HTTP requests up front, but you won't have to continually download and parse the inline markup defining those reusable components.

And really, thinking about reusable components is a good way to think about structuring any aspect of your project so that's a benefit above and beyond leveraging the browser's cache.

Complexity

While I've actually tried to limit the complexity of the SVG code samples you've seen so far in this book, you have already seen some very *busy* examples of SVG. In fact, when working with anything more complicated than a handful of `rect`, `circle`, or `text` elements, the size and/or readability of SVG code can go downhill very quickly. This is especially true of generated code where it's not really meant for human consumption.

This complexity can be a problem in two separate ways: a more complicated authoring environment and a slowdown in the rendering and performance of your page.

Authoring

SVG documents can grow quite large, even for simple images. Depending on the number of effects and the number of elements, the markup used to draw an SVG image could quickly overwhelm everything else on the page. For that reason, it's worth keeping large SVG elements as separate document fragments and pulling them into your documents as needed. Depending on how they're being used, this might be with the `use` element inside a containing SVG document or might be a case of importing a document fragment using your page composition tool of choice. There are a large number of server-side and/or client-side solutions for bringing together pieces of markup and text together (for example, JavaScript template solutions, CMSs, blog platforms, and server-side scripting languages, such as PHP), so I'm not going to create an example of potentially limited use. I'll trust you'll leverage the one closest to your heart.

You'd still have to deal with it when inspecting the page, but it's much nicer than having 500 lines of markup in a 700-line file being taken up by an SVG illustration showing a supply chain diagram or something similar.

The Document Object Model

In addition to problems with authoring, you can also run into browser performance problems with very complicated SVG. This is true whichever way you're importing them, since even SVG imported as an `img src` is more than just a collection of pixels, but this can become more acute if you're already doing a lot of interaction with the DOM. In general, the number of elements in your document directly affects the speed and responsiveness of the page (`https://developers.google.com/web/fundamentals/performance/rendering/avoid-large-complex-layouts-and-layout-thrashing`). When you have many hundreds or many thousands of potentially interactive SVG elements on the page, each of which has to be calculated (some with very complicated calculations under the hood) and rendered by the browser, things can slow down very quickly indeed.

Most of the time, you're not going to run into performance problems of this sort. At least I hope you are not. It *is* possible, however, so keep the possibility filed away and hopefully, you'll never have to use the knowledge.

Summary

In this chapter, you learned about working with SVG in the context of an HTML document. First, you learned about SVG accessibility with both inline SVG elements and SVG images as the `src` of an `img` element. This includes details on the `alt` attribute for `img` elements and details of the `title` and `desc` elements in inline SVG.

Following that you learned about the solutions for responsive images and how using SVG can greatly simplify the implementation of even the most complicated responsive image use case. Finally, you learned some other aspects of inline SVG to pay attention to when implementing these solutions in the real world.

Next up, we'll look at the important intersection of CSS and SVG. The next chapter will build on everything we've learned and will introduce some powerful new tools for you to add to your SVG toolbox.

Working with SVG and CSS

5

This chapter will focus on the intersection between SVG and CSS. While JavaScript is the most powerful tool for working with SVG, SVG without CSS wouldn't be nearly as popular as it has become. SVG, as you've learned, is well-suited for the modern web and is often the best answer to an RWD question. Because of that, it's been wholeheartedly embraced by designers and developers for producing images for the web.

This preference for SVG is a good one for the web as a whole and should be cultivated. This chapter will hopefully illustrate why.

In this chapter, we'll learn about the following:

- Using CSS background images
- How to optimize data URIs for SVG
- SVG sprites versus icon fonts
- How the different ways of embedding SVG interact with CSS
- Using common CSS properties to manipulate SVG
- Using SVG-specific CSS properties to manipulate SVG
- Basic CSS animations and transitions with SVG

CSS background images

You've already seen examples of using CSS for background images all the way back in Chapter 1, *Introducing Scalable Vector Graphics*. This section will add some more details to using SVG in this way.

In this initial, basic example, we add an SVG image of a stylized letter **R** as the background image of a div. One important aspect is setting the background-size property. The natural size of the SVG image is 458 by 392. In this case it's set to be half that size in order to fit into the size of the div:

```
<!doctype html>
<html lang="en">
    <head>
        <meta charset="utf-8">
        <title>Mastering SVG- CSS Background Images</title>
        <style type="text/css">
          .logo{
            width: 229px;
            height: 196px;
            background: url(icon.svg);
            background-repeat: no-repeat;
            background-size: 229px 196px;
          }
        </style>
    </head>
    <body>
        <div class="logo">
        </div>
    </body>
</html>
```

Rendered in the browser, we get the following:

Other than providing for high pixel density displays (which *is* a great feature), this doesn't get you much beyond what a PNG provides.

In an environment where relative units are being used, you can leverage SVG's ability to scale with `contain` or `cover` as the value of `background-size` to really take advantage of SVG. In the following example, the same previous logo is applied as a background image, alongside some text. All of the metrics are relative, using the root em (rem) unit. The background image is set with a `background-size` value of `contain`. `contain` ensures that the logo will be shown, *in its entirety*, constrained by the height and width of the containing element. Since we're using an SVG image as the background image, the base font for the document (and therefore the calculation of the *root em*) could scale from 16 pixels (the browser default) to 1,600 pixels and the SVG background would be able to scale to match:

```
<!doctype html>
<html lang="en">
    <head>
        <meta charset="utf-8">
        <title>Mastering SVG- Relative Background Images </title>
        <link href="https://fonts.googleapis.com/css?
         family=Raleway:600" rel="stylesheet">
        <style type="text/css">
          .logo{
            width: 14.3rem;
            height: 14.3rem;
            background: url(icon.svg);
            background-repeat: no-repeat;
            background-size: contain;
            background-position-y: 2.5rem;
          }
          h1 {
            font-family: Raleway, sans-serif;
            font-size: 2rem;
          }
        </style>
    </head>
    <body>
      <div class="logo">
      <h1>Rob Larsen</h1>
    </div>
    </body>
</html>
```

Rendered in the browser, we get the following:

There's not much here that's new, but it's such an important use for SVG on the modern web it's worth taking some time to reinforce the pattern.

Data URLs for SVG background images

If you're performance-minded, you might be wondering about the technique of embedding a background image directly in your CSS via a data: URL. Data URLs allow you to embed files directly into a document via a special `data:` URL. This technique allows you to save an HTTP request.

When working with binary formats such as JPGs or PNGs, the image data needs to be `base64`-encoded. While this will work with SVG images, it's actually faster (`https://css-tricks.com/probably-dont-base64-svg/`) to embed the SVG images as an SVG source. This works because, in addition to `base64`-encoded data, you can directly embed text. SVG is, of course, a text format. You just need to do a couple of things to the SVG to make it work properly. You should read the full article by Taylor Hunt for the details (`https://codepen.io/tigt/post/optimizing-svgs-in-data-uris`) but the basic steps are:

- Use single quotes for attribute values
- URL-encode any non-safe characters (<, >, #, and so on)
- Double quote the data URL

Converting the initial example, we get code that looks as follows:

```
<!doctype html>
<html lang="en">
    <head>
        <meta charset="utf-8">
        <title>Mastering SVG- CSS Background Images with Data
```

```
       URLs</title>
       <style type="text/css">
         .logo{
           width: 229px;
           height: 196px;
           background: url("data:image/svg+xml,%3Csvg
xmlns='http://www.w3.org/2000/svg' height='392' width='458'%3E%3Cg
stroke='%23000' stroke-width='14.17'%3E%3Cpath d='M96.42 60.2s14 141.5-58
2891145.5-18.4 55.4-276.7z' fill='%23000012'/%3E%3Cpath d='M145.42
1881108.5 171.6 189.2 24.4-123.4-196z' fill='%23000012'/%3E%3Cpath
d='M70.12 43.7s14 141.5-58 2891145.5-18.4 55.4-276.7z'
fill='%23e9c21b'/%3E%3Cpath d='M59.02 23.61116.2 237.2c-.1 0
411.3-239.1-116.2-237.2z' fill='%23000012'/%3E%3Cpath d='M119.12
171.61108.5 171.6 189.2 24.4-123.4-196z' fill='%233fc4eb'/%3E%3Cpath
d='M32.62 7.11116.2 237.2S560.22 5.2 32.62 7.1z'
fill='%2359ea39'/%3E%3C/g%3E%3C/svg%3E");
           background-repeat: no-repeat;
           background-size: 229px 196px;
         }
       </style>
     </head>
     <body>
       <div class="logo">
       </div>
     </body>
   </html>
```

While this is actually pretty straightforward to prep by hand (the example here was hand-coded), there are some tools available that can do this for you if you're looking to squeeze out all the bytes. There's a node module (https://www.npmjs.com/package/mini-svg-data-uri) and a SASS function (https://codepen.io/jakob-e/) that can help you build this capability into your workflow.

SVG sprites and icon sets

This section isn't strictly about CSS, but does discuss a replacement for a common CSS-driven solution for adding icons to applications so this seems such as the best place to discuss it.

If you're reading this book you're probably somewhat familiar with the idea of icon fonts such as GLYPHICONS (http://glyphicons.com/) or Font Awesome (https://fontawesome.com/icons?from=io). If you're not, they are fonts that, instead of representing characters that can be read as language (as in, the characters that you're reading right now), they present different images that can be used as icons for a site or application.

For example, you could create an interface for a video player using *Font Awesome* without having to design a single element.

The following code sample shows what that implementation might look such as. In addition to Font Awesome, the following example uses Bootstrap styles.

The basic pattern for Font Awesome is to include the icons as an empty element. In this case an i. Each one has two common classes: `fa` and `fa-2x`. These indicate that the element is a Font Awesome icon and that it should render at `2x` the normal size. After that, the individual icons are added with `fa-`classes that indicate the type of icon to be used:

```
<!doctype html>
<html lang="en">
    <head>
        <meta charset="utf-8">
        <title>Mastering SVG- Font Awesome</title>
        <link rel="stylesheet"
href="https://maxcdn.bootstrapcdn.com/bootstrap/4.0.0/css/bootstrap.min.css
" integrity="sha384-
Gn5384xqQ1aoWXA+058RXPxPg6fy4IWvTNh0E263XmFcJlSAwiGgFAW/dAiS6JXm"
crossorigin="anonymous">
        <link href="font-awesome.min.css" rel="stylesheet" />
    </head>
    <body>
        <div style="text-align: center">
            <button class="btn btn-link"><i class="fa fa-2x fa-backward
              "></i></button>
            <button class="btn btn-link"><i class="fa fa-2x fa-fast-
              backward"></i></button>
            <button class="btn btn-link"><i class="fa fa-2x fa-play">
              </i></button>
            <button class="btn btn-link"><i class="fa fa-2x fa-fast-
              forward"></i></button>
            <button class="btn btn-link"><i class="fa fa-2x fa-
              forward"></i></button>
        </div>
    </body>
</html>
```

Rendered in the browser, it looks as follows:

That's all very clean and easy to understand. Because of that, these icon fonts are very popular. I've used them in multiple environments and I am impressed with their general ease of use and the ability they offer to get up and running very quickly.

That said, there are downsides to using icon fonts. Two prominent downsides are:

- Accessibility: There are ways to do icon fonts well with regard to accessibility (`https://www.filamentgroup.com/lab/bulletproof_icon_fonts.html`), but out of the box, you're inserting gibberish characters into an empty element. Screen readers can read that nonsense, creating a confusing experience for users who rely on **Assistive Technology** (**AT**) to browse the web.
- Semantics: Empty elements are *empty.* Icon fonts using `i` or `span` don't really hold any meaning.

There are other issues including the finicky nature of loading web fonts in general and problems for dyslexic users (`https://cloudfour.com/thinks/seriously-dont-use-icon-fonts/`).

The good news is, if you're interested in better semantics, better accessibility and more straightforward implementation, there's an SVG alternative to icon fonts: using *SVG sprites*. To be fair, SVG sprites aren't a perfect solution either as the most elegant variation on them requires an IE/Edge-shaped workaround,. But for certain configurations (specifically single-page apps) SVG sprites are a great choice for icon delivery.

Let's take a look at how it works.

For this example, we're going to use Front Awesome v5 which provides SVG Versions of all of their icons to replicate the previous set of controls.

Here's how the same controls are implemented using SVG sprites.

First, let's look at a detail of the sprite file itself. In it, all of the icons are defined as a `symbol` element that corresponds to the same name referenced via the class name for the CSS icon. Each `symbol` element includes the accessible `title` element.

Each of the icons in the set is represented in the file `fa-solid.svg`:

```
<symbol id="play" viewBox="0 0 448 512">
  <title id="play-title">play</title>
  <path d="M424.4 214.7L72.4 6.6C43.8-10.3 0 6.1 0 47.9V464c0 37.5
   40.7 60.1 72.4 41.31352-208c31.4-18.5 31.5-64.1 0-82.6z"></path>
</symbol>
```

In the HTML file, things are slightly different, but all in all the pattern is much the same. We still link to Bootstrap for convenience. We no longer link to anything from Font Awesome in the head. We just have a small block of CSS to size the icons on our page. In a real-world example, you might do a bit more to style these, but for now this is enough to make it functional.

In the body of the document, we have a new pattern. Instead of the `button.btn > i.fa` pattern, we have `button.btn > svg > use`, with the use pointing to a specific symbol in the `fa-solid.svg` file.

Other than that, we have an Internet Explorer shaped wrinkle. Internet Explorer won't allow you to `use` an element from an external document. The script *svg4everybody* polyfills that shortcoming and allows you to link to external SVG in IE:

```
<html lang="en">
<head>
  <meta charset="utf-8">
  <title>Mastering SVG- Font Awesome</title>
  <link rel="stylesheet"
    href="https://maxcdn.bootstrapcdn.com/bootstrap/4.0.0-
    beta.3/css/bootstrap.min.css" integrity="sha384-
    Zug+QiDoJOrZ5t4lssLdxGhVrurbmBWopoEl+M6BdEfwnCJZtKxi1KgxUyJq13dy"
    crossorigin="anonymous">
  <style>
    .btn svg{
      height: 2em;
      width: 2em;
      fill: #007bff;
    }
  </style>
</head>
<body>
  <div>
    <button aria-label="rewind" class="btn btn-link">
      <svg xmlns="http://www.w3.org/2000/svg" role="img">
        <use xlink:href="fa-solid.svg#backward"></use>
      </svg>
    </button>
    <button aria-label="skip to previous track" class="btn btn-link">
      <svg xmlns="http://www.w3.org/2000/svg" role="img">
        <use xlink:href="fa-solid.svg#fast-backward"></use>
      </svg>
    </button>
    <button aria-label="play" class="btn btn-link">
      <svg xmlns="http://www.w3.org/2000/svg" role="img">
        <use xlink:href="fa-solid.svg#play"></use>
```

```
      </svg>
    </button>
    <button aria-label="skip to next track" class="btn btn-link">
      <svg xmlns="http://www.w3.org/2000/svg" role="img">
        <use xlink:href="fa-solid.svg#fast-forward"></use>
      </svg>
    </button>
    <button aria-label="fast forward" class="btn btn-link">
      <svg xmlns="http://www.w3.org/2000/svg" role="img">
        <use xlink:href="fa-solid.svg#forward"></use>
      </svg>
    </button>
  </div>
  <script src="svg4everybody.min.js"></script>
  <script>svg4everybody();</script>
</body>

</html>
```

I mentioned how single-page apps can be treated differently. If you're working on a single-page application and want to use SVG icons, you can *inline* the symbols in your page and use them without any polyfill script in all modern browsers. With single-page apps you might be inlining things such as CSS already to save on HTTP requests, so adding a section of SVG inline in your document can be part of the same process.

I'm not going to detail how this might work from a build or page creation perspective, since there are many ways to do this (either as part of a build process or through a server-side templating system), but the output might look something such as the following code sample.

The biggest difference is the definition of the symbols in the inline svg element at the top of the body. This adds complexity to the page, but saves on HTTP requests. So if you're building a single-page app and don't need to rely on caching a separate sprite file, this is going to be slightly faster.

Other than that, the references are directly to a document fragment of the same page, as opposed to linking to a separate file. This means we don't need svg4everybody and Internet Explorer is happy to support use:

```
<!doctype html>
<html lang="en">

<head>
  <meta charset="utf-8">
  <title>Mastering SVG- Font Awesome</title>
  <link rel="stylesheet"
```

```
    href="https://maxcdn.bootstrapcdn.com/bootstrap/4.0.0-
    beta.3/css/bootstrap.min.css" integrity="sha384-
    Zug+QiDoJOrZ5t4lssLdxGhVrurbmBWopoE1+M6BdEfwnCJZtKxi1KgxUyJq13dy"
    crossorigin="anonymous">
  <style>
    .btn svg {
      height: 2em;
      width: 2em;
      fill: #007bff;
    }
  </style>
</head>

<body>
  <svg xmlns="http://www.w3.org/2000/svg" style="display:none">
    <defs>
      <symbol id="play" viewBox="0 0 448 512">
        <title id="play-title">play</title>
        <path d="M424.4 214.7L72.4 6.6C43.8-10.3 0 6.1 0 47.9V464c0
          37.5 40.7 60.1 72.4 41.3l352-208c31.4-18.5 31.5-64.1
0-82.6z"></path>
      </symbol>
      <symbol id="fast-backward" viewBox="0 0 512 512">
        <title id="fast-backward-title">fast-backward</title>
        <path d="M0 436V76c0-6.6 5.4-12 12-12h40c6.6 0 12 5.4 12
          12v151.9L235.5 71.4C256.1 54.3 288 68.6 288 96v131.9L459.5
          71.4C480.1 54.3 512 68.6 512 96v320c0 27.4-31.9 41.7-52.5
          24.6L288 285.3V416c0 27.4-31.9 41.7-52.5 24.6L64 285.3V436c0
          6.6-5.4
          12-12 12H12c-6.6 0-12-5.4-12-12z"></path>
      </symbol>
      <symbol id="fast-forward" viewBox="0 0 512 512">
        <title id="fast-forward-title">fast-forward</title>
        <path d="M512 76v360c0 6.6-5.4 12-12 12h-40c-6.6 0-12-5.4-12-
          12V284.1L276.5 440.6c-20.6 17.2-52.5 2.8-52.5-24.6V284.1L52.5
          440.6C31.9 457.8 0 443.4 0 416V96c0-27.4 31.9-41.7 52.5-
          24.6L224 226.8V96c0-27.4 31.9-41.7 52.5-24.6L448 226.8V76c0-
          6.6 5.4-12 12-12h40c6.6 0 12 5.4 12 12z"></path>
      </symbol>
      <symbol id="forward" viewBox="0 0 512 512">
        <title id="forward-title">forward</title>
        <path d="M500.5 231.4l-192-160C287.9 54.3 256 68.6 256 96v320c0
          27.4 31.9 41.8 52.5 24.6l192-160c15.3-12.8 15.3-36.4 0-49.2zm-
          256 0l-192-160C31.9 54.3 0 68.6 0 96v320c0 27.4 31.9 41.8 52.5
          24.6l192-160c15.3-12.8 15.3-36.4 0-49.2z"></path>
      </symbol>
      <symbol id="backward" viewBox="0 0 512 512">
        <title id="backward-title">backward</title>
```

```
        <path d="M11.5 280.6l192 160c20.6 17.2 52.5 2.8 52.5-24.6V96c0-
        27.4-31.9-41.8-52.5-24.6l-192 160c-15.3 12.8-15.3 36.4 0
        49.2zm256 0l192 160c20.6 17.2 52.5 2.8 52.5-24.6V96c0-27.4-
        31.9-41.8-52.5-24.6l-192 160c-15.3 12.8-15.3 36.4 0 49.2z"></path>
      </symbol>
    </defs>
  </svg>
  <div>
    <button aria-label="rewind" class="btn btn-link">
      <svg xmlns="http://www.w3.org/2000/svg" role="img">
        <use xlink:href="#backward"></use>
      </svg>
    </button>
    <button aria-label="skip to previous track" class="btn btn-link">
      <svg xmlns="http://www.w3.org/2000/svg" role="img">
        <use xlink:href="#fast-backward"></use>
      </svg>
    </button>
    <button aria-label="play" class="btn btn-link">
      <svg xmlns="http://www.w3.org/2000/svg" role="img">
        <use xlink:href="#play"></use>
      </svg>
    </button>
    <button aria-label="skip to next track" class="btn btn-link">
      <svg xmlns="http://www.w3.org/2000/svg" role="img">
        <use xlink:href="#fast-forward"></use>
      </svg>
    </button>
    <button aria-label="fast forward" class="btn btn-link">
      <svg xmlns="http://www.w3.org/2000/svg" role="img">
        <use xlink:href="#forward"></use>
      </svg>
    </button>
  </div>
</body>

</html>
```

As with icon fonts, SVG sprites are fully customizable with CSS. You've already seen an example where we changed the size and color of the icons in the preceding examples. As you read through the rest of the chapter, you'll encounter the many ways that you can manipulate SVG with CSS. It's quite a powerful combination!

Styling inline SVG

This section is going to focus on some of the many ways you can manipulate inline SVG elements with CSS. This section will not be exhaustive, but will cover many of the most common properties that you'll use when working with SVG.

These fall into two classes of properties:

- CSS properties that you're probably familiar with from working with CSS and HTML, and that will also work with SVG
- CSS properties that are specific to SVG itself

Let's start with the familiar CSS properties.

Using common CSS properties to manipulate SVGs

This section is going to focus on common CSS properties that work with SVG. With a couple of exceptions, most of the ones you'll actually pay attention to are related to text.

Basic font properties

If you've worked with CSS for any length of time, you've likely manipulated the font face and style for an element. Those same properties are available for SVG elements.

The following code sample shows four `text` elements. The first shows no styles applied to it and shows the default rendering of a `text` element in SVG. The next three elements are enhanced by CSS styles. The first class `text` adds the excellent Raleway typeface (available as a Google web font) and a new `font-size` (2em). The next two classes, `text-italic` and `text-bold`, build on that with the use of `font-style` and `font-weight` respectively:

```
<!doctype html>
<html lang="en">
    <head>
        <meta charset="utf-8">
        <title>Mastering SVG- CSS Font Properties</title>
        <link href="https://fonts.googleapis.com/css?
         family=Raleway:400" rel="stylesheet">

        <style type="text/css">
          .text {
```

```
      font-family: Raleway, sans-serif;
      font-size: 2em;
    }
    .text-italic {
      font-style: italic;
    }
    .text-bold {
      font-weight: bold;
    }
  </style>
</head>
<body>
  <svg xmlns="http://www.w3.org/2000/svg" role="img" width="800"
    height="250" viewBox="0 0 800 250">
    <text x="25" y="50">
      Default text format
    </text>
    <text x="25" y="100" class="text">
      font-family: Raleway, sans-serif;
      font-size: 2em;
    </text>
    <text x="25" y="150" class="text text-italic">
      font-style: italic;
    </text>
    <text x="25" y="200" class="text text-bold">
      font-weight: bold;
    </text>
  </svg>
</body>
</html>
```

Rendered in the browser, you can see the result as follows:

Default text format

font-family: Raleway, sans-serif; font-size: 2em;

font-style:italic;

font-weight:bold;

In case you were wondering, the shorthand properties also work as well. So simply defining a font property is supported, as the following code sample shows:

```
<!doctype html>
<html lang="en">
    <head>
        <meta charset="utf-8">
        <title>Mastering SVG- CSS Font Shorthand</title>
        <link href="https://fonts.googleapis.com/css?
         family=Raleway:400" rel="stylesheet">
        <style type="text/css">
          .text {
            font: 2em bold Raleway, sans-serif;
          }
        </style>
    </head>
    <body>
      <svg xmlns="http://www.w3.org/2000/svg" role="img" width="800"
      height="250" viewBox="0 0 800 250">
        <text x="25" y="50">
          Default text format
        </text>
        <text x="25" y="100" class="text">
          font: 2em bold Raleway, sans-serif;
        </text>
      </svg>
    </body>
</html>
```

This renders in the browser as follows:

Default text format

font: 2em bold Raleway, sans-serif;

Text properties

The next set of CSS properties supported in SVG all relate to blocks of text. So not just the individual glyph, as defined by the font properties, but the way that a larger grouping of glyphs fit together.

The following code sample illustrates several of them. The first class, text, again changes the font-family and font-size.

Following that, we have several other classes that show SVG support for text properties. The first illustrates support for direction, which allows you to define blocks of text that will work properly in languages that is read right-to-left (for example, Farsi, Arabic, and Hebrew). This example simply anchors the English-based property definition to the right side of the box. Following that, we set the letter-spacing (tracking) property to a roomy 1em, add an underline using text-decoration, and set the word-spacing to 2em:

```
<!doctype html>
<html lang="en">
    <head>
        <meta charset="utf-8">
        <title>Mastering SVG- CSS Text Properties</title>
        <link href="https://fonts.googleapis.com/css?
         family=Raleway:400" rel="stylesheet">

        <style type="text/css">
          .text {
            font-family: Raleway, sans-serif;
            font-size: 1.5em;
          }
          .text-direction {
            direction: rtl;
          }
          .text-letter-spacing {
            letter-spacing: 1em;
          }
          .text-decoration {
            text-decoration: underline;
          }
          .text-word-spacing {
            word-spacing: 2em;
          }
        </style>
    </head>
    <body>
      <svg xmlns="http://www.w3.org/2000/svg" role="img" width="500"
        height="300" viewBox="0 0 500 300">
```

```
          <text x="475" y="50" class="text text-direction">
            direction: rtl;
          </text>
          <text x="25" y="100" class="text text-letter-spacing">
            letter-spacing: 1em;
          </text>
          <text x="25" y="150" class="text text-decoration">
            text-decoration: underline;
          </text>
          <text x="25" y="200" class="text text-word-spacing">
            word-spacing: 2em;
          </text>
        </svg>
      </body>
  </html>
```

Rendered in the browser, that sample looks as follows:

Miscellaneous CSS properties

The final example in this section shows support for the cursor, display, and visibility properties. Of these, the most useful will be cursor. In this example, we change the `cursor` of a `rect` element to be the help cursor. Drag handles, resize handles, clickable pointers, and so on are all going to be common values used in interactive SVG.

Following that we use the `display` and `visibility` properties to hide elements. While the differences between the two are obvious in HTML, there's less practical difference between the two properties in SVG. In HTML elements with `display:none` are not factored into the rendering of the document. They do not effect the overall flow of the document. They're in the DOM and are accessible from JavaScript but they're, in effect, ignored by the rendering engine. Elements set with `visibility:hidden`, on the other hand, remain part of the flow of the document. A 200-pixel high `div` will still take up 200 pixels. It will just do so invisibly.

Since most elements in SVG are positioned with (x, y) properties on a coordinate system, the differences between the two might be subtle. SVG elements with `visibility:hidden` normally don't have any flow to interrupt (`tspan` would be one exception) so there's no practical difference in layout. The one difference is in the way JavaScript events are handled. We'll look at this in more depth later, both in the next section and in the later JavaScript chapters. But depending on how the `pointer-events` property is set, `visibility:hidden` elements might still interact with the user through JavaScript events. By default they will not, but it's still possible:

```
<!doctype html>
<html lang="en">
    <head>
        <meta charset="utf-8">
        <title>Mastering SVG- CSS Misc Properties</title>
        <link href="https://fonts.googleapis.com/css?
         family=Raleway:400" rel="stylesheet">

        <style type="text/css">
          .help {
            cursor: help;
          }
          .display-none {
            display: none;
          }
          .visibility-hidden {
            visibility: hidden;
          }
        </style>
    </head>
    <body>
      <svg xmlns="http://www.w3.org/2000/svg" role="img" width="500"
        height="300" viewBox="0 0 500 300">
        <rect x="10" y="0" width="100" height="100" fill="red"
          class="help"></rect>
        <rect x="120" y="120" height="100" width="100" fill="blue"
          class="display-none"></rect>
        <rect x="240" y="120" height="100" width="100" fill="blue"
           class="visibility-hidden"></rect>
      </svg>
    </body>
</html>
```

Rendered in the browser, when hovering over the element with the mouse cursor this sample looks as follows:

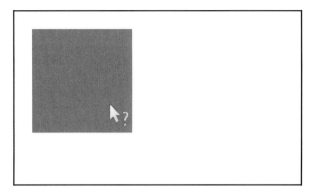

 If you're familiar with CSS, then you'll know there are other possible values for `display`. While I'm sure there are valid use cases for setting an SVG element to have another `display` value, it's not going to be something you'll commonly do, so I'm not going to talk about that here.

Using SVG-specific CSS properties to manipulate SVGs

This section will talk about the different CSS properties that you can use to work with SVG. Most of these properties have already been seen in previous chapters as attributes of specific SVG elements. You'll find that the combination of these representational attributes and the possibility of using CSS for sharing styles across SVG elements and SVG documents represents a powerful combination.

 CSS properties will override presentation attributes, but will not override `style` attributes (which really just means that SVG + CSS behaves the way you would expect it to if you're familiar with the way that CSS specificity works (`https://css-tricks.com/specifics-on-css-specificity/`)).

Color and painting properties

This first example illustrates the ability to change the fill of an element. The `fill` property accepts any valid CSS color value (`https://developer.mozilla.org/en-US/docs/Web/CSS/color_value`), as well as a link to a paint server (for example, a `pattern` defined in a `defs` section). `fill-opacity` changes the opacity of the fill itself (as the alpha value in an `rgba` color definition does) and not the whole element, as the CSS `opacity` property would.

In this example, we define four classes. The first two, `red-fill` and `blue-fill`, define two different primary colors, red and blue, for fills. The third, `half-opacity`, defines `50%` opacity. The final one, `gradient`, defines the fill as a link to a paint server defined in the SVG element.

They're then applied with the same `class` attribute you would use with a regular HTML element:

```
<!doctype html>
<html lang="en">
    <head>
        <meta charset="utf-8">
        <title>Mastering SVG- CSS Fill Properties</title>
        <link href="https://fonts.googleapis.com/css?
          family=Raleway:400" rel="stylesheet">

        <style type="text/css">
          .red-fill {
            fill: red;
          }
          .blue-fill {
            fill: blue;
          }
          .half-opacity{
            fill-opacity: .5;
          }
          .gradient{
            fill: url(#linear);
          }
        </style>
    </head>
    <body>
      <svg xmlns="http://www.w3.org/2000/svg" role="img" width="550"
        height="300" viewBox="0 0 550 300">
        <defs>
          <linearGradient id="linear">
              <stop offset="5%" stop-color="green"/>
              <stop offset="95%" stop-color="gold"/>
```

```
            </linearGradient>
        </defs>
        <rect x="10" y="0" width="100" height="100" class="red-fill">
        </rect>
        <rect x="120" y="0" height="100" width="100" class="blue-fill">
        </rect>
        <rect x="230" y="0" height="100" width="100" class="blue-fill
         half-opacity" ></rect>
        <rect x="340" y="0" height="100" width="100" class="gradient">
        </rect>
    </svg>
  </body>
</html>
```

Rendered in the browser, we get the following result:

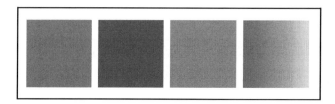

Stroke properties

Another very useful set of properties that are available to manipulate SVG from CSS are related to strokes. All of the stroke properties are available as CSS properties. Similar to the `fill` properties, these are going to come in very handy in creating consistent interfaces and visualizations.

This example shows the usage of `stroke` and `stroke-width` as part of a base `stroke` class. This sets up a common stroke style so that we can apply the other stroke manipulation properties to our examples. Following that, we set the two dash properties, `stroke-dashoffset` and `stroke-dasharray`, and apply those to the first two `rect` elements using the `stroke-dasharray` and `stroke-dashoffset` classes. After that, we apply `stroke-linecap` to a `line` element using the `stroke-linecap-join` class. Following that, we apply the `stroke-linejoin-round` class to a final `rect` element.

The `property`/`value` pairs match the same patterns you learned about in Chapter 2, *Getting Started with Authoring SVG*, when you initially learned about these presentation attributes.

All of these are available as CSS properties, which should help you to create consistent reusable stroke patterns for elements in your SVG document:

```
<!doctype html>
<html lang="en">
    <head>
        <meta charset="utf-8">
        <title>Mastering SVG- CSS Stroke Properties</title>
        <link href="https://fonts.googleapis.com/css?
         family=Raleway:400" rel="stylesheet">

        <style type="text/css">
            .stroke {
                stroke-width: 10px;
                stroke: royalblue;
            }
            .stroke-dasharray {
                stroke-dasharray: 10;
            }
            .stroke-dashoffset {
                stroke-dashoffset: 25;
            }
            .stroke-linecap-square {
                stroke-linecap: square;
            }
            .stroke-linejoin-round{
                stroke-linejoin: round;
            }
            .stroke-opacity{
                stroke-opacity: .5;
            }
        </style>
    </head>
    <body>
      <svg xmlns="http://www.w3.org/2000/svg" width="550" height="300"
      viewBox="0 0 550 300">
        <rect x="50" y="15" width="300" height="50" fill="none"
        class="stroke stroke-dasharray"></rect>
        <rect x="50" y="80" width="300" height="50" fill="none"
        class="stroke stroke-dasharray stroke-dashoffset"></rect>
        <line x1="50" y1="160" x2="350" y2="160" class="stroke stroke-
          linecap-square"></line>
        <rect x="50" y="180" width="300" height="50" fill="none"
        class="stroke stroke-linejoin-round"></rect>
      </svg>
    </body>
</html>
```

Rendered in the browser, the preceding code produces the following output:

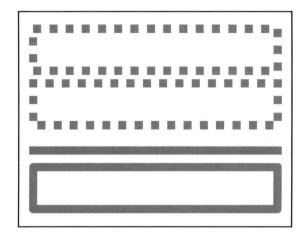

Text properties

This section will introduce some SVG-specific text properties. The first few examples deal with the baseline of text in SVG. Depending on the sort of work you're doing, you may never have to tweak a text element's baseline (the visual plane on which a line of text sits). But you *may* have to, especially if you're doing work with multi-lingual layouts or complicated text-based illustrations (like a logo). So it's worth introducing you to these properties. The baseline related properties are `alignment-baseline`, `dominant-baseline`, and `baseline-shift`.

In addition to those, this section will also look at the `text-anchor` property, which changes the anchor point of a `text` element.

As a brief note about the baseline properties, there's more to them than this, but the following description will give you enough of a foundation to get what's going on in the code sample. This is *probably* enough for you to get by using these properties:

- `dominant-baseline` is used to adjust the baseline for a `text` element
- `alignment-baseline` is used to adjust the baseline for a child element relative to the baseline of its parent `text` element
- `baseline-shift` is probably the most useful, providing the common *subscript* and *superscript* functionality by shifting the dominant baseline up or down

`dominant-baseline` and `alignment-baseline` accept similar values. The two used here are *hanging,* which drops the text off the bottom of the text box, and *middle,* which centers the text vertically on the bottom of the text box. In this example `dominant-baseline` is applied to `text` elements with the two different values and `alignment-baseline` is applied to two different child `tspan` elements with the two different values.

Following that, the common superscript and subscript patterns are created with the `super` and `sub` values of `baseline-shift`.

Finally, the `text-anchor` property is illustrated by three different values applied to a text element centered in the middle of the viewport. `text-anchor` aligns text to different points in the text box: `start`, `middle`, and to `end` of the sentence.

The code sample that follows illustrates the usage of these baseline attributes as well as the usage of the `text-anchor` property:

```
<!doctype html>
<html lang="en">

<head>
    <meta charset="utf-8">
    <title>Mastering SVG- SVG-specific CSS Text Properties</title>
    <link href="https://fonts.googleapis.com/css?family=Raleway:400"
      rel="stylesheet">

    <style type="text/css">
     .text {
         font-family: Raleway, sans-serif;
         font-size: 1.5em;
     }
     .dominant-hanging {
         dominant-baseline: hanging;
     }
     .dominant-middle {
         dominant-baseline: middle;
     }
     .alignment-hanging {
         alignment-baseline: hanging;
     }
     .alignment-middle {
         alignment-baseline: middle;
     }
     .sub {
        baseline-shift: sub;
     }
     .super {
```

```
            baseline-shift: super;
        }
        .text-anchor-start{
            text-anchor:start;
        }
        .text-anchor-middle{
            text-anchor:middle;
        }
        .text-anchor-end{
            text-anchor:end;
        }
        </style>
    </head>

    <body>
        <svg xmlns="http://www.w3.org/2000/svg" width="400" height="550"
          viewBox="0 0 400 550">
            <rect width="400" height="25" x="0" y="0" fill="#cccccc" />
            <rect width="400" height="25" x="0" y="25" fill="#efefef" />
            <rect width="400" height="25" x="0" y="50" fill="#cccccc"/>
            <rect width="400" height="25" x="0" y="75" fill="#efefef"/>
            <rect width="400" height="25" x="0" y="100" fill="#cccccc"/>
            <rect width="400" height="25" x="0" y="125" fill="#efefef"/>
            <rect width="400" height="25" x="0" y="150" fill="#cccccc"/>
            <rect width="400" height="25" x="0" y="175" fill="#efefef"/>
            <rect width="400" height="25" x="0" y="200" fill="#cccccc"/>
            <rect width="400" height="25" x="0" y="225" fill="#efefef"/>
            <rect width="400" height="25" x="0" y="250" fill="#cccccc"/>
            <rect width="400" height="25" x="0" y="275" fill="#efefef"/>
            <rect width="400" height="25" x="0" y="300" fill="#cccccc"/>
            <rect width="400" height="25" x="0" y="325" fill="#efefef"/>
            <rect width="400" height="25" x="0" y="350" fill="#cccccc"/>
            <rect width="400" height="25" x="0" y="375" fill="#efefef"/>
            <rect width="400" height="25" x="0" y="400" fill="#cccccc"/>
            <rect width="400" height="25" x="0" y="425" fill="#efefef"/>

            <line x1="200" y1="300" x2=
            "200" y2="325" stroke="red"></line>
            <line x1="200" y1="350" x2=
            "200" y2="375" stroke="red"></line>
            <line x1="200" y1="400" x2=
            "200" y2="425" stroke="red"></line>
            <text class="text dominant-hanging" x="50"
              y="25">Hanging</text>
            <text class="text dominant-middle" x="50" y="75">Middle</text>
            <text class="text" x="50" y="125">Text <tspan class="alignment-
            hanging">Hanging</tspan></text>
            <text class="text" x="50" y="175">Text <tspan class="alignment-
```

```
    middle">Middle</tspan></text>
    <text class="text" x="50" y="225">Super<tspan
    class="super">sup</tspan></text>
    <text class="text" x="50" y="275">Sub<tspan
    class="sub">sub</tspan></text>
    <text class="text text-anchor-start" x="200" y="325">Text
      Anchor Start</text>

    <text class="text text-anchor-middle" x="200" y="375">Text
      Anchor Middle</text>

    <text class="text text-anchor-end" x="200" y="425">Text Anchor
      End </text>
  </svg>
</body>

</html>
```

Rendered in the browser, these effects are visible in the following screenshot:

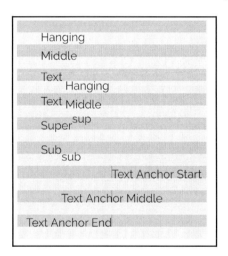

The darker bands show the initial textbox based on the *x, y* position of the text element. You can see how hanging and middle clearly shift the baseline of the font in reference to the *x, y* position.

The text-anchor example is illustrated with the addition of a line that indicates the (x, y) position of those text elements. They are placed at the center of the SVG element, which illustrates the effect of that property on a text element.

Compositing properties

Browser support for the compositing properties is pretty crummy at present. Microsoft doesn't have full support for the `clip` properties, at the time of writing, and mask property support is terrible across the board). That's unfortunate, as they'd present powerful options for defining and reusing clip-paths and masks.

The one working example I'm going to show illustrates how to define a `clip-path` using CSS. There are two variations. The first simply references a `clipPath` element by `id`. This is straightforward and works in modern browsers.

The second example allows for greater separation of concerns. Instead of having to define an element with a path to use for clipping, you can provide polygon coordinates directly to CSS. `polygon`, `circle`, and `inset` are available values for this property. This syntax replaces the now deprecated `clip` property. If you're familiar with `clip`, you should note a couple of things. First, notice that there is no direct replacement for the `rect` value. Thankfully, as we show here, polygon is more than enough to replace `rect`. Secondly, `clip-path` does *not* require an element to be absolutely positioned (although, that's not a particular concern when using this property in SVG).

The syntax for the polygon value is slightly different from the one used for a `polygon` element's `path` attribute. Instead of the commas being arbitrary and there just for legibility (as is the case with a d attribute of a path element), the pairs of points in this CSS property need to be comma-separated and require units. Otherwise, it works the same way as a `polygon` in SVG.

This example replicates the rectangle seen in the `clipPath` example by mapping out the points as a `polygon`:

```
<!doctype html>
<html lang="en">

<head>
    <meta charset="utf-8">
    <title>Mastering SVG- CSS Compositing Properties</title>
    <link href="https://fonts.googleapis.com/css?family=Raleway:400"
      rel="stylesheet">

    <style type="text/css">
      .clip-url{
        clip-path: url(#box);
      }
      .clip-polygon {
        clip-path: polygon(50% 0, 100% 0, 100% 100%, 50% 100%, 50% 0)
```

```
      }
    </style>
  </head>
  <body>
    <svg xmlns="http://www.w3.org/2000/svg" width="240" height="240"
      viewBox="0 0 240 240" version="1.1">
      <defs>
        <clipPath id="box" maskUnits="userSpaceOnUse" x="0" y="0"
          width="240" height="240">

            <rect x="120" y="0" width="240" height="240" fill="red" >
            </rect>
        </clipPath>
        <polygon id="star" points="95,95 120,5 150,95 235,95 165,150
          195,235 120,180 50,235 75,150 5,95"></polygon>
      </defs>
      <use href="#star" fill="red"></use>
      <use href="#star" fill="black" class="clip-url"></use>
    </svg>
    <svg xmlns="http://www.w3.org/2000/svg" width="240" height="240"
      viewBox="0 0 240 240" version="1.1">
      <defs>
        <polygon id="star" points="95,95 120,5 150,95 235,95 165,150
          195,235 120,180 50,235 75,150 5,95"></polygon>
      </defs>
      <use href="#star" fill="red"></use>
      <use href="#star" fill="black" class="clip-polygon"></use>
    </svg>
  </body>
</html>
```

Rendered in the browser, you get the following output:

As I mentioned, support for the `mask` properties is problematic, so I don't have fully realized examples. There are three patterns that are defined:

- The first is similar to the `clip-path` property. You can define a `mask-image` property and pass a mask image into it via a `url`:

```
.mask{
    mask-image: url(mask.svg);
}
```

- The second option is to use a portion of a linked image using a fragment identifier:

```
.mask-fragment{
    mask-image: url(mask.svg#fragment);
}
```

- The third, and most interesting option, would allow you to create masks in the property value:

```
.mask-image {
    mask-image: linear-gradient(rgba(0, 0, 0, 1.0),
transparent);
}
```

This technology isn't ready for prime time yet, but it's good to know what's on the horizon, especially as it would allow you to reuse masks defined in a central place using nothing but a CSS class.

Interactivity properties

The final CSS property we're going to look at is the `pointer-events` property. The `pointer-events` property indicates whether or not an SVG element can become the target of pointer events (inclusive of all inputs, including mouse, pen, or touch inputs).

The basic way to implement `pointer-events` is to turn them on or off. The following example shows this in action. This example will also include a little bit of JavaScript, so you can get a small head start on Chapter 6, *JavaScript and SVG*, where we'll dive headlong into manipulating SVG with JavaScript.

In this sample, we have two `rect` elements. One is set with a class of `pointer-default`. This class has a single property, `pointer-events` set to `visiblePainted`. `visiblePainted` is the default value for `pointer-events` on an SVG element. It indicates that the entire visibly painted area of the element should accept mouse events. That means both the border and the fill.

The second `rect` has a class of `pointer-none`. The value of its single property, `pointer-events`, is `none`. This indicates that the element should not receive mouse events.

At the bottom of the page there's a small JavaScript block that shows the property in action. It also illustrates the sort of differences you might encounter when working with SVG and JavaScript. In it, we use some core **Document Object Model (DOM)** methods to attach a click event handler to each of the `rect` elements. First, we use `document.querySelectorAll` to get a reference to all of the `rect` elements on the page. If you're unfamiliar with it, `querySelectorAll` can be thought of as a standardized, browser-native version of the famous jQuery interface. You pass in a CSS selector and it returns a static `nodeList` containing the results of your query.

We immediately loop through the array-like `nodeList` with the convenience method, `forEach`, and attach event handlers to each of the nodes. This event handler is designed to change the text of the adjacent `text` element whenever a square is clicked.

 If you're used to using `innerHTML` to set text content, you will notice the property `textContent` used here instead. Why? SVG doesn't have an `innerHTML` (*which makes sense, since it's not HTML*).

Running this in the browser, you'll see that only clicks on the `rect` with the default `pointer-events` value will change the text. The `rect` with `pointer-events` set to `none` doesn't do anything:

```
<!doctype html>
<html lang="en">

<head>
    <meta charset="utf-8">
    <title>Mastering SVG- CSS Compositing Properties</title>
    <link href="https://fonts.googleapis.com/css?family=Raleway:400"
      rel="stylesheet">

    <style type="text/css">
      .pointer-default {
        pointer-events: visiblePainted;
      }
```

```
      .pointer-none {
        pointer-events: none;
      }
    </style>
  </head>
  <body>
    <svg xmlns="http://www.w3.org/2000/svg" width="500" height="250"
    viewBox="0 0 500 250" version="1.1">
      <rect x="10" y="10" width="100" height="100" class="pointer-
        default" fill="red"></rect>
      <rect x="120" y="10" width="100" height="100" class="pointer-
        none" fill= "red"></rect>
      <text x="10" y="150" id="text"></text>
  </svg>
  <script>
    document.querySelectorAll("rect").forEach(function(element){
      let classname = element.className.baseVal;
      element.addEventListener("click", ()=>{
        document.getElementById("text").textContent= `clicked
          ${classname}`
      });
    });
  </script>
  </body>
</html>
```

The following illustration shows the page after both rect elements were clicked:

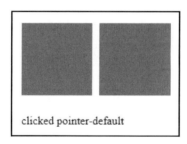

clicked pointer-default

The following table illustrates the other possible values for this property. They offer a lot of control in the way you can interact with SVG elements. Depending on how much precise interactivity you're planning on doing, you might end up taking advantage of that precision:

Property	Definition
visiblePainted	The element can be targeted if the visibility property is set to visible and the pointer is over a *painted area*. With this value the painted area includes the stroke (if it's set to a value other than none) and the fill (if it's set to a value other than none).
visibleFill	The element can be targeted if the visibility property is set to visible and the pointer is over the interior (the fill area), whether or not the fill is set.
visibleStroke	The element can be targeted if the visibility property is set to visible and the pointer is over the perimeter (the stroke area), whether or not the stroke is set.
visible	The element can be targeted if the visibility property is set to visible and the pointer is over the interior or perimeter, whether or not the fill or stroke are set.
painted	The element can be targeted if the visibility property is set to visible and the pointer is over a *painted area*. With this value the painted area includes the stroke (if it's set to a value other than none) and the fill (if it's set to a value other than none. The value of the visibility property isn't taken into account.
fill	The element can be targeted if the pointer is over the interior (the fill area), whether or not the fill is set. The value of the visibility property isn't taken into account.
stroke	The element can be targeted if the pointer is over the perimeter (the stroke area), whether or not the fill is set. The value of the visibility property isn't taken into account.
all	The element can be targeted if the pointer is over the interior or perimeter of the element. The values of the stroke, fill, and visibility properties aren't taken into account.
none	The element does not receive pointer events.

Styles in standalone SVG images

While all the examples so far have been about inline SVG inside an HTML document, you can also use CSS within a standalone SVG image. The following SVG image shows using CSS to adjust the display of multiple SVG `text` elements. Interesting details include the **character data** (`<![CDATA[ ]]>`) block wrapping the styles contained in the `style` element:

If you haven't dealt with a lot of XML (and it's not nearly as common as it once was, so that might be the case), CDATA is used to indicate to the XML parser that the section might contain characters that could be interpreted as XML, but shouldn't be. JavaScript (with the prevalence of < and >) is the most common use case (and the one you'll know if you were building websites in 1999) but CSS could potentially fall into the same trap, so it's good to use it here as well.

The next thing to note is the absence of external style sheets. If you're going to create an SVG image that will be imported as an `img src` or as a background image in CSS, it needs to be entirely self-contained.

Other than that, this works much like the HTML and CSS combination that's likely familiar to you:

```
<?xml version="1.0" encoding="UTF-8"?>
  <svg xmlns="http://www.w3.org/2000/svg" width="250" height="250"
viewBox="0 0 250 250" version="1.1">
  <style>
    <![CDATA[
        text {
          font-family: Verdana, Geneva, sans-serif;
          fill: slategray;
        }
        .palatino{
          font-family: Palatino, "Palatino Linotype", "Palatino LT
          STD", "Book Antiqua", Georgia, serif;
        }
```

```
    .big-green{
      fill: forestgreen;
      font-size: 2rem;
      opacity: .75;
    }
    .huge-blue{
      fill: dodgerblue;
      font-size: 4rem;
    }
    .medium-deep-pink{
      fill: deeppink;
      font-size: 1.5rem;
    }
    .bigger {
      font-size: 6rem;
    }
    .text-anchor-middle{
      text-anchor: middle;
    }
    .text-baseline-middle{
      dominant-baseline: middle;
    }
    .half-opacity{
      opacity: .5;
    }
  ]]>
</style>
    <text x="20" y="20" class="big-green">Styles</text>
    <text x="-10" y="50" class="huge-blue palatino">Styles</text>
    <text x="66" y="40" class="medium-deep-pink half
     opacity">Styles</text>
    <text x="77" y="77" class="big-green">Styles</text>
    <text x="55" y="66">Styles</text>
    <text x="100" y="125" class="medium-deep-pink
     bigger">Styles</text>
    <text x="175" y="33" class="big-green">Styles</text>
    <text x="220" y="44" class="huge-blue half-
      opacity">Styles</text>
    <text x="-20" y="244" class="huge-blue bigger half-
      opacity">Styles</text>
    <text x="120" y="120" class="medium-deep-pink">Styles</text>
    <text x="14" y="166" class="big-green palatino">Styles</text>

    <text x="136" y="199" class="huge-blue palatino half-
      opacity">Styles</text>
    <text x="170" y="144" class="huge-blue">Styles</text>
    <text x="-40" y="144" class="huge-blue half-
      opacity">Styles</text>
```

```
        <text x="143" y="24" class="big-green">Styles</text>
        <text x="125" y="125" class="bigger text-anchor-middle text-
          baseline-middle">Styles</text>
    </svg>
```

Rendered in the browser, this image looks as follows:

Basic CSS animations and transitions with SVG

One of the most interesting ways to work with SVG and CSS is with CSS *animations* and *transitions*.

- **Animations**: This allow you to assign animations to elements. These animations are defined as a series of changes to CSS properties.
- **Transitions**: This allow you to control the time it takes for CSS property changes to take effect. Instead of immediately changing, they *transition* between states.

These are a very powerful set of features and are an important conceptual and technical addition to your SVG toolkit.

CSS animations

CSS animations in SVG work the same way as they do in HTML, with the addition of the ability to use the SVG-specific properties.

Basic animation format

The basic pattern is as follows. SVG is simple. It's a single `rect` element. The CSS has two interesting components. The first is the class `rect`, which references one property, `animation`. `animation`; this is a shorthand property that maps to a whole series of `animation`-properties. In this case, we're setting two of them. The first of the mapped properties is `animation-name`, which references the animation defined in the `@keyframes` animation named `movement`. The second one we're setting is the `animation-duration`, which we set to three seconds (`3s`). The `@keyframes` animation is where the magic happens. In it, we set two sets of keyframes. The first set marks the initial (`0%`) and final state (`100%`) of the animation with the same property, a CSS `transform` with a `translate` function set to (`0,0`). This is the initial (and finishing) state. We're going to animate against the `transform` property in the next keyframe. In it, set for the middle of the animation (`50%`), we translate the `rect` 400 pixels to the right:

```
<!doctype html>
<html lang="en">

<head>
    <meta charset="utf-8">
    <title>Mastering SVG- CSS animation</title>

    <style type="text/css">
    .rect {
      animation: movement 3s;
    }

    @keyframes movement {
      0%, 100% {
        transform: translate(0, 0);
      }
      50% {
        transform: translate(400px, 0);
      }
    }
    </style>
</head>
<body>
  <svg xmlns="http://www.w3.org/2000/svg" width="500" height="100"
    viewBox="0 0 500 100" version="1.1">
    <rect x="0" y="0" width="100" height="100" class="rect">
  </svg>
</body>
</html>
```

The effect is that the rectangle slowly moves from left to right and then back again as follows:

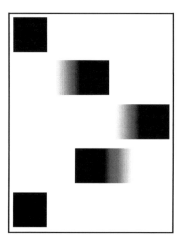

Animating a clip path

One relatively simple example (from a CSS perspective) of how powerful animations can be with SVG is animating a clip path. Using the polygon option we just learned about, you can animate between two (or more) shapes defined as a clip-path. If they have the *same number of points*, the browser will smoothly animate between positions defined as keyframes in your animation.

The following example shows just that. In this example we create a class stars:

- stars has one animation property. It references the @keyframe stars block defined later on in the style sheet.
- The second argument you're already familiar with, animation-duration. Once again this is set to three seconds.
- The third property is potentially new to you. The property value infinite maps to the animation-iteration-count property.
- animation-iteration-count accepts either a number indicating the specific number of times an animation should run or the keyword infinite, which indicates that the animation should play forever.

The `@keyframes` follow the same pattern as the previous animation. We have equivalent starting and finishing states (0% and 100%). These are defined as a polygon `clip-path` that illustrates a star. The mid-point of the animation (50%), redefines the polygon as a square. Since the number of points needs to be equivalent between the states of an animation, this means that we're defining many more than four points to animate between these states:

```
<!doctype html>
<html lang="en">

<head>
    <meta charset="utf-8">
    <title>Mastering SVG- CSS animation</title>

    <style type="text/css">
    .stars {
      animation: stars 3s infinite;
    }

    @keyframes stars {
      0%, 100% {
        clip-path: polygon(95px 95px, 120px 5px, 150px 95px, 235px
          95px, 165px 150px, 195px 235px, 120px 180px, 50px 235px,75px
          150px, 5px 95px)
      }
      50% {
        clip-path: polygon(10px 10px, 120px 10px, 230px 10px, 230px
          120px, 230px 180px, 230px 230px, 120px 230px, 10px 230px, 10px
          180px, 10px 120px)
      }
    }
    </style>
</head>
<body>
  <svg xmlns="http://www.w3.org/2000/svg" width="240" height="240"
    viewBox="0 0 500 500" version="1.1">
    <image href="take-2-central-2017.jpg" width="1000" height="500"
      x="0" y="0" class="stars"></image>
  </svg>
</body>
</html>
```

The following time-lapse screenshot shows how the animation unfolds over the three seconds that it runs. Be sure to run it in a supporting browser to see how interesting this effect can be:

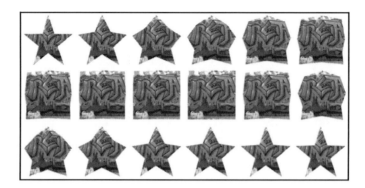

Animating multiple properties and assigning multiple animations to an element

Two more things to note about animations are as follows:

- You can animate multiple CSS properties at one time
- You can also apply multiple animations to the same element

The following code sample shows how these two features work. There are three important sections. The first is the single class, `rect`. It has *two* comma-separated arguments for the `animation` property, the animations `box` and `change-color-and-fade`. `box` defines two square `clip-path` properties, one `50` pixels from the edge of the rectangle, the other `10` pixels in from the edge. `change-color-and-fade` changes the background color from red to blue and the opacity from `.5` to `1`:

```
<!doctype html>
<html lang="en">

<head>
  <meta charset="utf-8">
  <title>Mastering SVG- CSS animation</title>
  <style type="text/css">
    svg {
      background: lightgray;
    }
    .rect {
      animation: box 3s infinite, change-colors-and-fade 3s infinite;
```

```
      }
    @keyframes box {
      0%,
      100% {
        clip-path: polygon(50px 50px, 200px 50px, 200px 200px, 50px
        200px)
      }
      50% {
        clip-path: polygon(10px 10px, 240px 10px, 240px 240px, 10px
        240px)
      }
    }
    @keyframes change-colors-and-fade {
      0%,
      100% {
        opacity: .5;
        fill: rgb(255, 0, 0);
      }
      50% {
        opacity: 1;
        fill: rgb(0, 0, 255);
      }
    }
  </style>
</head>

<body>
  <svg xmlns="http://www.w3.org/2000/svg" width="250" height="250"
  viewBox="0 0 250 250" version="1.1">
    <rect x="0" y="50" width="250" height="50" fill="gray"></rect>
    <rect x="0" y="0" width="250" height="250" class="rect"></rect>
  </svg>
</body>

</html>
```

Run in the browser, the animation goes through the following stages:

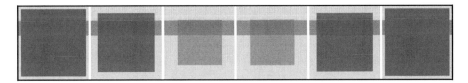

CSS transitions

The final CSS property we're going to look at in this chapter is the CSS `transition` property. `transition` allows you to define the way that the browser animates between changes in property values. Instead of the properties changing immediately, they can transition more smoothly.

The following example shows how this works. In it we have a small, single-value bar chart that fills up when the user hovers over it, showing imaginary progress against a goal.

The CSS is full of classes to define the text. You'll notice many properties you've learned about throughout this chapter. In addition to those, which you should have at least some familiarity with after working with them in this chapter, there are classes that define the bar chart, one of which is more interesting than the other.

The first, `the-bar`, defines the outline of the bar chart. The second, `fill-the-bar`, defines the *progress* part of the bar. It has no stroke and a green fill. The interesting part for our purposes is the `transition` property. `transition` is a shorthand property for a group of related `transition`-properties. In this case we're using `transition-property` (`transform`) and `transition-duration` (`3s`). This indicates that the browser should watch for changes to the `transform` property on this element and transition the changes to that property over three seconds. Also in this class we define a `scaleY` `transform` with a value of `1` and anchor the `transform` to the `bottom` of the element with `transform-origin`. We need a baseline `scaleY` so the browser has a matching property to animate against. `fill-the-bar:hover` changes the scale to `7.5` which, given the way this is configured, fills up the bar to `75%` of the goal:

```
<!doctype html>
<html lang="en">
<head>
  <meta charset="utf-8">
  <title>Mastering SVG- CSS Transitions</title>
  <link href="https://fonts.googleapis.com/css?family=Raleway:400"
   rel="stylesheet">

  <style type="text/css">
    .text {
      font-family: Raleway, sans-serif;
      font-size: 1.5em;
    }
```

```css
    .smaller-text {
      font-size: 1em;
    }

    .the-bar {
      stroke: black;
      stroke-width: 2px;
      fill: none;
    }

    .fill-the-bar {
      transition: transform 2s;
      transform: scaleY(1);
      transform-origin: bottom;
      stroke: none;
      fill: green;
      cursor: pointer;
    }

    .fill-the-bar:hover {
      transform: scaleY(7.5);
    }

    .dominant-baseline-hanging {
      dominant-baseline: hanging;
    }

    .dominant-baseline-middle {
      dominant-baseline: middle;
    }

    .text-anchor-end {
      text-anchor: end;
    }
  </style>
</head>

<body>
  <svg xmlns="http://www.w3.org/2000/svg" width="250" height="500"
  viewBox="0 0 250 500" version="1.1">
    <text class="text" x="10" y="25">Our Progress</text>
    <text x="90" y="50" class="dominant-baseline-hanging smaller-text
    text-anchor-end">100%</text>
    <text class="text smaller-text text-anchor-end" x="90" y="250">0%
    </text>
    <text class="text smaller-text text-anchor-end dominant-baseline-
    middle" x="90" y="150">50%</text>
```

```
    <rect x="100" y="50" height="200" width="50" class="the-bar">
    </rect>
    <rect class="fill-the-bar" x="100" y="230" height="20" width="50"
    fill="green"></rect>
  </svg>
</body>

</html>
```

Run in the browser; the transition grows slowly until it fills the appropriate space:

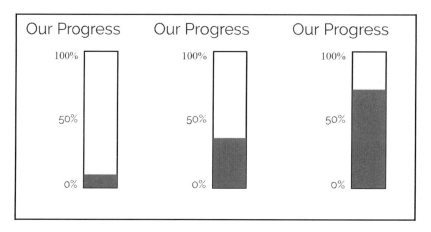

Summary

You've learned a lot in this chapter. CSS is one of the linchpin technologies for making fast, maintainable modern websites and applications, and understanding the intersection between SVG and CSS is important.

The chapter started with details about the common use case of using SVG for CSS background images, including interesting details about using SVG data URLs.

Following that, you learned about SVG sprites and icon sets and how and why they can be used in place of the common font icon sets so popular on the web today.

Following that, you learned about styling inline SVG, including detailed ways to manipulate the font and the flow of lines of text. Following that, you learned about many SVG-specific properties including those controlling the fill, stroke, and text of elements. After that, you learned about some cutting edge compositing properties, such as clip-path and mask-image, which are powerful, even if browser support isn't fully there yet.

After that, you learned about using CSS to improve consistency and ease of authoring in standalone SVG images.

Finally, you learned about basic CSS animations and transitions with SVG, a powerful pattern to add interactivity and movement to your sites and applications.

Next up, we'll take all that we've learned about getting SVG onto the page and making sure it looks right, and we'll add JavaScript to the mix, so we can start to interact with SVG in increasingly interesting ways.

JavaScript and SVG 6

You've learned quite a bit in this book so far about SVG. You've spent a lot of time looking at the details of the SVG specification and the different ways in which SVG can interact with CSS and HTML. Hopefully, it's been as interesting for you as it is for me.

As interesting as it has all been, it's *this* chapter where we'll put *all* the tools together to really unlock the power of SVG. Adding JavaScript to the mix opens up a huge number of new possibilities.

Granted, there are many web developers and designers who will never do animation, dynamic visualizations, or other interactive work with SVG. For them, getting a full understanding of the way that SVG itself works as markup and how it fits in with other static web technologies is incredibly valuable. This is especially true of the intersection between SVG and CSS that we just learned about in detail.

That said, the most exciting thing about SVG is how easily it works with JavaScript to enhance the interactivity of your site. All of these open web technologies are designed to work together in ways that create something greater than the sum of the individual specifications. Even though there are separate experts working on all of these various technologies, they do so out in the open (for the most part) and are, generally, part of larger organizations such as Microsoft, Google, or Mozilla and therefore have a real desire to make sure that these technologies work together in the best possible way.

The intersection of SVG and JavaScript is definitely one such case.

In this chapter, we'll learn about the low-level interface between JavaScript and SVG. This includes the DOM interface to SVG. This is important stuff, even though we're also going to learn about libraries and frameworks for working with SVG. Even if you've been doing web development for a while and are familiar with JavaScript and the DOM, the differences between the regular HTML DOM and the interface to SVG elements is important. If you're not so familiar with raw DOM manipulations (and many developers who started in the jQuery era and later are not), then this chapter will give you a whole set of useful skills.

In this chapter, we'll learn about the following:

- The basic DOM interface to SVG-basic accessing and manipulating SVG elements in JavaScript
- SVG-specific DOM interfaces
- Working with SVG and CSS dynamically

JavaScript Versions and tools

Before we get into the code, I think it's important to go over different JavaScript Versions and how they'll be used in the book. I'd also like to go over how I'll present examples that require tooling.

JavaScript Versions

As you may be aware, there's been a lot of work over the past few years around evolving the JavaScript programming language. Some of this work is really, really great. So great, in fact, that the dominant libraries and frameworks on the web right now are idiomatically written in versions and variations of JavaScript that aren't universally available in web browsers. Working in bleeding-edge versions of the language, including framework-specific extensions, is possible because of the use of a transpiler (`https://scotch.io/tutorials/javascript-transpilers-what-they-are-why-we-need-them`), a piece of software that takes software code written in one language (or in this case, a version of a language) and outputs code in another language (in this case an older, fully supported version of the language). This transpilation step allows us to write our applications in whatever flavor of JavaScript we prefer and then convert it into browser-standard JavaScript that can run anywhere.

This section outlines the different Versions of JavaScript you will encounter in this book. The next section will talk a little bit about how we'll present the tooling required to use a transpiler in order to make your bleeding-edge code run in common web browsers.

As a note, this is the broadest possible introduction to this topic. Additional details, as they arise, will be covered in the course of the book, but even that will only scratch the surface of this far-ranging topic.

While I have called and will continue to call the language JavaScript throughout the book, that trademarked name (trademarked by Oracle, which got the trademark from Sun Microsystems, who in turn got the trademark from Netscape) is not the official name of the language. The language is officially called **ECMAScript**, based on Ecma (`https://www.ecma-international.org/`), the organization which hosts the standards body that writes the specification.

ECMAScript 5

ECMAScript 5 (ES5) is the most fully supported version of the language in browsers today and is the version that is targeted by transpilers because it will run anywhere. Standardized in 2009, as of the time of writing this version has full support in over 90% of browsers out there and has partial support in around 97%. With the addition of ES5 polyfills (`https://github.com/es-shims/es5-shim`) you can get near-universal coverage targeting ES5. Some code, specifically the Angular 1 and jQuery sections in Chapter 7, *Common JavaScript Libraries and SVG*, will be written directly as ES5. This is because most people will be familiar with Angular 1 and jQuery as ES5 style interfaces. The comment at the top of the file, as follows, indicates this version is being used:

```
/*
ECMAScript 5
*/
```

ECMAScript 2015

ECMAScript 2015 was formerly known as **ECMAScript 6 (ES6)**. This version, finalized in 2015, is the version making its way into browsers now. It's got partial support across all the latest versions of the major browsers (Edge, Firefox, Chrome, and Safari.) In general, the JavaScript code written in this book, with the exception of the previously mentioned examples, will use ES6. With the exception of the *React* section, which uses more advanced features and some React-specific extensions, the features used are all supported in the latest Versions of Chrome, Edge, and Firefox. So if you're using one of those browsers, you won't have to actually run a transpiler for these samples. If you're looking to move this code into production, that's another story, which is outside the scope of this book.

The comment at the top of the file, as follows, indicates this version is being used:

```
/*
ECMAScript 6
*/
```

TypeScript

The Angular (https://angular.io/) section will be written in TypeScript (https://www.typescriptlang.org/). Typescript is a superset of JavaScript that adds certain optional features, most notably static typing (https://www.typescriptlang.org/docs/handbook/basic-types.html), through the use of type annotations. TypeScript is used by the Angular team to add some core features to the development environment for Angular. Because not everyone has experience in TypeScript, TypeScript language features in the examples will be pointed out, to keep confusion to a minimum.

The good news on that front is that once the script is up and running, the body of any Angular component can be written as plain old JavaScript.

Tooling

Up until this point, we haven't had to do much in terms of tooling. Almost all the examples will work when served off the local file system, as written.

That won't necessarily be the case going forward. In the simplest case, any examples that require making HTTP requests, for example, will rely on the node package serve (https://www.npmjs.com/package/serve) in order to set up a simple local server.

The React and Angular examples, in particular, require even more extensive tooling. At a minimum you will need to have Node.js (https://nodejs.org/en/) installed and you'll have to follow a few steps to get set up. In the end you'll have a local web server running, and several processes which will watch for changes to your JavaScript or Typescript files. When you make changes, the related processes will catch the changes and perform actions (transpiling the code from Typescript to JavaScript, for example) to ensure that the code is updated on the local server.

There'll be instructions for getting up and running with the code samples in each of the respective sections.

Additionally, remember that all of the working code is available on GitHub (https://github.com/roblarsen/mastering-svg-code).

After all of that, let's look at some code that doesn't require anything other than a newer web browser to run locally.

The DOM interface to SVG

The DOM is an API for accessing, updating, creating, and deleting the elements, properties, and content of XML-based documents. This includes documents in related, but not strict XML, grammars such as the latest HTML specification.

For the average developer, doing a ton of pure DOM manipulation is pretty rare these days. jQuery took care of that many years ago and it's never come back into fashion. I can say from experience that it's still useful to know how DOM manipulation works under the hood so that you can code yourself out of a bind when you run into something the library or framework you're using doesn't provide.

It also illustrates the possibilities of what's available when working with different technologies. It's one thing to have access to something that a library or framework author finds interesting, but if you're familiar with the underlying code, you're only limited by your imagination and what's available in your target browsers.

The SVG DOM builds on the Dom Level 2 Specification (`https://www.w3.org/TR/2000/REC-DOM-Level-2-Core-20001113/core.html`). It supports most of what anyone with DOM and HTML experience would expect and adds several sets of SVG-specific interfaces that you can use to manipulate SVG documents.

This section will go through the basic classes of SVG-specific DOM methods and illustrate their usage. Unless you're writing a library, you won't need to know everything about these lower-level tools. This chapter will serve as an introduction so you have a good introduction to them and know what to look for.

Initial exploration

To get started, let's look at some DOM methods and properties that are available on an arbitrary (and common) SVG element, `rect`. To do this, you might go to the `SVGRectElement` element documentation (`https://developer.mozilla.org/en-US/docs/Web/API/SVGRectElement`). That would be a good option.

You might also inspect a `rect` element directly, using the developer tools of your browser of choice. That will look something like the following screenshot. This will be the way many of you interface with the available methods and properties of SVG elements:

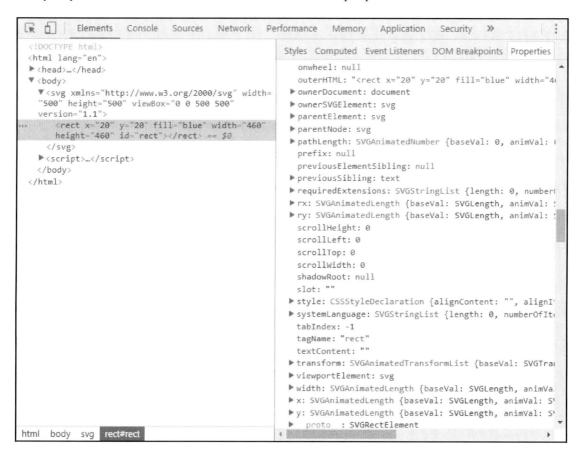

While these are common, you could also do something like the following, which is a nice step towards scripting SVG.

In this code sample we get access to the `rect` element with `document.getElementById` and store it in a variable, `rect`. `document.getElementById` is one of the common DOM accessor methods that you'll use to access DOM elements both in SVG and in HTML itself. You'll see more examples of its use throughout the chapter.

Following that, we then loop through the properties of the `rect` loop using a simple `for...in` loop, writing the variables and properties out to the console using bracket notation where `prop` is the name of a property or method on the `rect` element:

```
<!doctype html>
<html lang="en">

<head>
    <meta charset="utf-8">
    <title>Mastering SVG- SVG Basic SVG DOM Manipulation</title>
</head>

<body>
    <svg xmlns="http://www.w3.org/2000/svg" width="500" height="500"
     viewBox="0 0 500 500" version="1.1">
        <rect x="20" y="20" fill="blue" width="460" height="460"
         id="rect"></rect>
    </svg>
    <script>
    /*
        ES6
    */
        document.addEventListener("DOMContentLoaded", ()=>
            const rect = document.getElementById("rect");
            for (let prop in rect){
                let val = rect[prop];
                console.log(`${prop} = ${val}`);
            }
        });
    </script>
</body>

</html>
```

The output is shown in the following screenshot. You'll notice that the first few properties and methods are all SVG-specific. This list continues on for several screens past the ones in the following screenshot, but the first ones in the list are all SVG specific. This is because the `for...in` loop starts with the innermost properties of the `SVGRectElement` and then works its way up the prototype chain to the properties of the `SVGGeometryElement`, all the way up to `SVGElement`, `Element`, and `Node` (the most generic DOM interface). Of these properties, some are very obvious and immediately useful such as `x`, `y`, `width`, and `height`.

Others might not be as obviously useful, such as `getBBox` or `isPointInFill` (although you might be able to guess what they can do), but you can start to see that there's a lot available for you to work with when you have access to an element:

```
x = [object SVGAnimatedLength]
y = [object SVGAnimatedLength]
width = [object SVGAnimatedLength]
height = [object SVGAnimatedLength]
rx = [object SVGAnimatedLength]
ry = [object SVGAnimatedLength]
pathLength = [object SVGAnimatedNumber]
isPointInFill = function isPointInFill() { [native code] }
isPointInStroke = function isPointInStroke() { [native code] }
getTotalLength = function getTotalLength() { [native code] }
getPointAtLength = function getPointAtLength() { [native code] }
transform = [object SVGAnimatedTransformList]
nearestViewportElement = [object SVGSVGElement]
farthestViewportElement = [object SVGSVGElement]
requiredExtensions = [object SVGStringList]
systemLanguage = [object SVGStringList]
getBBox = function getBBox() { [native code] }
getCTM = function getCTM() { [native code] }
getScreenCTM = function getScreenCTM() { [native code] }
className = [object SVGAnimatedString]
dataset = [object DOMStringMap]
style = [object CSSStyleDeclaration]
ownerSVGElement = [object SVGSVGElement]
viewportElement = [object SVGSVGElement]
tabIndex = -1
onabort = null
onblur = null
oncancel = null
oncanplay = null
oncanplaythrough = null
```

Console | What's New ✕ | Search

Taking that basic foundation and the idea of exploration, let's start to build a small application that lets you manipulate an SVG canvas in simple ways. The next section will focus on building out a small tool, step-by-step, that will allow you to add simple SVG elements to an SVG canvas (`text`, `rect`, and `circle`) and manipulate them in different ways. This small demo will be easy to digest and will demonstrate a number of different ways to interact with SVG.

The SVG DOM manipulator

The app we're going to build will allow you to click and add three different kinds of SVG element to an SVG canvas. The interface will allow you to click on the item you want to add (rect, circle, or text) and then you will be able to click on the canvas and add that element to the screen at those particular (x, y) coordinates. With that element selected, you will then be able to edit it by changing several available properties.

This example will use Bootstrap to simplify laying out the different form fields and to create a simple modal to edit the properties. Because of that, jQuery will also be included, although, for this version of the demo at least, jQuery interactions will be kept to a minimum; we'll focus on raw DOM manipulations.

When it's complete, it will look as shown in the following screenshot, which shows the SVG canvas at the top of the screen, bordered in black. After that there are simple instructions and then at the bottom of the screen there are three buttons that allow you to select a rectangle, a circle, or a text element to add to the canvas:

This time, instead of adding the entire code sample at once and explaining the whole thing, as we've been doing so far in the book, we are going to build the sample and discuss each code block as we go through the example.

Let's start with the skeleton of the page. This initial state doesn't have any JavaScript in it at all, but it does provide us with some structure and some tools we'll use later.

In the `head` we link to Bootstrap from a **Content Delivery Network (CDN)**, we link to the Raleway font from Google fonts and then set up some basic styles for our page, adding Raleway as the body font, putting a border around our canvas SVG element, and then changing the color of our SVG sprite buttons.

In the body, we set the page up to be responsive, using Bootstrap's utility classes to create a fluid layout that fills the entire screen width. The SVG element will scale to fit this Bootstrap container.

The layout has two sections: the target SVG element, where the drawings will happen, and a second section for the UI controls. The UI controls, for now, are just three `button` elements wrapped around SVG sprites.

Next, we have a hidden SVG element featuring a series of `symbol` elements, defining our sprites.

Finally, we link out to some third party JavaScript in order to wire up some of the Bootstrap functionality:

```
<!doctype html>
<html lang="en">

<head>
  <meta charset="utf-8">
  <title>Mastering SVG- SVG Basic The DOM Manipulator</title>
  <link rel="stylesheet"
   href="https://maxcdn.bootstrapcdn.com/bootstrap/4.0.0/css/bootstrap.
    min.css" integrity="sha384-
    Gn5384xqQ1aoWXA+058RXPxPg6fy4IWvTNh0E263XmFcJlSAwiGgFAW/dAiS6JXm"
    crossorigin="anonymous">
  <link href="https://fonts.googleapis.com/css?family=Raleway"
    rel="stylesheet">
  <style type="text/css">
    body {
      font-family: Raleway, sans-serif;
    }
    svg.canvas {
      border: 1px solid black;
    }
```

```
      button svg {
        fill: cornflowerblue;
        stroke: cornflowerblue;
        max-width: 50px;
      }
  </style>
</head>

<body>

  <div class="container-fluid">
    <div class="row">
        <div class="col-12">
            <svg xmlns="http://www.w3.org/2000/svg" viewBox="0 0 500
              200" version="1.1" id="canvas" class="canvas">
            </svg>
        </div>
    </div>
    <div class="row">
      <div class="col-5 offset-2">
        <h2>Pick an SVG element to add to the canvas. </h2>
        <p>Click on an item to select it and then click on the canvas
              to place it in the SVG element.</p>
      </div>
    </div>
    <div class="row">
      <div class="col-4 text-center">
        <button class="btn btn-link" title="click to add a circle">
          <svg xmlns="http://www.w3.org/2000/svg" role="img">
            <use xlink:href="#circle"></use>
          </svg>
        </button>
      </div>
      <div class="col-4 text-center" title="click to add a square">
        <button class="btn btn-link">

          <svg xmlns="http://www.w3.org/2000/svg" role="img">
            <use xlink:href="#square"></use>
          </svg>
        </button>
      </div>
      <div class="col-4 text-center">
        <button class="btn btn-link" title="click to add a text box">
          <svg xmlns="http://www.w3.org/2000/svg" role="img">
            <use xlink:href="#text"></use>
          </svg>
        </button>
      </div>
```

```
    </div>
  </div>


  <svg xmlns="http://www.w3.org/2000/svg" style="display:none">
    <defs>
      <symbol id="circle" viewBox="0 0 512 512">
        <circle cx="256" cy="256" r="256"></circle>
      </symbol>
      <symbol id="square" viewBox="0 0 512 512">
        <rect x="6" y="6" height="500" width="500"></rect>
      </symbol>
      <symbol id="text" viewBox="0 0 512 512">
        <rect x="6" y="106" height="300" width="500" fill="none"
            stroke-width="10px"></rect>
        <text x="6" y="325" font-size="150">TEXT</text>
      </symbol>
      <!--
      Font Awesome Free 5.0.2 by @fontawesome - http://fontawesome.com
      License - http://fontawesome.com/license (Icons: CC BY 4.0,
        Fonts: SIL OFL 1.1, Code: MIT License)
      -->
      <symbol id="edit" viewBox="0 0 576 512">
          <title id="edit-title">Edit</title>
          <path d="M402.6 83.2l90.2 90.2c3.8 3.8 3.8 10 0 13.8L274.4
            405.6l-92.8 10.3c-12.4 1.4-22.9-9.1-21.5-21.5l10.3-
            92.8L388.8 83.2c3.8-3.8 10-3.8 13.8 0zm162-22.9l-48.8-
            48.8c-15.2-15.2-39.9-15.2-55.2 0l-35.4 35.4c-3.8 3.8-3.8 10
            0 13.8l90.2 90.2c3.8 3.8 10 3.8 13.8 0l35.4-35.4c15.2-15.3
            15.2-40 0-55.2zM384 346.2V448H64V128h229.8c3.2 0 6.2-1.3
            8.5-3.5l40-40c7.6-7.6 2.2-20.5-8.5-20.5H48C21.5 64 0 85.5 0
            112v352c0 26.5 21.5 48 48 48h352c26.5 0 48-21.5 48-
            48V306.2c0-10.7-12.9-16-20.5-8.5l-40 40c-2.2 2.3-3.5 5.3-
            3.5 8.5z"></path>
      </symbol>
    </defs>
  </svg>
  <script>

  </script>
  <script src="https://code.jquery.com/jquery-3.2.1.slim.min.js"
      integrity="sha384-
KJ3o2DKtIkvYIK3UENzmM7KCkRr/rE9/Qpg6aAZGJwFDMVNA/GpGFF93hXpG5KkN"
    crossorigin="anonymous"></script>
  <script
   src="https://cdnjs.cloudflare.com/ajax/libs/popper.js/1.12.9/umd/pop
    per.min.js" integrity="sha384-
```

```
    ApNbgh9B+Y1QKtv3Rn7W3mgPxhU9K/ScQsAP7hUibX39j7fakFPskvXusvfa0b4Q"
    crossorigin="anonymous"></script>
  <script
    src="https://maxcdn.bootstrapcdn.com/bootstrap/4.0.0/js/bootstrap.mi
    n.js" integrity="sha384-
    JZR6Spejh4U02d8jOt6vLEHfe/JQGiRRSQQxSfFWpi1MquVdAyjUar5+76PVCmYl"
    crossorigin="anonymous"></script>
</body>

</html>
```

Now that we've taken a look at the basics of the page, let's start to add some interactivity.

 Although we have jQuery on the page, I'm not going to use it for any of the DOM manipulations so that we can look at the raw interactions. We will look at jQuery and SVG in `Chapter 7`, *Common JavaScript Libraries and SVG*, so don't fret.

The first thing we'll do is create a few event handlers to handle the different interactions. The first event handlers we'll add are `click` event handlers on the buttons. The idea is that you click on the button to load an SVG element onto your cursor, and then you click once more to place it on the canvas. This code doesn't yet handle adding the element to the SVG canvas, but it does illustrate a couple of wrinkles when working with SVG and JavaScript.

This is an instance where some things you might know from old-school DOM manipulation might fail you. If you've been manipulating the HTML DOM directly for any length of time, you might be used to working with the `Element.className` property. On HTML elements, the `className` property is a `read/write` string that maps to the `class` attribute on the HTML element. In that context, you can manipulate the string and changes are reflected in the DOM.

The DOM interface `SVGElement` does have a `className` property, but it isn't a simple string. Its an `SVGAnimatedString` property with two string values, `AnimVal` and `BaseVal`. Because of that extra layer, and because the interface for my chosen alternative is modern and much clearer, I decided to use the `SVGElement.classList` property to manipulate the CSS classes instead. `classList` is a structured interface to the CSS classes on an element. Accessed directly, `classList` is `readonly`, but there are methods available to query and manipulate the list of classes.

Let's dive into this code to see how that works.

We start the whole thing by adding a function that fires on the DOMContentLoaded event. This event fires a function when the DOM has been read by the browser. This is the safest place to start to manipulate the DOM if you're looking to use an element on the page when the markup is read by the browser. Then we set two local references, one to document via the variable doc and the other to the SVG canvas itself, via the canvas variable.

We create local references to DOM properties and elements because DOM lookups can be slow. Saving a local reference to DOM properties and elements is a common performance pattern.

Then we get the collection of buttons, using querySelectorAll, and loop through each of them in turn, adding a click event handler to each button. Inside the body of the click event handlers, we initially set two local references, classlist as a reference to the target SVG element's classList, and a const, referencing the type of element that has been requested. This type is being passed in via a data-* attribute on the use element. data-* is a method for storing arbitrary data on a DOM element.

We then use that type and a simple if...else statement to ensure that the proper classes are on the target SVG element. In the first if block, we test to see if the current classes match the current type and that it has the active class. If they match the current type and the element has the active class, we remove the classes. This action is for cases where we've already loaded the cursor with a specific type and want to reset it by clicking on the same button. The next block checks to see if the cursor is active but isn't the currently selected type. In that case, we remove all of the type classes to ensure we clear the selected type, and then add the currently selected one back in. In the final block, the cursor isn't active, so we just add the active class and the type class, loading up the cursor:

```
/*
Ecmascript 6
*/
document.addEventListener("DOMContentLoaded", () => {
  let doc = document;
  let canvas = doc.getElementById("canvas");
  doc.querySelectorAll(".controls .btn").forEach((element) => {
    element.addEventListener("click", (event) => {
      let classlist = canvas.classList;
      const type = event.srcElement.dataset.type;
      if (classlist.contains("active") && classlist.contains(type)){
        classlist.remove("active",type);
      }
      else if (classlist.contains("active")){
        classlist.remove("circle","text","square");
        classlist.add(type);
```

```
    } else {
      classlist.remove("circle","text","square");
      classlist.add("active",type);
    }
  });
 });
});
```

The CSS for the active cursors is as follows. In the new CSS we simply pass a URL reference to a PNG to the cursor property for each of the active cursors:

```
svg.canvas.active.square{
  cursor:url(square.png), crosshair;
}
svg.canvas.active.circle{
  cursor:url(circle.png), crosshair;
}
svg.canvas.active.text{
  cursor:url(text.png), crosshair;
}
```

A cursor loaded with a circle element looks like the following screenshot:

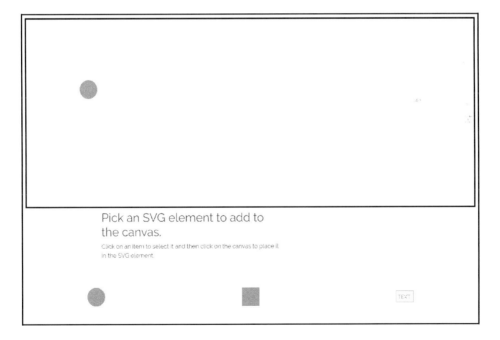

Next up we'll go through the process of adding elements on click to the target SVG element. The function `add` is where the magic happens. In it we first set a number of variables. We start with five consts. The first is a reference to the `document`, stored as `doc`, the second is a reference to the target SVG element, stored as `canvas`, the third is the target SVG's `classList`, stored as `classes`, then there's a reference to the SVG namespace URL, stored as **namespace** (**NS**), and finally there's an `SVGpoint`, created and stored as `point`. The first three should be straightforward; the usage of the `NS` variable will be explained shortly.

`point` is used immediately. This is one major difference between regular DOM manipulation and working with the SVG DOM, so let's take a look at what's going on there. The basic purpose of this code is to transform the screen coordinates from the click event to the proper (potentially transformed or scaled) coordinates inside the SVG element. If you've been paying attention to the way that SVG scales, in general, and the way that transforms work with SVG elements, you should be able to see how, depending on the way the document is set up, the screen pixels may or may not match up to the user units within the SVG document. Since we've got a static `viewbox` set to 500 user units and an SVG element that scales to fit the entire page, we are going to need to use some SVG tools to access the current transformation matrix and apply that matrix to the point of the click.

To do this, we have a couple of steps that we need to go through. `point` is created via `createSVGPoint`, which is a method that returns a point in the current SVG coordinate system. The initial return value has two properties, `x` and `y`, set to zero. We immediately populate that variable with the mouse coordinates of the click event. These are available as part of the event object that's automatically passed in as an argument to the function as `event.offsetX` and `event.offsetY`. Next we use the `getScreenCTM()` method to get the inverse of the **Current user unit Transformation Matrix** (**CTM**). The CTM represents the transformation steps required to convert from the screen coordinate system to the one in the SVG document. Calling the `inverse()` method returns the steps required to move from the SVG user unit coordinate system to the one on the screen. Applying that matrix to the `(x, y)` points defined in point, therefore, shifts the points to the correct place in the SVG document.

Finally, we create an empty variable, `elem`, which is going to be filled later with the element we're looking to add to the document.

Next, we actually create the element.

If the class active is on the target SVG element, then we're going to add an element to it. No matter which type of element we're trying to create, the pattern is the same:

1. We test which type of element is active.
2. We create the element.
3. We set a couple of properties on it before adding it to the DOM.

Again, if you're familiar with DOM manipulations, then you'll notice some differences here. This is where the NS variable comes into play. Since this isn't pure HTML and is, in fact, an entirely different document definition, we need to supply that namespace in order to create the element properly. So, instead of document.createElement, we have to use document.createElementNS and we pass in a second argument referencing the SVG namespace via the NS variable.

Once the element is created, we set the relevant attributes using elem.setAttribute. For the rect we set x, y, width, and height. For the circle we set r, cx, and cy. For the text element we set x, y and then set the text content using elem.textContent, which is a new wrinkle if you're used to updating text and/or HTML nodes with innerHTML. As mentioned previously, there is no innerHTML of an SVG element.

Once the elem is defined with the baseline attributes, we insert it into the document using the appendChild method. Finally, we remove the "active" class from the target SVG element, which will prevent further elements being added accidentally:

```
function add(event) {
    const classes = canvas.classList;
    const NS = canvas.getAttribute('xmlns');
    const point = canvas.createSVGPoint()
    point.x = event.offsetX;
    point.y = event.offsetY;
    const svgCoords =
    point.matrixTransform(canvas.getScreenCTM().inverse());
    let elem;
    if (classes.contains("active")) {
      if (classes.contains("square")) {
        elem = doc.createElementNS(NS, "rect");
        elem.setAttribute("x", svgCoords.x);
        elem.setAttribute("y", svgCoords.y);
        elem.setAttribute("width", 50);
        elem.setAttribute("height", 50);

      } else if (classes.contains("circle")) {
        elem = doc.createElementNS(NS, "circle");
        elem.setAttribute("r", 10);
        elem.setAttribute("cx", svgCoords.x);
```

```
          elem.setAttribute("cy", svgCoords.y);
      } else if (classes.contains("text")) {
        elem = doc.createElementNS(NS, "text");
        elem.setAttribute("x", svgCoords.x);
        elem.setAttribute("y", svgCoords.y);
        elem.textContent = "TEXT"
      }
      elem.setAttribute("fill", "#ff8000");
      canvas.appendChild(elem);
      classes.remove("active");
    }
  }
```

This is a newly added square element on the SVG canvas as follows:

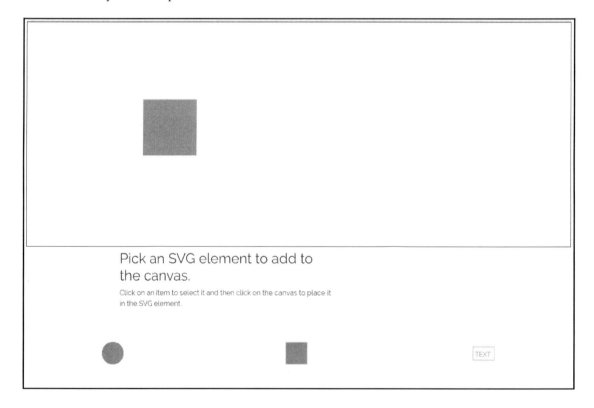

While we now have events bound to the document and can add elements to the screen, this demo isn't done just yet. What we need to do to finish this off is to allow the user to update the elements that have been placed on the target SVG element. While we could do that in increasingly complicated ways (clicking and dragging, drawing new elements with the mouse or with your finger, copying and pasting elements) for the sake of this demo, we're simply going to allow the user to click on the SVG element and open up a small Bootstrap modal which will allow them to edit basic SVG properties. This will illustrate manipulating the underlying DOM properties without getting into too much depth on any one set of interactions. This is especially key since many of the most complicated interactions are better handled by a separate library or framework anyway. As you'll see, doing this stuff entirely by hand can be cumbersome even in the best of circumstances.

So let's get that started. The first thing we'll do is update the add function with one line. This line adds the click event handler to elem, which will fire the edit function. So, looking at the bottom of the add function, we can see the new code:

```
elem.setAttribute("fill", "#ff8000");
canvas.appendChild(elem);
classes.remove("active");
elem.addEventListener("click", edit, false);
```

Before we look at the edit function, let's look at the modal markup. If you've worked with Bootstrap before, this should be familiar. If not, the basics are pretty straightforward. The pattern of the Bootstrap modal wrapper class and modal- classes adds the Bootstrap modal layout, and the classes also indicate that the Bootstrap JavaScript should bind Bootstrap-specific events to this particular element. We'll see one of these events in action shortly.

Each of the modals has an id to reference from our functions as well as specific form fields required to update the selected elements.

The first modal is used to edit the rect elements. It has an input of type color to allow the user to choose a new color for the background, two inputs of type number to update the x and y coordinates, and two number inputs to update the height and width of the element.

 Inputs of type number and type color are newer, HTML5 input types.

The second modal is used to edit the `circle` elements. It provides a `color input` to change the background color, two `number inputs` to change the `cx` and `cy` attributes, and a final `number input` to change the radius of the circle.

The final modal is used to edit the `text` elements. It provides a `color input` to change the color of the text, two `number inputs` to change the `x` and `y` positions of the element, and a `text input` to change the actual text of the `text` element:

```
<div class="modal" tabindex="-1" role="dialog" id="rect-edit-modal">
    <div class="modal-dialog" role="document">
      <div class="modal-content">
        <div class="modal-header">
          <h5 class="modal-title">Edit your element</h5>
          <button type="button" class="close" data-dismiss="modal"
            aria-label="Close">
            <span aria-hidden="true">&times;</span>
          </button>
        </div>
        <div class="modal-body">
          <div class="row">
            <div class="col-4">
              <label for="rect-color">Background color:</label>
            </div>
            <div class="col-8">
              <input type="color" id="rect-color">
            </div>
          </div>
          <div class="row">
            <div class="col-2">
              <label for="rect-x">x:</label>
            </div>
            <div class="col-4">
              <input type="number" id="rect-x" class="form-control">
            </div>
            <div class="col-2">
              <label for="rect-y">y:</label>
            </div>
            <div class="col-4">
              <input type="number" id="rect-y" class="form-control">
            </div>
          </div>
          <div class="row">
            <div class="col-2">
              <label for="rect-width">width:</label>
            </div>
            <div class="col-4">
              <input type="number" id="rect-width" class="form-
```

```
              control">
          </div>
          <div class="col-2">
            <label for="rect-height">height:</label>
          </div>
          <div class="col-4">
            <input type="number" id="rect-height" class="form-
              control">
          </div>
        </div>
      </div>
      <div class="modal-footer">
        <button type="button" class="btn btn-primary" id="rect-
          save">Save changes</button>
        <button type="button" class="btn btn-secondary" data-
          dismiss="modal">Close</button>
      </div>
    </div>
  </div>
</div>
<div class="modal" tabindex="-1" role="dialog" id="circle-edit-
  modal">
  <div class="modal-dialog" role="document">
    <div class="modal-content">
      <div class="modal-header">
        <h5 class="modal-title">Edit your element</h5>
        <button type="button" class="close" data-dismiss="modal"
            aria-label="Close">
          <span aria-hidden="true">&times;</span>
        </button>
      </div>
      <div class="modal-body">
        <div class="row">
          <div class="col-4">
            <label for="circle-color">Background color:</label>
          </div>
          <div class="col-8">
            <input type="color" id="circle-color">
          </div>
        </div>
        <div class="row">
          <div class="col-2">
            <label for="cirlce-cx">cx:</label>
          </div>
          <div class="col-4">
            <input type="number" id="circle-cx" class="form-control">
          </div>
          <div class="col-2">
```

```
        <label for="circle-cy">cy:</label>
      </div>
      <div class="col-4">
        <input type="number" id="circle-cy" class="form-control">
      </div>
    </div>
    <div class="row">
      <div class="col-2">
        <label for="circle-radius">radius:</label>
      </div>
      <div class="col-4">
        <input type="number" id="circle-radius" class="form-
          control">
      </div>

    </div>
  </div>
  <div class="modal-footer">
    <button type="button" class="btn btn-primary" id="circle-
      save">Save changes</button>
    <button type="button" class="btn btn-secondary" data-
      dismiss="modal">Close</button>
  </div>
  </div>
  </div>
</div>
<div class="modal" tabindex="-1" role="dialog" id="text-edit-modal">
  <div class="modal-dialog" role="document">
    <div class="modal-content">
      <div class="modal-header">
        <h5 class="modal-title">Edit your element</h5>
        <button type="button" class="close" data-dismiss="modal"
          aria-label="Close">
          <span aria-hidden="true">&times;</span>
        </button>
      </div>
      <div class="modal-body">
        <div class="row">
          <div class="col-4">
            <label for="text-color">Color:</label>
          </div>
          <div class="col-8">
            <input type="color" id="text-color">
          </div>
        </div>
        <div class="row">
          <div class="col-2">
            <label for="text-x">x:</label>
```

```
      </div>
      <div class="col-4">
        <input type="number" id="text-x" class="form-control">
      </div>
      <div class="col-2">
        <label for="text=y">y:</label>
      </div>
      <div class="col-4">
        <input type="number" id="text-y" class="form-control">
      </div>
    </div>
    <div class="row">
      <div class="col-2">
        <label for="text-text">content:</label>
      </div>
      <div class="col-10">
        <input type="text" id="text-text" class="form-control">
      </div>

    </div>
  </div>
  <div class="modal-footer">
    <button type="button" class="btn btn-primary" id="text-
      save">Save changes</button>
    <button type="button" class="btn btn-secondary" data-
      dismiss="modal">Close</button>
  </div>
    </div>
  </div>
</div>
```

Now let's take a look at the `edit` function. Most of the interesting stuff here happens based on the `event argument`. `event` has references to all sorts of information about the event being fired. `edit` checks the `event.srcElement.nodeName` to see what kind of element has been clicked. The function then does three things for each of the element types.

1. It opens the correct editing modal using the `$().modal` method called with the `"show"` option.
2. It stores a reference to the current element using the jQuery `$().data()` method. `$().data` allows you to bind arbitrary data to an element. We'll look at more jQuery features in `Chapter 7`, *Common JavaScript Libraries and SVG*, but since we are already using jQuery to get to the Bootstrap methods, let's use `$().data()` here for the sake of convenience.

3. It loads up the current values from the clicked element and loads them into the form fields. There are multiple instances of this, but for the most part they follow the same pattern. The `form` field is referenced via `id` and the value is set using the current value accessed by `event.srcElement.getAttribute`. The one exception is the text value of the text element that is accessed by the `event.srcElement.textContent` attribute.

So, as soon as the element is clicked, the modal is opened and populated with the current values ready to be manipulated:

```
function edit(event) {
  let elem = event.srcElement;

  if (event.srcElement.nodeName.toLowerCase() === "rect") {
    $("#rect-edit-modal").modal("show").data("current-element",
      elem);
    document.getElementById("rect-color").value =
      elem.getAttribute("fill");
    document.getElementById("rect-x").value =
      elem.getAttribute("x");
    document.getElementById("rect-y").value =
      elem.getAttribute("y");
    document.getElementById("rect-width").value =
      elem.getAttribute("width");
    document.getElementById("rect-height").value =
      elem.getAttribute("height");
  }
  else if (event.srcElement.nodeName.toLowerCase() === "circle") {
    $("#circle-edit-modal").modal("show").data("current-element",
      elem);
    document.getElementById("circle-color").value =
      elem.getAttribute("fill");
    document.getElementById("circle-cx").value =
      elem.getAttribute("cx");
    document.getElementById("circle-cy").value =
      elem.getAttribute("cy");
    document.getElementById("circle-radius").value =
      elem.getAttribute("r");
  }
  else if (event.srcElement.nodeName.toLowerCase() === "text") {
    $("#text-edit-modal").modal("show").data("current-element",
      event.srcElement);
    document.getElementById("text-color").value =
      elem.getAttribute("fill");
    document.getElementById("text-x").value =
      elem.getAttribute("x");
    document.getElementById("text-y").value =
```

```
        elem.getAttribute("y");
      document.getElementById("text-text").value =
        elem.textContent;
    }
  }
```

The following is what an opened modal looks like:

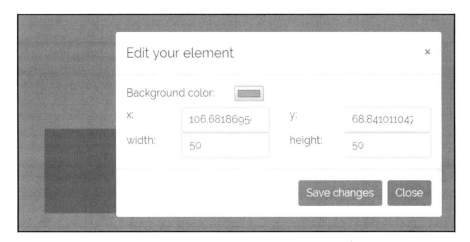

To capture the changes, we need to add some more event handlers to the document and a few more functions to save the data. This is done by adding some click handlers to the three modals save buttons and defining three different functions to handle the changes.

As you can see in the next sample, the event handlers are straightforward. You get a reference to each of the save buttons with `document.getElementById`, and using `addEventListener` add the correct save handler to each of the elements:

```
document.getElementById("rect-save").addEventListener("click",
  rectSave);
document.getElementById("circle-save").addEventListener("click",
circleSave);
document.getElementById("text-save").addEventListener("click",
  textSave);
```

The various save functions are also pretty straightforward. They all initially hide the opened modal using the $.modal() method with the hide argument passed in. After that the function stores a reference to the currently clicked element using the get signature of the $().data() method and stores it as a local variable elem. Then, depending on the type, the function accesses values from the form and sets the new values on the selected element. rectSave accesses the fill, x, y, height, and width attributes. circleSave accesses the fill, cx, cy, and r attributes. textSave accesses the fill, x, y, and text attributes:

```
function rectSave() {
    $("#rect-edit-modal").modal("hide");
    let elem = $("#rect-edit-modal").data("current-element")
    elem.setAttribute("fill", document.getElementById("rect-
    color").value);
    elem.setAttribute("x", document.getElementById("rect-
    x").value);
    elem.setAttribute("y", document.getElementById("rect-
    y").value);
    elem.setAttribute("height", document.getElementById("rect-
    height").value);
    elem.setAttribute("width", document.getElementById("rect-
    width").value);
}
function circleSave() {
    $("#circle-edit-modal").modal("hide");
    let elem = $("#circle-edit-modal").data("current-element")
    elem.setAttribute("fill", document.getElementById("circle-
    color").value);
    elem.setAttribute("cx", document.getElementById("circle-
    cx").value);
    elem.setAttribute("cy", document.getElementById("circle-
     cy").value);
    elem.setAttribute("r", document.getElementById("circle-
    radius").value);
}
function textSave() {
    $("#text-edit-modal").modal("hide");
    let elem = $("#text-edit-modal").data("current-element")
    elem.setAttribute("fill", document.getElementById("text-
    color").value);
    elem.setAttribute("x", document.getElementById("text-
    x").value);
    elem.setAttribute("y", document.getElementById("text-
    y").value);
    elem.textContent = document.getElementById("text-text").value;
}
```

Running the edit function against a `text` element looks as shown in the following screenshot:

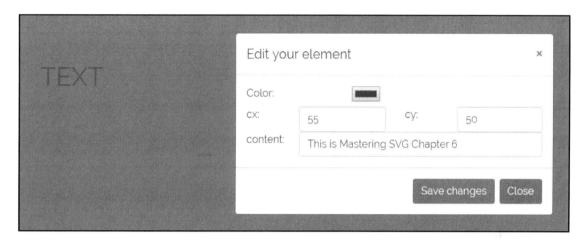

Applying those values produces the following output:

This is Mastering SVG Chapter 6

While there are many, many more features we could add to this small SVG editing demo, this example is both simple enough to understand in a single chapter and also allows us to illustrate the basic patterns used to add, access, and update SVG elements on screen. If you've had some experience with raw DOM manipulations in the past, this should all be familiar to you. If you haven't, it's a useful set of skills to have, and the basic pattern you've seen here is the way that this all works in both the SVG and HTML realms. Once you have access to an element, you can then access and update its properties and call various methods on it to adjust it on the screen. With this foundation, you'll be able to solve problems that might not be easily solved by a library or framework in both SVG and HTML

Summary

In this chapter, you created a small application that allows you to add and edit SVG elements on a target SVG canvas. Working your way through this application, you learned about a wide variety of DOM features and functionality, including:

- Two different ways to access DOM elements, using `document.getElementById` and `document.querySelectorAll`
- How to insert SVG elements using `document.createElementNS` and `appendChild`
- How to bind events to HTML and SVG elements using `addEventListener`
- How to get, set, and remove CSS classes from an SVG element using the `classList` interface
- How to manipulate common SVG properties using `getAttribute` and `setAttribute`
- How to convert between the browser coordinate system and the SVG element coordinate system by using the `getScreenCTM` method to get the inverse of the Current user unit *Transformation Matrix*
- How to set the text content of an SVG text element using `textContent`

Together with the lessons you've already learned in this book, the lessons you learned in this chapter will mean you are ready to work with SVG at a very high level across a large variety of tasks. If you're comfortable with the raw DOM interface, the patterns of creating, accessing, and manipulating DOM elements are all you need to build the most complicated web apps and visualizations.

Taking that foundation, we're going to now apply everything we've learned so far to other libraries and frameworks so that you can take advantage of the power and convenience that libraries such as jQuery, React, and D3, and frameworks such as Angular, provide on top of the raw DOM interface.

Common JavaScript Libraries and SVG

7

Now that you've taken a look at the raw DOM interface to SVG, it's time to look at the interface between SVG and some of the more common JavaScript libraries and frameworks. Taking the lessons learned from Chapter 6, *JavaScript and SVG*, we'll look at some of the quirks present in getting SVG to work properly with jQuery, AngularJS (1.*), Angular (2+), and ReactJS. These examples will not be very deep, but should all illustrate the basic issues present in working with SVG and these other codebases. The goal here won't be to introduce you fully to these libraries and frameworks. There will be just enough of an introduction to get you up and running, and then each section will deal with the specifics of that library, or framework and SVG.

In this chapter, we will cover:

- Working with the ever-popular jQuery library and SVG
- The interface between Angular 1 and Angular (2+) and SVG
- SVG and ReactJS, the popular library from Facebook

Manipulating SVG with jQuery

The first library we'll look at is jQuery. jQuery isn't as hot as it once was, but it's still the most popular JavaScript library on the planet, and understanding the quirks of using SVG with jQuery is still potentially useful.

Since jQuery functions as a friendly replacement for common DOM interactions, this section will feature a jQuery-based rewrite of the DOM manipulator demo we worked on in Chapter 6, JavaScript and SVG.

It uses the exact same markup, so the only place we need to look at in this chapter is the script block at the bottom.

This code will be written in idiomatic jQuery/ES5.

The first thing we'll look at is the function we'll fire on jQuery's equivalent of the `DOMContentLoaded` event, `$(document).ready()`. `$(document).ready()` takes a function as an argument. As the name implies, that function will be executed when the document's DOM content has finished loading.

While you could pass in a function expression, we're going to define a traditionally-named function called `init` to pass into `$(document).ready()`.

In it, we set a few event handlers. The first is a `click` event handler for our buttons. It fires the `loadCursor` function. The second through fourth event handlers create `save` events for each of the different SVG element types. The last one adds the `add` function to the `#canvas` element so that clicks on the canvas element will know to drop the chosen SVG elements onto the page:

```
function init() {
    $(".controls .btn").on("click", loadCursor);
    $("#rect-save").on("click", rectSave);
    $("#circle-save").on("click", circleSave);
    $("#text-save").on("click", textSave);
    $("#canvas").on("click", add);
}
$().ready(init);
```

Now that we've taken a look at the function that kicks off the application, let's look at the other functions in turn. First we'll look at the new version of the `add` function. `add` has one major wrinkle and then several smaller ones.

We start off by grabbing a loaded jQuery reference to the `$("#canvas")` SVG element. After that, the initialization is similar to the vanilla JavaScript Version of the function.

This includes one major wrinkle, where the expected behavior from jQuery fails. While the common jQuery element creation methods like `$("<rect>")` work with SVG elements and will insert the `<rect>` element into the page, they still need to be created with the proper namespace. Without the namespace, as you learned in the previous chapter, they will be treated by browsers like arbitrary HTML elements and won't render as expected. So, like the vanilla JS example, we need to add the namespace to the element creation. So we do that with the same `elem = doc.createElementNS(NS, "rect");` pattern we used in the JavaScript-only example. Once the element is created, it can be inserted into the DOM and manipulated with jQuery as normal.

After the elements are created, the individual options for the square, circle, and text are all handled similarly to the JavaScript-only example. In this case we just use the jQuery convenience methods $().hasClass() and $().attr() to test the class name and set the various attributes.

Finally, we use a few more jQuery convenience methods to add the element to the $canvas element, remove the "active" class, and add the click event handler to edit the elements:

```
function add($event) {
    var $canvas = $("#canvas");
    var elem;
    var doc = document;
    var NS = canvas.getAttribute('xmlns');
    var point = canvas.createSVGPoint();
    var $elem;
    point.x = $event.offsetX;
    point.y = $event.offsetY;
    var svgCoords =
      point.matrixTransform(canvas.getScreenCTM().inverse());
    if ($canvas.hasClass("active")) {
      if ($canvas.hasClass("square")) {
        elem = doc.createElementNS(NS, "rect");
        $elem = $(elem).attr({
          "x": svgCoords.x,
          "y": svgCoords.y,
          "width": 50,
          "height": 50
        });

      } else if ($canvas.hasClass("circle")) {
        elem = doc.createElementNS(NS, "circle");

        $elem = $(elem).attr({
          "cx": svgCoords.x,
          "cy": svgCoords.y,
          "r": 10
        });
      } else if ($canvas.hasClass("text")) {
        elem = doc.createElementNS(NS, "text");
        $elem = $(elem).attr({
          "x": svgCoords.x,
          "y": svgCoords.y,
          "width": 50,
          "height": 50
        });
        $elem.text("TEXT");
```

```
    }
    $elem.attr("fill", "#ff8000");
    $canvas.append($elem);
    $canvas.removeClass("active");
    $elem.on("click", edit);
  }
}
```

The three edit functions again follow the same pattern as the vanilla JS example. In each function we get a loaded jQuery reference to the `target` element and store it as `$elem`. We then use the jQuery method `$().prop`, which looks up object properties, to test for the `nodeName` of the calling object. We then show the correct modal, with the Bootstrap modal method called with the `"show"` argument, and set the current element with the jQuery `$().data` method. `$().data`, as you'll remember from Chapter 6, *JavaScript and SVG*, gets and sets arbitrary data on an element. We then use a combination of the `$().val()` method, which gets or sets the value of form inputs, and the `$().attr()` method, which gets or sets an element attribute, to populate the form values. `$().val()` is used here to set the values of the forms by reading the value of the SVG elements with `$().attr()`, called a `getter` (with no arguments) and using that value as `$().val()`'s argument:

```
function edit($event) {
    var $elem = $($event.target);
    if ($elem.prop("nodeName") === "rect") {
      $("#rect-edit-modal").modal("show").data("current-element",
        $elem);

      $("#rect-color").val($elem.attr("fill"));
      $("#rect-x").val($elem.attr("x"));
      $("#rect-y").val($elem.attr("y"));
      $("#rect-width").val($elem.attr("width"));
      $("#rect-height").val($elem.attr("height"));
    }
    else if ($elem.prop("nodeName") === "circle") {
      $("#circle-edit-modal").modal("show").data("current-element",
        $elem);
      $("#circle-color").val($elem.attr("fill"));
      $("#circle-cx").val($elem.attr("cx"));
      $("#circle-cy").val($elem.attr("cy"));
      $("#circle-radius").val($elem.attr("r"));
    }
    else if ($elem.prop("nodeName") === "text") {
      $("#text-edit-modal").modal("show").data("current-element",
        $elem);
      $("#text-color").val($elem.attr("fill"));
      $("#text-x").val($elem.attr("x"));
```

```
    $("#text-y").val($elem.attr("y"));
    $("#text-text").val($elem.text());
  }
}
```

Finally, we have the various `save` methods. These follow the same pattern as the previous examples. It's the same basic workflow as the vanilla JS example, but once again we are able to use the full suite of jQuery convenience methods against our SVG elements: using the Bootstrap method to hide the modal, grabbing a reference to the current element using the `$().data()` method, and then setting attributes with the `$().attr()` method, called a setter, and `$().val()` called a getter, as the argument:

```
function rectSave() {
  $("#rect-edit-modal").modal("hide");
  var $elem = $("#rect-edit-modal").data("current-element");
  $elem.attr({
    "fill": $("#rect-color").val(),
    "x": $("#rect-x").val(),
    "y": $("#rect-y").val(),
    "height": $("#rect-height").val(),
    "width": $("#rect-width").val()
  });
}
function circleSave() {
  $("#circle-edit-modal").modal("hide");
  var $elem = $("#circle-edit-modal").data("current-element");
  $elem.attr({
    "fill": $("#circle-color").val(),
    "cx": $("#circle-cx").val(),
    "cy": $("#circle-cy").val(),
    "r": $("#circle-radius").val()
  });
}
function textSave() {
  $("#text-edit-modal").modal("hide");
  var $elem = $("#text-edit-modal").data("current-element");
  $elem.attr({
    "fill": $("#text-color").val(), "x": $("#text-x").val(),
    "y": $("#text-y").val()
  });
  $elem.text($("#text-text").val());
}
```

As you can see, with the exception of element creation, working with SVG and jQuery is straightforward. Element creation requires using a standard DOM method, but every other interaction with SVG elements can use the appropriate jQuery methods.

Working with AngularJS and SVG

Now it's time to look at using SVG inside more complete application frameworks. We're going to start with AngularJS, the original Version of Google's wildly popular application framework. While AngularJS (Angular 1.*) is old in the context of web frameworks, it remains popular and in use in many environments. It's also familiar to many people and is widely deployed, so taking a brief look at how to work with SVG inside an AngularJS application is useful from multiple perspectives.

This and the following examples will be simpler than the jQuery and pure JavaScript demos. There are two reasons for this. The first is that you've seen a lot of details, under the hood, about how SVG and JavaScript interact in the DOM. You're actually ready to tackle SVG DOM manipulation on your own, so going over a wide number of variations in the different frameworks might not even be that beneficial. Covering the basics should give you enough to go off on your own.

Secondly, we don't want too much detail about the actual libraries and frameworks. Keeping the introduction to each to a minimum means we can focus on the SVG portion of the discussion. To that end, we'll look at the simplest possible demo that will show the two most important aspects of working with an element in an application: inserting dynamic SVG elements into the DOM, and manipulating them via user interaction.

The demos will look as follows:

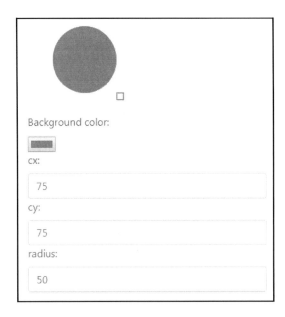

This code will be written in idiomatic ES5.

The code follows. All the code for this example is in a single HTML file. This isn't normally the way that you'd build an AngularJS application, but it works fine for this example.

The document `head` sets the application up with the necessary scripts and styles. We link to Bootstrap, jQuery and Angular:

```
<head>
  <link rel="stylesheet"
   href="https://maxcdn.bootstrapcdn.com/bootstrap/4.0.0/css/bootstrap.
    min.css" integrity="sha384-
    Gn5384xqQ1aoWXA+058RXPxPg6fy4IWvTNh0E263XmFcJlSAwiGgFAW/dAiS6JXm"
    crossorigin="anonymous">
  <link rel="stylesheet" href="style.css" />
  <script src="https://code.jquery.com/jquery-3.3.1.min.js"
          integrity="sha256-
          FgpCb/KJQlLNfOu91ta32o/NMZxltwRo8QtmkMRdAu8="
          crossorigin="anonymous"></script>
  <script
   src="https://ajax.googleapis.com/ajax/libs/angularjs/1.6.10/angular.
    min.js"></script>
</head>
```

The interesting stuff starts with the `body` element. That's where we set up our Angular application. The `ng-app` attribute indicates that Angular should process the `body` element and all of its children, applying Angular's special parsing rules to the markup contained within. We'll see more about what the `ng-app` value `"angularSVG"` references shortly.

The markup that follows is where we wire up the UI to use Angular features and functionality. Angular uses a combination of special attributes and custom HTML elements to create dynamic interfaces.

The most important piece, from our perspective, is the use of the `ng-attr` prefix to `fill`, `cx`, `cy`, and `r` attributes. Angular allows you to reference variables in the current controller's scope in the markup and, as long as it's wrapped in the `{{}}` pattern, Angular will replace that reference with the value from the model. It's a live reference and it will automatically update in a regular cycle.

This very convenient feature *does not* play well with certain SVG attributes. While the following will eventually work after you play around with the application and the values are converted from the Angular tokens to numerical values, it will *error* when the document loads:

```
<circle
        fill="{{fill}}"
        cx="{{cx}}"
        cy="{{cy}}"
        r="{{r}}" />
```

The error can be seen in the following screenshot. The SVG parser is expecting a `length` value and is instead getting a string:

```
Error: <circle> attribute cx: Expected length, "{{cx}}".    7-2-SVG-Angular-DOM-Manipulator.html:22
Error: <circle> attribute cy: Expected length, "{{cy}}".    7-2-SVG-Angular-DOM-Manipulator.html:22
Error: <circle> attribute r: Expected length, "{{r}}".      7-2-SVG-Angular-DOM-Manipulator.html:22
```

Fixing this requires the use of the `ng-attr` prefix. This prefix indicates to Angular that the `allOrNothing` flag should be used during the interpolation step. In plain English, this means that if the value of the attribute is `undefined`, the attribute is not rendered into the document. Once it has a value it is rendered as normal.

The second interesting part of this markup is the custom HTML element, `angular-rect`. `angular-rect` is what's called a **directive** in Angular. A directive is Angular's mechanism for creating custom HTML elements and attributes that allow you to expand and enhance common HTML elements and documents with reusable code blocks of your own design. While this one will be very simple, as you'll see shortly, this custom element will succinctly illustrate the way that Angular directives work with SVG.

The only other interesting part of the markup is the use of the `ng-model` attribute to bind JavaScript variable values to the elements in the form field. This special AngularJS attribute wires up two-way data-binding between the markup and the Angular controller. We'll soon see the way these variables are set in the controller, but just keep in mind the idea that once this connection is set, AngularJS keeps it alive and will update the values in the SVG elements whenever the `form` field is updated:

```
<body ng-app="angularSVG">
  <div ng-controller="circleController" class="container">
    <svg xmlns="http://www.w3.org/2000/svg" width="150" height="150"
      viewBox="0 0 150 150" version="1.1">
      <circle
      ng-attr-fill="{{fill}}"
      ng-attr-cx="{{cx}}"
```

```
      ng-attr-cy="{{cy}}"
      ng-attr-r="{{r}}" />
      <angular-rect></angular-rect>
  </svg>
  <div class="row">
    <div class="col-4">
      <label>Background color:</label>
    </div>
    <div class="col-8">
      <input type="color" ng-model="fill" id="circle-color">
    </div>
  </div>
  <div class="row">
    <div class="col-2">
      <label>cx:</label>
    </div>
    <div class="col-4">
      <input type="number" ng-model="cx" id="circle-cx" class="form-
        control">
    </div>
    <div class="col-2">
      <label>cy:</label>
    </div>
    <div class="col-4">
      <input type="number" ng-model="cy" id="circle-cy" class="form-
        control">
    </div>
  </div>
  <div class="row">
    <div class="col-2">
      <label>radius:</label>
    </div>
    <div class="col-4" height="{{cx}}">
      <input type="number" ng-model="r" id="circle-radius"
        class="form-control">
    </div>
  </div>
</div>
```

The JavaScript is very simple. Just a few lines of JavaScript allow you to wire up the values of the form fields to dynamically adjust the height, width, and fill color of the circle. The first piece, the `angular.module()` method call, creates an Angular app called "angularSVG". It's this reference that Angular looks for in the markup in order to know whether or not there's an Angular app on the page. If it finds that value in an `ng-app`, it parses that markup and applies Angular-based magic to the page.

Following that, there's our small controller definition, `circleController`.
`circleController` has one argument, the angular `$scope` variable. `$scope`, if you're not
familiar with Angular, can be thought of as a managed alias for the `this` value of a
function. It's the internal state of the controller, and the properties and methods in `$scope`
are available to both the JavaScript code and to the Angular aware markup.

Inside the controller, all we do is set some variables on the `$scope`. These serve as our
baseline values for the circle, and because they're bound to the Angular `$scope`, they
automatically become live, two-way links to the corresponding values in both the circle,
and the form fields.

After that we create a simple Angular directive, `angularRect`, which does nothing but
insert a `rect` element into the SVG DOM. We won't go into the complexities of Angular
directives here, but there is one specific detail that is important for SVG elements. The
`templateNamespace` property of the return object indicates to Angular that the directive
should be treated as SVG. Without it, like jQuery's common DOM creation pattern and the
DOM method `document.createElement`, the directive will be inserted into the
document, but it will not be created as a proper SVG element. It'll be there, but it won't
actually show up as a square when it's rendered:

Angular uses the JavaScript friendly camelCase inside JavaScript and then
kebab case when the elements are inserted into the document.

```
<script>
    angular.module('angularSVG', [])
        .controller('circleController', function ($scope) {
            $scope.cx = 75;
            $scope.cy = 75;
            $scope.r = 50;
            $scope.fill = "#ff0000";
        }).directive('angularRect', function() {
            return {
                restrict: 'E',
                templateNamespace: 'svg',
                template: '<rect x="125" y="125" width="10" height="10"
                 stroke="blue" fill="none"></rect>',
                replace: true
            };
    });
    </script>
```

Running that in the browser and then adjusting the values looks like the following screenshots. The initial screenshot shows the demo loaded with the initial values:

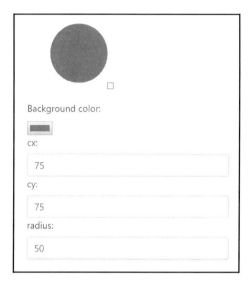

This second screenshot shows the values adjusted and the circle element changed in a corresponding manner:

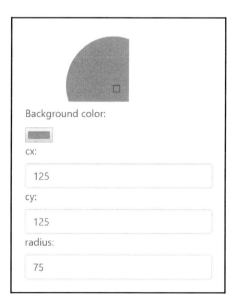

Now that we've looked at AngularJS, let's take a look at the new evolution of Angular, Angular 2.+. Known as just Angular, this iteration of the framework is very different and very powerful.

Let's take a quick look.

Manipulating SVG with Angular

Moving on from AngularJS, let's take a look at the modern evolution of Angular. Angular 2.+ (referred to *just as Angular*) is a thoroughly modern framework. It's traditionally written in TypeScript, a super-set of JavaScript that adds optional features that Angular takes advantage of to add some incredibly convenient features and functionality to the library.

Getting started with Angular

Since Angular is a newer framework and has a much larger footprint, we'll go through a little bit of the setup to get you going. The code in the downloaded examples will work, but knowing how you get there is pretty useful. So, let's get set up.

This Angular example will replicate the exact same demo that the AngularJS example provided redone using Angular code. As you've probably already sensed and will continue to learn, the basic issues with dynamic SVG are the same no matter what library or framework you're using; the solutions are just slightly different.

 You can use whatever text editor you like for the Angular sample, but I suggest using Microsoft's VS Code. It's free, well-supported, updated frequently, and plays very well with TypeScript.

Installing Node, npm, and Angular Cli

Before you can start to work with Angular, you need to be set up with the tools needed to actually run the code. The foundation of everything is Node.js and Node's package manager, `npm`. So you should install those first if you haven't already. The easiest way to do that is to head on over to `nodejs.org` and download the installer for your operating system.

Once you've done that, you can go ahead and install the Angular **Command Line Utility (CLI)**. Angular CLI makes it very easy to get up and running with an Angular project, as you'll see in short order. The following command will install Angular CLI globally on your machine:

```
rob@Rivendell MINGW64 ~/Documents/GitHub/mastering-svg-code/7 -- SVG and JavaScr
ipt Frameworks and Libraries (master)
$ npm install -g @angular/cli
```

1. Once it's installed, it's time to create a project using the `ng new` command. `ng new` will create a new folder with everything you need to get an Angular project up and running. We won't go into all the details but after running this command, you should be all set to start working with your application:

```
$ ng new angular-svg
  create angular-svg/e2e/app.e2e-spec.ts (293 bytes)
  create angular-svg/e2e/app.po.ts (208 bytes)
  create angular-svg/e2e/tsconfig.e2e.json (235 bytes)
  create angular-svg/karma.conf.js (923 bytes)
  create angular-svg/package.json (1316 bytes)
  create angular-svg/protractor.conf.js (722 bytes)
  create angular-svg/README.md (1026 bytes)
  create angular-svg/tsconfig.json (363 bytes)
  create angular-svg/tslint.json (2985 bytes)
  create angular-svg/.angular-cli.json (1288 bytes)
  create angular-svg/.editorconfig (245 bytes)
  create angular-svg/.gitignore (516 bytes)
  create angular-svg/src/assets/.gitkeep (0 bytes)
  create angular-svg/src/environments/environment.prod.ts (51 bytes)
  create angular-svg/src/environments/environment.ts (387 bytes)
  create angular-svg/src/favicon.ico (5430 bytes)
  create angular-svg/src/index.html (297 bytes)
  create angular-svg/src/main.ts (370 bytes)
  create angular-svg/src/polyfills.ts (2667 bytes)
  create angular-svg/src/styles.css (80 bytes)
  create angular-svg/src/test.ts (1085 bytes)
  create angular-svg/src/tsconfig.app.json (211 bytes)
  create angular-svg/src/tsconfig.spec.json (304 bytes)
```

2. The next step is to go into the folder you just created and run `npm install`:

```
rob@Rivendell MINGW64 ~/Documents/GitHub/mastering-svg-code/7 -- SVG and JavaScr
ipt Frameworks and Libraries (master)
$ cd angular-svg/

rob@Rivendell MINGW64 ~/Documents/GitHub/mastering-svg-code/7 -- SVG and JavaScr
ipt Frameworks and Libraries/angular-svg (master)
$ npm install
```

npm install will ensure that all your dependencies are installed in node_modules and your application will be ready to run.

3. The following screenshot from VS Code shows the layout of the application after it's been initialized and npm install has been run:

4. Since we're using Bootstrap for this Version of the Demo as well, we need to make sure that it's available. That's done by running

```
npm install --save bootstrap
```

which will install Bootstrap into your `node_modules`:

```
MINGW64:/c/Users/rob/Documents/GitHub/mastering-svg-code/7 -- SVG a...    —    □    ✕

rob@Rivendell MINGW64 ~/Documents/GitHub/mastering-svg-code/7 -- SVG and JavaScr
ipt Frameworks and Libraries/angular-svg (master)
$ npm install bootstrap

> node-sass@4.8.3 install C:\Users\rob\Documents\GitHub\mastering-svg-code\7 --
SVG and JavaScript Frameworks and Libraries\angular-svg\node_modules\node-sass
> node scripts/install.js

Cached binary found at C:\Users\rob\AppData\Roaming\npm-cache\node-sass\4.8.3\wi
n32-x64-57_binding.node

> uglifyjs-webpack-plugin@0.4.6 postinstall C:\Users\rob\Documents\GitHub\master
ing-svg-code\7 -- SVG and JavaScript Frameworks and Libraries\angular-svg\node_m
odules\webpack\node_modules\uglifyjs-webpack-plugin
> node lib/post_install.js


> node-sass@4.8.3 postinstall C:\Users\rob\Documents\GitHub\mastering-svg-code\7
 -- SVG and JavaScript Frameworks and Libraries\angular-svg\node_modules\node-sa
ss
> node scripts/build.js

Binary found at C:\Users\rob\Documents\GitHub\mastering-svg-code\7 -- SVG and Ja
vaScript Frameworks and Libraries\angular-svg\node_modules\node-sass\vendor\win3
2-x64-57\binding.node
Testing binary
Binary is fine
npm WARN bootstrap@4.1.3 requires a peer of jquery@1.9.1 - 3 but none is install
ed. You must install peer dependencies yourself.
npm WARN bootstrap@4.1.3 requires a peer of popper.js@^1.14.3 but none is instal
led. You must install peer dependencies yourself.
npm WARN optional SKIPPING OPTIONAL DEPENDENCY: fsevents@1.1.3 (node_modules\fse
vents):
npm WARN notsup SKIPPING OPTIONAL DEPENDENCY: Unsupported platform for fsevents@
1.1.3: wanted {"os":"darwin","arch":"any"} (current: {"os":"win32","arch":"x64"}
)

+ bootstrap@4.1.3
added 1134 packages in 70.155s

rob@Rivendell MINGW64 ~/Documents/GitHub/mastering-svg-code/7 -- SVG and JavaScr
ipt Frameworks and Libraries/angular-svg (master)
$
```

You can then wire it up in `angular-cli.json`. `angular-cli.json` is where you configure different aspects of your Angular CLI installation. In this case all we need to do is add Bootstrap CSS to the styles property so that it will be bundled with the rest of the application:

 Under the hood, Angular CLI uses Webpack to bundle scripts and styles and process them in a number of ways to ready them for delivery to your development server as well as to production environments. One of the greatest benefits of using Angular CLI is that it smoothes out the complexity of working with Webpack. Webpack is incredibly powerful but has a steep learning curve. Angular CLI makes it just work.

```
"apps": [
  {
    "root": "src",
    "outDir": "dist",
    "assets": [
      "assets",
      "favicon.ico"
    ],
    "index": "index.html",
    "main": "main.ts",
    "polyfills": "polyfills.ts",
    "test": "test.ts",
    "tsconfig": "tsconfig.app.json",
    "testTsconfig": "tsconfig.spec.json",
    "prefix": "app",
    "styles": [
      "../node_modules/bootstrap/dist/css/bootstrap.css",
      "styles.css"
    ],
    "scripts": [],
    "environmentSource": "environments/environment.ts",
    "environments": {
      "dev": "environments/environment.ts",
      "prod": "environments/environment.prod.ts"
    }
  }
],
```

Running the application in this simple state will allow us to start developing the application and testing against a development server running locally. This is done using the `ng serve` command. It's called here with the `--open` option which will open a web browser after the code is compiled:

```
MINGW64:/c/Users/rob/Documents/GitHub/mastering-svg-code/7 -- SVG a...    —    □    ✕
```
```
rob@Rivendell MINGW64 ~/Documents/GitHub/mastering-svg-code/7 -- SVG and JavaScr
ipt Frameworks and Libraries (master)
$ cd angular-svg/

rob@Rivendell MINGW64 ~/Documents/GitHub/mastering-svg-code/7 -- SVG and JavaScr
ipt Frameworks and Libraries/angular-svg (master)
$ ng serve --open
** NG Live Development Server is listening on localhost:4200, open your browser
on http://localhost:4200/ **
webpack: wait until bundle finished: /
Date: 2018-09-13T02:06:37.837Z
Hash: e095674f8dc1a09984d3
Time: 16679ms
chunk {inline} inline.bundle.js (inline) 3.85 kB [entry] [rendered]
chunk {main} main.bundle.js (main) 24.8 kB [initial] [rendered]
chunk {polyfills} polyfills.bundle.js (polyfills) 548 kB [initial] [rendered]
chunk {styles} styles.bundle.js (styles) 529 kB [initial] [rendered]
chunk {vendor} vendor.bundle.js (vendor) 6.76 MB [initial] [rendered]

webpack: Compiled successfully.
```

This will auto-reload the code in the browser whenever changes are made to the code.

So, with that, it's time to actually start writing some TypeScript and interacting with SVG.

The first thing we'll do is edit the main module for the application. `app.module.ts` is the root module for the application and it's where all the parts of the application are wired together. Most of this is automatically wired up by `Angular CLI`. All we need to do is import the `FormsModule` from an Angular core, using the new ES6 module pattern (`import module from src`). Then we add it to the `imports` array of the `@NgModule` decorator. This allows the directives and properties of the `FormsModule` to be available inside this application:

```
import { BrowserModule } from '@angular/platform-browser';
import { NgModule } from '@angular/core';
import { FormsModule } from '@angular/forms';
import { AppComponent } from './app.component';


@NgModule({
  declarations: [
    AppComponent,
    AngularRectComponent
```

```
  ],
  imports: [
    BrowserModule,
    FormsModule
  ],
  providers: [],
  bootstrap: [AppComponent]
})
export class AppModule { }
```

Following that, we'll completely edit the `app.component.ts` file to represent our (simple) component. In it, we import `Component` and `FormsModule` from Angular, do some standard housekeeping in the `@Component` decorator, and then we export the `AppComponent` class which ships with four properties set. This pattern deserves some explanation since it's probably familiar but different enough that it might be a head-scratcher. For starters, all of these are created with the `public` keyword. That indicates that these properties should be available outside the scope of the class. Next is the variable name itself, followed by a colon and a type annotation, indicating the expected type of the variable. TypeScript allows you to create custom types based on other TypeScript classes, but for our purposes, we're just using standard JavaScript primitives, `number` and `string`. Finally we set default values for all of them so that our application has something to hang onto:

```
import { Component } from '@angular/core';
import { FormsModule } from '@angular/forms';

@Component({
  selector: 'app-root',
  templateUrl: './app.component.html',
  styleUrls: ['./app.component.css']
})
export class AppComponent {
  public cx:number = 75;
  public cy:number = 75;
  public r:number = 50
  public color:string = "#cc0000";
}
```

Next we have the markup, which is similar to the previous example. It's all contained in `app.component.html`. There are some similarities to the AngularJS Version. For example the dynamic attributes have to be similarly handled, you still can't bind directly to SVG attributes without causing an error, so you still have to manage them explicitly. In this case you use the `attr.` prefix instead of the `ng-attr-` prefix you used in AngularJS. You'll also notice the square brackets surrounding the attributes.

Using the simple square brackets `[]` indicates that this is a one-way data binding; the template reads from the component properties we previously defined. Later on, in the inputs, we see an example of explicit two-way data binding with the square bracket/parenthesis `[()]` syntax surrounding the attribute. `ngModel` is the directive we were importing with `FormsModule`. It allows us to do two-way data binding from a form element to the properties of a component. This way the entries in the form are, once again, represented in the attributes of the SVG `circle` element and it displays changes as updates are made to the `form` fields:

```
<div class="container">
  <svg xmlns="http://www.w3.org/2000/svg" width="150" height="150"
viewBox="0 0 150 150" version="1.1">
    <svg:circle
    [attr.fill]="color"
    [attr.cx]="cx"
    [attr.cy]="cy"
    [attr.r]="r" />
  </svg>
  <div class="row">
    <div class="col-4">
      <label>Background color:</label>
    </div>
    <div class="col-8">
      <input type="color" [(ngModel)]="color" id="circle-color">
    </div>
  </div>
  <div class="row">
    <div class="col-2">
      <label>cx:</label>
    </div>
    <div class="col-4">
      <input type="number" id="circle-cx" [(ngModel)]="cx" class="form-
        control">
    </div>
    <div class="col-2">
      <label>cy:</label>
    </div>
    <div class="col-4">
      <input type="number" id="circle-cy" [(ngModel)]="cy" class="form-
        control">
    </div>
  </div>
  <div class="row">
    <div class="col-2">
      <label>radius:</label>
    </div>
    <div class="col-4">
```

```
      <input type="number" id="circle-radius" [(ngModel)]="r"
        class="form-control">
    </div>
  </div>
</div>
```

There's only one more thing we need to do to get this Angular example to match the previous example in AngularJS, and that is to add a sub-component that represents the small blue `rect` element. There are a couple of interesting wrinkles with this. The first is an illustration of the power of Angular CLI. With Angular CLI if you need to wire up a component, you can do so with the `ng new` command. In our case we'll run `ng new component angular-rect`, which will generate the various files that make up an Angular component and will actually wire the component up into `app.module.ts`:

```
rob@Rivendell MINGW64 ~/Documents/GitHub/mastering-svg-code/7 -- SVG and JavaScr
ipt Frameworks and Libraries/angular-svg (master)
$ ng generate component angular-rect
  create src/app/angular-rect/angular-rect.component.html (31 bytes)
  create src/app/angular-rect/angular-rect.component.spec.ts (664 bytes)
  create src/app/angular-rect/angular-rect.component.ts (292 bytes)
  create src/app/angular-rect/angular-rect.component.css (0 bytes)
  update src/app/app.module.ts (435 bytes)

rob@Rivendell MINGW64 ~/Documents/GitHub/mastering-svg-code/7 -- SVG and JavaScr
ipt Frameworks and Libraries/angular-svg (master)
$ |
```

You can see what `app.module.ts` looks like in the following updated code sample where the new `AngularRectComponent` component is imported and added to the `@NgModule` declarations:

```
import { BrowserModule } from '@angular/platform-browser';
import { NgModule } from '@angular/core';
import { FormsModule } from '@angular/forms';
import { AppComponent } from './app.component';
import { AngularRectComponent } from './angular-rect/angular-
rect.component';

@NgModule({
  declarations: [
    AppComponent,
    AngularRectComponent
  ],
  imports: [
    BrowserModule,
    FormsModule
```

```
    ],
    providers: [],
    bootstrap: [AppComponent]
})
export class AppModule { }
```

There are a couple more wrinkles, related directly to SVG, that need pointing out to get this custom element onto the page. The first is the requirement of adding the `svg:` prefix to the elements in the `angular-rect` component. This indicates to Angular that, you guessed it, it should use the SVG namespace when creating these elements:

```
<svg:rect x="125" y="125" width="10" height="10" stroke="blue"
fill="none"></svg:rect>
```

The next wrinkle is a two-parter. With a component made up of simple HTML elements, you could do something like this, which is similar to what you saw in AngularJS. You would add the element to the page as follows:

```
<angular-rect></angular-rect>
```

Which will render, in the live view in the Web **Inspector**, the following:

```
<angular-rect _ngcontent-c0="" _nghost-c1=""><rect _ngcontent-c1=""
fill="none" height="10" stroke="blue" width="10" x="125" y="125"></rect>
</angular-rect>
```

That looks fine from a markup perspective, but in the browser, the blue rectangle is missing. The whole element isn't rendering, even though it's in the DOM.

In HTML5, this sort of thing will work because the HTML5 parser has been designed to be forgiving of unknown elements (as well as poorly formed markup) and you can manipulate custom elements with CSS. SVG, on the other hand, remains a strict XML grammar, so unless the element is in the SVG specification, or you can point to an XML-based **Document Type Definition** (**DTD**) that defines that particular element, it won't render properly. Thankfully, there's an SVG-shaped solution that works perfectly well with a feature of Angular components. You can use Angular's ability to bind custom components to attributes with the generic `g` element to create much the same effect.

The following code sample shows how this is done.

First, let's look at the `angular-rect` component itself. The only thing to note, as most of the file is just boilerplate, is that the selector in the `@Component` decorator is wrapped in square brackets `[]`. Since it's wrapped in square brackets, that indicates to the parser that it's an attribute selector, as opposed to the common element selector you saw with the app component itself. That means that Angular will look for the presence of `angular-rect` as an attribute of an element and will replace that with our new custom component:

```
import { Component, OnInit } from '@angular/core';

@Component({
  selector: '[angular-rect]',
  templateUrl: './angular-rect.component.html',
  styleUrls: ['./angular-rect.component.css']
})
export class AngularRectComponent implements OnInit {

  constructor() {}

  ngOnInit() {}

}
```

Next, we'll see how that works with the markup. We, once again, add the `svg:` prefix to the `g` element and then we simply add the `angular-rect` attribute and the component renders properly:

```
<svg xmlns="http://www.w3.org/2000/svg" width="150" height="150"
viewBox="0 0 150 150" version="1.1">
  <svg:circle
  [attr.fill]="color"
  [attr.cx]="cx"
  [attr.cy]="cy"
  [attr.r]="r" />
  <svg:g angular-rect></svg:g>
</svg>
```

And that's that for Angular.

Working with React and SVG

The final library we're going to look at is React. React is a very popular library that came along just as AngularJS was getting long in the tooth and before Angular was ready for prime-time. It's very popular in some circles. It's based on ES6 with some extensions specific to React.

Much of it will look familiar to you, just based on what you've seen so far in this chapter and especially if you've done any serious web application development.

Getting started with React is less straightforward than getting up and running with Angular. Angular, under the hood, is probably more complicated, but Angular CLI smooth out a lot of the issues so you never (or rarely) actually see the complexity as a developer. React is more of a library than a complete framework, so you can end up having to make a lot more decisions in order to get up and running. Thankfully, while there are many ways to get there and none are as central to the project as Angular CLI is to Angular (they're tightly coupled in the documentation and community), there are ways to do it just as simply as Angular CLI. Perhaps even simpler since there's nothing to even install.

Assuming you have Node Version >6 installed on your machine, all you need to do to create the simple application used in the demo code is to run a single command:

```
$ npx create-react-app react-svg
```

create-react-app is a utility from Facebook that spins up a fully functional React app. Running it looks like the following two screenshots (the full scroll would take up many pages of the book).

It's very cool. It creates the folder, downloads all of the dependencies and installs everything, giving you a series of commands to run in order to interact with your newly minted React application:

Continued result:

```
MINGW64:/c/Users/RLARSEN/Documents/GitHub/mastering-svg-code/7 -- SVG an...

├─ webpack-dev-server@2.9.4
├─ webpack-manifest-plugin@1.3.2
├─ webpack@3.8.1
├─ websocket-extensions@0.1.3
├─ whatwg-fetch@2.0.3
├─ whatwg-url@4.8.0
├─ whet.extend@0.9.9
├─ which@1.3.0
├─ widest-line@2.0.0
├─ window-size@0.1.0
├─ wordwrap@0.0.2
├─ wrap-ansi@2.1.0
├─ write-file-atomic@2.3.0
├─ write@0.2.1
├─ xml-name-validator@2.0.1
├─ xtend@4.0.1
└─ yargs-parser@5.0.0
Done in 184.92s.

Success! Created react-svg at C:\Users\RLARSEN\Documents\GitHub\mastering-svg-co
de\7 -- SVG and JavaScript Frameworks and Libraries\react-svg
Inside that directory, you can run several commands:

  yarn start
    Starts the development server.

  yarn build
    Bundles the app into static files for production.

  yarn test
    Starts the test runner.

  yarn eject
    Removes this tool and copies build dependencies, configuration files
    and scripts into the app directory. If you do this, you can't go back!

We suggest that you begin by typing:

  cd react-svg
  yarn start

Happy hacking!

RLarsen@RLARSEN MINGW64 ~/Documents/GitHub/mastering-svg-code/7 -- SVG and JavaS
cript Frameworks and Libraries (master)
$ |
```

Looking deeper, it creates a directory that looks like the following screenshot. It contains the `node_modules` folder with all of the dependencies, `public`, which is where the transpiled files live (and are served from when you browse your working code) and `src`, which is where all the source files for your application live. The other files are all standard files for a `git/npm/yarn-based project`:

> Yarn is an alternative to npm. We won't go into the details of the differences between the two because it's out of the scope of this book and, to be honest, isn't all that interesting. Suffice to say, yarn is a parallel tool to npm so you will do the same things you would do with npm with yarn. The syntax is occasionally different and there is a different file created when doing `yarn install` (`yarn.lock`). But for the sake of this book you don't need to concern yourself with the differences.

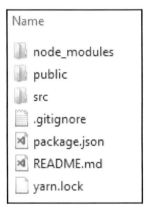

As previously mentioned, the application code is in `src`. You can see the layout of that folder in the following screenshot.

`App.css`, `App.js`, and `App.test.js` are where the heart of your application will live. The `index.js` file is the main entry point to your application and they Bootstrap your React application. `registerServiceWorker.js` is a file provided by the framework that serves assets from a local cache. However, you won't actually touch it in this simple app:

Running `yarn start` from the root of the project folder will compile all of the React code, and CSS, and will spin up a development server available at localhost:3000:

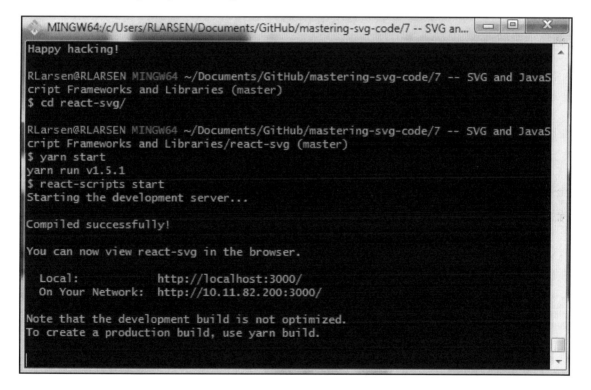

The starter app looks as follows, in case you were wondering. We will quickly blow that away:

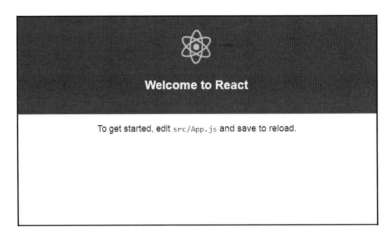

Before we get started with our dive into SVG and React, let's take a look at the basic React component spit out by `create-react-app`. You've seen it rendered previously; let's look at how it works.

The basic format of a React component is as follows. It's an ES6 module, with `import` statements, a class, and an export. There's one element specific to React that's worth noting.

The top of the file shows the ES6 imports. This can include CSS files (as we'll see in a minute) and SVG images. Webpack actually reads those import statements and optimizes those imports, much like Webpack worked with Angular decorators.

Following that we have the one class in the file. `App`, which extends the base `Component` class from React. It's got one method, `render()`, which uses an extension to JavaScript called JSX. JSX allows you to mix XML and JavaScript together. I honestly have never much liked this format and was practically shocked by it when they released it, but I've grown to appreciate the intent, even if I don't like it. JSX attributes are parsed as strings if they're quoted. Otherwise, they are treated as JavaScript expressions. In this case, the path to `logo.svg` is converted to a useful path and the logo is rendered in the browser.

Finally, we export the default class, `App`, which can then be imported by other applications:

```
import React, { Component } from 'react';
import logo from './logo.svg';
import './App.css';

class App extends Component {
```

```
    render() {
      return (
        <div className="App">
          <header className="App-header">
            <img src={logo} className="App-logo" alt="logo" />
            <h1 className="App-title">Welcome to React</h1>
          </header>
          <p className="App-intro">
            To get started, edit <code>src/App.js</code> and save to
              reload.
          </p>
        </div>
      );
    }
  }

  export default App;
```

Quickly, since there's not a lot that we actually do with it, let's take a look at index.js. This will show us how the application gets loaded.

There are several ES6 module imports at the top of the file. React and ReactDOM are core, driving the basic React library and adding in the ReactDOM interface. They drive the majority of what we're going to do with this little demo.

The imports also include the index.css file.

Other than that, we import two pieces of JavaScript: App, which is the module we're going to do our work in, and the previously mentioned registerServiceWorker, which we won't work with at all.

Once everything is imported, we run two small functions. ReactDOM.render is called with two arguments, <App />, indicating the custom element created by the App component, and document.getElementById("root"), which indicates the node that should receive the new element:

```
import React from 'react';
import ReactDOM from 'react-dom';
import './index.css';
import App from './App';
import registerServiceWorker from './registerServiceWorker';

ReactDOM.render(<App />, document.getElementById('root'));
registerServiceWorker();
```

Now that we've taken a quick look at the basic React architecture, let's take a look at our demo.

In addition to the basic React app, Bootstrap is also installed into this project by running the following command. We are going to do another version of the simple form / SVG demo we've been doing and it makes sense to continue to use the same markup:

```
npm install --save bootstrap
```

Let's look at our App.js. It starts with a couple of import statements. We pull in React and component from React. Then we pull in two CSS files, our own custom App.css and the Bootstrap CSS we just installed, linking to the files in the project's node_modules. Finally, we import our standalone ReactRect component from the rect module.

Then we have the App class definition. It's really got just a couple of things going on. In the constructor, we create a base state object with default values of our standard SVG properties, cx, cy, r, and color. And then we set a method, handleChange, to handle changes to the underlying model.

The method is simple. It takes the event object in, creates a target constant with the event.target, and then further inspects that object to get the name and value of the input. It then uses the method setState (inherited from props) to set the value of the application's state.

Following that is the render function.

Looking through it you'll notice there's not much that you need to do to get React to properly render the SVG.

First we set local variables for the various properties using the ES6 destructuring assignment pattern. Once those variables are set it's a simple matter of adding the variables that we need to have interpreted by React into bracket pairs { } in the appropriate attribute. The variable references in both the SVG elements and the form inputs are handled exactly the same way and don't require any special handling.

We simply bind the handleChange method to the onChange event, directly in the markup, and everything behaves as expected.

ReactRect, which we imported, is added to the SVG element. React handles importing that component, which we'll see shortly, and rendering it into the document:

Custom components need to start with a capital letter. Markup starting with a lowercase letter is interpreted as an HTML element.

```
import React, { Component } . from 'react';
import './App.css';
import 'bootstrap/dist/css/bootstrap.css';
import ReactRect from './rect';

class App extends Component {
  constructor(props) {
    super(props);
    this.state = {
      cx: 75,
      cy: 75,
      r: 50,
      color: "#cc0000"
    };
    this.handleChange = this.handleChange.bind(this);
  }
  handleChange(event) {
    const target = event.target;
    const value = target.value;
    const name = target.name;
    this.setState({
      [name]: value
    });
  }
  render() {
    const { cx,cy,r,color } = this.state;
    return (
      <div className="container">
      <svg xmlns="http://www.w3.org/2000/svg" width="150" height="150"
        viewBox="0 0 150 150" version="1.1">
        <circle
        r={r}
        cy={cy}
        cx={cx}
        fill={color}
        ></circle>
        <ReactRect></ReactRect>
      </svg>
      <div className="row">
        <div className="col-4">
          <label>Background color:</label>
        </div>
        <div className="col-8">
```

```
                <input type="color" id="circle-color" value={color}
                name="color"
                onChange={this.handleChange} />
            </div>
        </div>
        <div className="row">
          <div className="col-2">
            <label>cx:</label>
          </div>
          <div className="col-4">
            <input type="number" id="circle-cx" className="form-control"
              value={cx}
            name="cx"
            onChange={this.handleChange} />
          </div>
          <div className="col-2">
            <label>cy:</label>
          </div>
          <div className="col-4">
            <input type="number" id="circle-cy" className="form-control"
              value={cy}
            name="cy"
            onChange={this.handleChange} />
          </div>
        </div>
        <div className="row">
          <div className="col-2">
            <label>radius:</label>
          </div>
          <div className="col-4">
            <input type="number" id="circle-radius" className="form-
              control" value={r}
            name="r"
            onChange={this.handleChange} />
          </div>
        </div>
      </div>
    );
  }
}

export default App;
```

Our custom element is very simple. It's just a plain React component that returns our `rect` element:

```
import React, { Component } from 'react';
```

```
class ReactRect extends Component {
  render() {
    return (
      <rect x="125" y="125" width="10" height="10" stroke="blue"
        fill="none"></rect>

    );
  }
}

export default ReactRect;
```

As you can see, working with dynamic SVG and React is very straightforward. There was a concerted effort by the React team to ensure that SVG elements and attributes all worked, so this is down to their hard work. Thanks, React team!

Summary

In this chapter, you worked with four common libraries and frameworks, integrating these powerful tools with SVG.

Starting with jQuery and working your way through AngularJS, Angular, and React, you now have basic experience at integrating SVG with four of the most popular libraries and frameworks on the planet.

Specifically, you learned about setting up applications with each of the frameworks, how to create dynamic components that feature SVG elements and attributes, and how to manipulate those attributes in a dynamic way.

You also learned about the multiple gotchas when working with SVG and these libraries, including ways to ensure that elements are created properly in jQuery and ensuring that dynamic attributes are properly handled in the Angular frameworks.

8
SVG Animation and Visualizations

This chapter addresses the most dynamic and impressive use case for SVG: using SVG for data visualizations and animations. The tools you've already learned about, SVG, JavaScript, and CSS, and some new tools, will come together to create powerful options for you to build dynamic sites and applications.

In this chapter, we'll learn the following:

- How to produce a static data visualization using SVG, JavaScript, and structured data
- An overview of the general techniques for animating SVG
- Animating SVG with Vivus
- Animation with GSAP

After working through the examples in this chapter, you'll be able to create animations and data visualizations with SVG and will know about two of the best tools for working with SVG and animation.

Let's dive right in.

Creating an SVG data visualization

This first section is going to focus on putting together a basic data visualization using SVG and JavaScript. This particular visualization will focus on an illustration, the positive/negative variance from an average. In this case, it will illustrate the number of home runs hits, per season, by the baseball player David Ortiz in his career with the Boston Red Sox compared with his average number of home runs over his Red Sox career.

From 2003 until 2016 David Ortiz hit a minimum of 23 and a maximum of 54 home runs in a season while playing for the Red Sox. He averaged 34.5 per season. This visualization will show the relative positive/negative variance of his home run totals for every year against that 34.5 average. Years in which he hit more than the average will be in green. Years, where he hit less, will be in red.

The steps we'll need to go through are as follows:

1. We will take the data and get the total number of years, the total number of home runs, and then calculate the average.
2. We will loop through the data and calculate the positive/negative offset for each year.
3. We will calculate some metrics based on the available screen real estate.
4. We will draw a baseline, centered vertically on the screen.
5. We will draw a series of rectangles in the appropriate place, with the appropriate height to indicate the positive/negative variance, along with some simple labels indicating the year and number of home runs.
6. We will add a legend indicating the average number of home runs and number of years.

The final visualization will look like this:

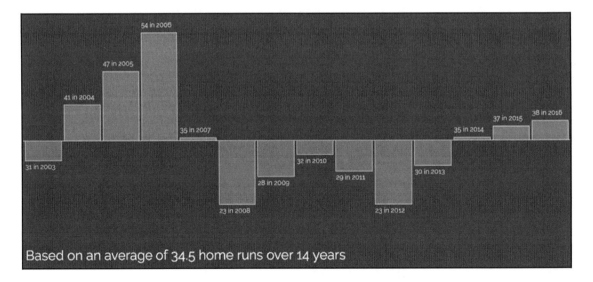

Now that we have the basics planned out, let's look at how this works in detail.

We'll start with the markup, which is very simple. We first include Bootstrap and the Raleway font as part of our standard template. Following that, we set the background of the SVG element and set the font family, size, and color of two different types of text element. Then we just include the target SVG element and the JavaScript file that runs the visualization:

```html
<!doctype html>
<html lang="en">

<head>
  <meta charset="utf-8">
  <title>Mastering SVG- SVG Data Visualization</title>
  <link rel="stylesheet"
   href="https://maxcdn.bootstrapcdn.com/bootstrap/4.0.0/css/bootstrap.
    min.css" integrity="sha384-
    Gn5384xqQ1aoWXA+058RXPxPg6fy4IWvTNh0E263XmFcJ1SAwiGgFAW/dAiS6JXm"
    crossorigin="anonymous">
  <link href="https://fonts.googleapis.com/css?family=Raleway"
    rel="stylesheet">
  <style type="text/css">
    body {
      font-family: Raleway, sans-serif;
    }
    svg.canvas {
     background: #0C2340;
    }
    text {
      font-family: Raleway, sans-serif;
      font-size: .75em;
      fill: #fff;
    }
    text.large {
      font-size: 1.5em;
    }
  </style>
</head>

<body>

  <div class="container-fluid">
    <div class="row">
      <div class="col-12">
        <svg xmlns="http://www.w3.org/2000/svg" viewBox="0 0 1000 450"
          width="1000" height="450" version="1.1" id="canvas"
            class="canvas">
```

```
        </svg>
      </div>
    </div>
  </div>
  <script src="scripts.js"></script>
</body>

</html>
```

The included JavaScript file is where the real work is done.

 This JavaScript file is written using several ES6 features.

`scripts.js` itself is basically one large function, `viz`.

At the top of `viz` we have the `data` variable. This variable is an array of JavaScript objects. Each object has two properties, `year` and `hrs`, indicating the year in question and the number of home runs Ortiz hit that year:

```
function viz() {
  /*
    ES6
  */
  const data = [
    {
      "year": 2003,
      "hrs": 31
    },
    {
      "year": 2004,
      "hrs": 41
    },
    {
      "year": 2005,
      "hrs": 47
    },
    {
      "year": 2006,
      "hrs": 54
    },
    {
      "year": 2007,
      "hrs": 35
    },
```

```
    {
      "year": 2008,
      "hrs": 23
    },
    {
      "year": 2009,
      "hrs": 28
    },
    {
      "year": 2010,
      "hrs": 32
    },
    {
      "year": 2011,
      "hrs": 29
    },
    {
      "year": 2012,
      "hrs": 23
    },
    {
      "year": 2013,
      "hrs": 30
    },
    {
      "year": 2014,
      "hrs": 35
    },
    {
      "year": 2015,
      "hrs": 37
    },
    {
      "year": 2016,
      "hrs": 38
    }
  ];
```

If you were running this visualization interactively, either accepting input from a user or inserting the result of a web service call to a statistical database into the visualization, you would just need to have the right structure (an array of objects) and format (`hrs` and `year`) and everything else would work itself out. Keep that in mind as we look at the variables and methods that populate the rest of the file.

Starting after `data`, there are several different variables we set that we'll use, in addition to `data`, throughout the visualization:

- `doc`: A reference to the document
- `canvas`: A reference the SVG element with an `id` of `#canvas`
- `NS`: A reference to the namespace derived from the SVG element
- `elem`: A placeholder variable for the elements we'll create

```
const doc = document;
const canvas = doc.getElementById("canvas");
const NS = canvas.getAttribute('xmlns');
let elem;
```

Next up are several utility methods we use to populate the visualization with values and elements.

The first, `addText`, lets us add the text labels to the visualization. It takes in a coordinates object, `coords`, the `text` to be entered, and then finally an optional CSS class, `cssClass`. We'll explore the use case for the CSS class argument in one of the examples. The first two arguments should be straightforward and are required.

Following `addText`, there is an `addLine` function that allows us to draw lines on the screen. It takes a coordinates object, `coords` (which in this case contains four coordinates) and an optional `stroke` color. You'll notice that the `stroke` is created with a default value in the function signature. If there is no stroke color provided, the `stroke` will be `#ff8000`.

Next up is the `addRect` function that allows us to add rectangles to the screen. It accepts a coordinates object, `coords`, which contains `height` and `width` properties, as well as optional `stroke` and `fill` colors.

Finally, there's a function, `maxDiffer`, which figures out the maximum difference between a set of positive/negative numbers. Getting this range and then using this maximum difference ensures that no matter how the numbers are spread, the maximum height needed above or below the baseline will fit into the screen:

```
function addText(coords, text, cssClass) {
  elem = doc.createElementNS(NS, "text");
  elem.setAttribute("x", coords.x);
  elem.setAttribute("y", coords.y);
  elem.textContent = text;
  if (cssClass){
    elem.classList.add(cssClass);
  }
  canvas.appendChild(elem);
```

```
  }
  function addLine(coords, stroke = "#ff8000") {
    elem = doc.createElementNS(NS, "line");
    elem.setAttribute("x1", coords.x1);
    elem.setAttribute("y1", coords.y1);
    elem.setAttribute("x2", coords.x2);
    elem.setAttribute("y2", coords.y2);
    elem.setAttribute("stroke", stroke);
    canvas.appendChild(elem);
  }
  function addRect(coords, fill = "#ff8000", stroke = "#ffffff") {
    elem = doc.createElementNS(NS, "rect");
    elem.setAttribute("x", coords.x);
    elem.setAttribute("y", coords.y);
    elem.setAttribute("width", coords.width);
    elem.setAttribute("height", coords.height);
    elem.setAttribute("fill", fill);
    elem.setAttribute("stroke", stroke);
    canvas.appendChild(elem);
  }
  function maxDiffer(arr) {
    let maxDiff = arr[1] - arr[0];
    for (let i = 0; i < arr.length; i++) {
      for (let j = i + 1; j < arr.length; j++) {
        if (arr[j] - arr[i] > maxDiff) {
          maxDiff = arr[j] - arr[i];
        }
      }
    }
    return maxDiff;
  }
```

After those utility functions, we have the code that defines the heart of the visualization. It happens in a function that runs on the DOMContentLoaded event.

As the function runs, we create multiple variables, holding different properties that we need to generate the visualization. Here's what they do:

- viewBox is a local reference to the SVG element's viewBox. We store this and the following DOM references locally so that we can save on the number of DOM lookups of the viewBox.
- width is a local reference to the width from the SVG element's viewBox.
- height is a local reference to the height from the viewBox.
- x is a local reference to the x point from the viewBox.

- y is a local reference to the y point from the `viewBox`.
- `padding` is an arbitrary constant that creates several padding calculations.
- `vizWidth` defines the visible width of the SVG canvas. This defines the area in which we can safely draw elements into the SVG element.
- `years` is a reference to the number of years in the data set.
- `total` is a calculated value that represents the total number of home runs hit over the full data set.
- `avg` is the average number of home runs hit per year, calculated by dividing the `total` by the number of `years`.
- `verticalMidPoint` represents the vertical mid-point of the SVG element. This is the line on which positive or negative variances are drawn.
- `diffs` is an array holding the positive and negative difference between the average number of home runs and the number of home runs hit in every year.
- `maxDiff` is the maximum difference between the average number of home runs and the number of home runs hit in a given year.
- `yInterval` is the number of pixels per home run. This ensures that the boxes scale properly, vertically, based on the number of home runs hit in any given year.
- `xInterval` is the number of pixels per year. This value allows us to evenly space boxes no matter how many years are in the data set:

```
document.addEventListener("DOMContentLoaded", () => {
  const viewBox = canvas.viewBox.baseVal;
  const width = viewBox.width;
  const height = viewBox.height;
  const x = viewBox.x;
  const y = viewBox.y;
  const padding = width / 200;
  const vizWidth = width - padding;
  const years = data.length;
  const total = data.reduce((total, item) => {
    return total + item.hrs;
  }, 0);
  const avg = total / years;
  const verticalMidPoint = (y + height) / 2;
  const diffs = data.map((item) => {
    return item.hrs - avg;
  });
  const maxDiff = maxDiffer(diffs);
  const yIntervals = verticalMidPoint / maxDiff;
  const xInterval = (vizWidth / years);
```

Following the creation of all those variables, we get to the business of drawing the different boxes and adding the labels. To do so, we use a `for...in` loop to loop through the array of `diffs`, doing two calculations that create two new variables, the `newX` and the `newY`. The `newX` is a regular interval based on the value of `i` multiplied by the `intervalX` variable we previously created. The `newY` variable is calculated by multiplying the value of `diffs[i]`, the current diff, by the `yInterval` constant. This gives us a distance to use to calculate the height of the rectangle in order to represent the number of home runs in each year.

Next, we test whether or not the current `diff` is greater or less than zero. If it's greater than zero, we want to draw a box that goes up from the `verticalMidPoint`. If the current `diff` is less than zero, then we draw a box that goes `down` from the `verticalMidPoint`. Since the direction of the rectangle and the associated anchor points for the box are different in each case, we need to handle them differently. We will also use different colors for the two variations in order to highlight the differences with a secondary indication.

While there are differences between the two branches of this `if`, both branches call `addRect` and `addText`. Let's look at the similarities and the differences between the two branches of the `if`.

For starters, each call to `addRect` follows the same pattern for the `x` and `width` properties. `x` is always the `newX` value added to the `padding` and the `width` is the `xInterval` value plus the `padding`.

The `y` and `height` values are handled differently by the two branches.

If the current difference is less than zero, then the new `y` coordinate is `verticalMidpoint`. This anchors the top of the box to the line that represents zero on the visualization and indicates that the box will hang below that line. If the current difference is greater than zero, then the `y` coordinate is set to be `verticalMidPoint` minus the `newY`. This sets the top of the new rectangle to be the value of `newY` above the line that indicates zero.

The `height`, if the current difference is less than zero, is the `newY` value passed into `Math.abs()`. You can't pass in a negative value to an SVG element, so the negative value needs to be converted to a positive value using `Math.abs()`. The `height`, in the case of a current diff, that's greater than zero, is just the `newY` value, since it's already a positive number.

The calls to `addText` in each branch of the `if` diverge on the placement of the `y` point. If the `newY` value is negative, then, once again, `Math.abs` has to convert the `newY` value to a positive number. Otherwise, it's passed through unchanged.

Following that, we add the zero line to the vertical mid-point with a call to `addLine`. The arguments passed in are the unchanged `x` and `width` from the `viewBox` for the leftmost and rightmost points and `verticalMidpint` for the `y` value for both points

Finally we add a little bit of text that explains the basics of the visualization. Here is where we use the optional `cssClass` argument to `addLine`, passing in `large` so that we can make slightly larger text. The `x` and `y` arguments leverage the `x` and `height` variables along with the `padding` variable to place the text slightly off the bottom left edge of the SVG element.

The final line of code simply calls the `viz()` function to kick off the visualization:

```
for (const i in diffs) {
    const newX = xInterval * i;
    const newY = diffs[i] * yInterval;
    if (diffs[i] < 0) {
      addRect({
        "x": newX + padding,
        "y": verticalMidPoint,
        "width": xInterval - padding,
        "height": Math.abs(newY),
      }, "#C8102E", "#ffffff");
      addText({
        "x": newX + padding,
        "y": verticalMidPoint + Math.abs(newY) + (padding * 3)
      }, `${data[i].hrs} in ${data[i].year}`);
    }
    else if (diffs[i] > 0) {
      addRect({
        "x": newX + padding,
        "y": verticalMidPoint - newY,
        "width": xInterval - padding,
        "height": newY,
      }, "#4A777A", "#ffffff");
      addText({
        "x": newX + padding,
        "y": verticalMidPoint - newY - (padding * 2)
      }, `${data[i].hrs} in ${data[i].year}`);
    }
    addLine({
      x1: x,
      y1: verticalMidPoint,
      x2: width,
      y2: verticalMidPoint
    }, "#ffffff");
    addText({
      "x": x + padding,
```

```
            "y": height - (padding * 3)
        }, `Based on an average of ${avg} home runs over ${years} years`,
            "large");
    }
  });


}
viz();
```

If this were a visualization destined for production, or for more general-purpose use, then there are still things that we'd want to do with it. Eagle-eyed readers will spot that we don't actually deal with the case where the number of home runs exactly equals the average number of home runs, for example. That said, for the purposes of this book, the detail here is enough to illustrate how one works with JavaScript, SVG, and data to tell the story of a data-set visually.

Now that we've looked at static visualizations, let's look at adding some movement to the screen. The next section will deal with multiple ways in which you can animate SVG in the browser.

General techniques for animating SVG

This section will introduce various general techniques for animating SVG. While there are different tools available to do this work (you'll meet two later on in this chapter), it's useful to know how these things are done without the aid of frameworks or libraries. This section will provide that foundation.

You've already previously seen some of these techniques, but it's good to look at them again, solely in the context of animation.

Animating with pure JavaScript

Before there were CSS keyframe animations and CSS transitions, two techniques we'll look at later in this chapter, we had to produce all of our animations and interesting effects in the browser by hand using JavaScript; updating properties in a loop and optimizing frame rates manually. Eventually, libraries such as jQuery came along and removed the need to know how this worked, by presenting animations as part of their API. Thankfully, these days, in addition to the animation methods available in your tool of choice, you can leverage CSS animations for many things we used to use JavaScript for so there's less and less need for people to learn these skills these days.

That said, there are places where CSS animations won't cut it, so there's some benefit to seeing how it works under the hood and without the aid of a library.

This simple animation will animate a circle element across an SVG element from left to right. We will need to calculate several metrics to create the animation, so even though it's simple, it will illustrate many of the challenges you might run into doing this sort of coding.

Let's look at the code.

There is nothing of interest in the head, so let's skip straight to the body of the page. The body has the standard Bootstrap markup we've been working with throughout the book. Inside the main div, we have an SVG element that contains a single circle element at 75, 225 with a 50-pixel radius. It's got an id of circle:

```
<div class="container-fluid">
  <div class="row">
    <div class="col-12">
      <svg xmlns="http://www.w3.org/2000/svg" viewBox="0 0 1000 450"
        width="1000" height="450" version="1.1" id="canvas"
         class="canvas">
        <circle cx="75" cy="225" r="50" fill="blue" id="circle">
      </circle>
      </svg>
    </div>
  </div>
</div>
```

The JavaScript is straightforward.

It consists of a single function added to the DOMContentLoaded event. That function does some familiar things. It creates local references to doc, canvas, and circle so that we can reference those elements easily throughout the animation. Following that there are several variables created to store properties of the viewBox: viewBox itself, height, width, and x. We then set two constants representing the number of seconds for the animation to run and the number of **frames per second (fps)** we're aiming for with our animation).

Following that we grab the current x value of the circle element as a variable, currX. After that we calculate the ending point, newX, by using the radius of the circle and multiplying it by 3. That gives us a comfortable ending point, visually.

Next we create some variables to run the animation. The first, `diffX`, is a calculation of the difference between the current x value and the target, `newX`, value. Then we take the `diffX`, divide it by the number of seconds, and multiply it by the number of frames per second. This will create three seconds' worth of intervals to animate by.

Finally we create the animated variable, `animX`, which is the variable we will work with in every frame as we animate the element across the screen.

Following that, there's a function that adjusts the position of the element on the screen every frame. It does three things. It adds the interval to the `animX` to move the element over by that calculated interval. It then sets the `cx` property of the element, moving it to its new position. Finally it calls itself recursively using `window.requestAnimationFrame`.

 `requestAnimationFrame` is a method that allows the browser to optimize the way that JavaScript animations are drawn onto the screen. The number of frames per second it's optimized to is usually `60`, but technically it will match the display refresh rate of the device.

All of that takes place inside an `if` block that stops the animation when it has completed. If `animX` is less than `newX`, then the code executes, calling `animate` again to kick off the next frame. If `animX` is greater than or equal to `newX`, then the animation stops:

```
document.addEventListener("DOMContentLoaded", () => {

const doc = document;
const canvas = doc.getElementById("canvas");
const circle = doc.getElementById('circle');
const viewBox = canvas.viewBox.baseVal;
const width = viewBox.width;
const height = viewBox.height;
const x = viewBox.x;
const padding = width / 200;
const seconds = 3;
const fps = 60;
let currX = circle.cx.baseVal.value;
let newX = width - (circle.r.baseVal.value * 3);
let diffX = newX - currX;
let intervalX = diffX / (fps * seconds);
let animX = currX;
function animate() {
    if (animX < newX) {
        animX = animX + intervalX;
        circle.setAttribute("cx", animX);
        window.requestAnimationFrame(animate);
    }
```

```
}
animate();
});
```

This isn't the most complicated animation, but using `window.requestAnimationFrame` means that it looks pretty good in the browser.

While there are other options for animating SVG, and you should learn about them and use them where appropriate, JavaScript is going to be the most powerful and ultimately the most flexible option out there. If your animation needs to work across the most possible browsers, then you're going to want to use JavaScript.

The good news is, as you'll see later on in the chapter, there are excellent tools to simplify animating with JavaScript.

Before we look at the first of several JavaScript libraries for working with SVG, let's look at the two other options for animating SVG, using core web technologies: CSS, and SMIL.

Animating with CSS

Animating SVG with CSS is straightforward in that it works the same way that CSS animations and transitions work with regular HTML elements. You define some CSS properties and, depending on whether or not you're using keyframe animation or transitions, you create specific CSS rules that handle how they are rendered over a period of time. The problem with the idea of that process being straightforward is that only presentation attributes, which drive much of SVG, that are also available as CSS properties can be manipulated with CSS. As you can see on the following website, the list, as defined in SVG 1.1, is missing many important properties: `https://www.w3.org/TR/SVG/propidx.html`. SVG 2.0 adds many more properties, but support for those new properties is not universal and, unfortunately, there isn't a proper compendium of what properties are supported where.

In other words, there are some potential rough edges using these technologies, depending on what your browser support matrix looks like.

Anyway, even with that somewhat rough story, it's still worth seeing these techniques in action.

There are three examples here. Two show animations similar to the previous JavaScript animation; they move a blue circle across the screen. They're implemented in two different ways. This illustrates the implementation differences you might see depending on what browsers you're targeting. The first example uses CSS transforms and CSS animation to translate the element across the screen. This technique has broader browser support. The second example uses the simpler approach of setting a transition on the cx property and then changing the value on hover of the SVG element. cx is available as a CSS property in Chrome, so in that browser this is the easier approach.

The third example shows a transition on the fill on an element, to illustrate an example where leaving the calculations to the browser and CSS is of great benefit. If it's not clear how you would animate from one color value to another, then you can probably see at least one great use case for leaving the heavy lifting to the browser.

Let's look at the examples in order.

The first example is simple. In it, we have the same markup as the previous JavaScript example, with one exception: setting the cx property via CSS. We do that in the #circle selector in the head of the document.

Additionally, we set a transition property on that selector, watching the cx property for changes and transitioning for three seconds when it changes. In the next selector, svg:hover #circle, we trigger the animation via a hover event on the parent SVG element, which sets the cx value to the final destination, 875 pixels.

With this CSS in place, when you mouse over the SVG element, the new cx is set and the browser will animate across the screen between 75 and 875 pixels on the *x* axis of the SVG element:

```
<!doctype html>
<html lang="en">

<head>
  <meta charset="utf-8">
  <title>Mastering SVG- SVG Animation with CSS</title>
  <link rel="stylesheet"
href="https://maxcdn.bootstrapcdn.com/bootstrap/4.0.0/css/bootstrap.m
    in.css" integrity="sha384-
    Gn5384xqQ1aoWXA+058RXPxPg6fy4IWvTNh0E263XmFcJlSAwiGgFAW/dAiS6JXm"
    crossorigin="anonymous">
  <style type="text/css">
    #circle {
      transition: cx 3s;
      cx: 75px;
    }
```

```
      svg:hover #circle {
        cx: 875px;
      }
    </style>

  </head>

  <body>

    <div class="container-fluid">
      <div class="row">
        <div class="col-12">
          <svg xmlns="http://www.w3.org/2000/svg" viewBox="0 0 1000 450"
           width="1000" height="450" version="1.1" id="canvas"
            class="canvas">
            <circle cy="225" r="50" fill="blue" id="circle"></circle>
          </svg>
        </div>
      </div>
    </div>


  </body>

</html>
```

This next example is set up similarly. It has exactly the same SVG markup as the previous example animated by JavaScript. The differences are once again in the CSS.

There are two sections of interest. The first section defines a two-keyframe animation called `animate-circle`. The first keyframe, at `0%`, has a `0px` translation across the X axis, using `transform: translateX`. The second keyframe, at `100%`, increases that transformation to `800px`.

Then, in the `#circle` selector, we define the `animation` property with the named animation, a duration of three seconds and linear easing. Then we set the `animation-fill-mode` to forwards, which indicates that the animation should run forwards once and complete, keeping the animated element at its final state.

When this runs, the circle smoothly animates across the screen:

```
<!doctype html>
<html lang="en">

<head>
  <meta charset="utf-8">
  <title>Mastering SVG- SVG CSS Animation</title>
```

```
<link rel="stylesheet"
 href="https://maxcdn.bootstrapcdn.com/bootstrap/4.0.0/css/bootstrap.
  min.css" integrity="sha384-
  Gn5384xqQ1aoWXA+058RXPxPg6fy4IWvTNh0E263XmFcJlSAwiGgFAW/dAiS6JXm"
  crossorigin="anonymous">
<style type="text/css">
  @keyframes animate-circle {
    0% {
      transform: translateX(0)
    }
    100% {
      transform: translateX(800px)
    }
  }

  #circle {
    animation: animate-circle 3s linear;
    animation-fill-mode: forwards;
  }
</style>

</head>

<body>

  <div class="container-fluid">
    <div class="row">
      <div class="col-12">
        <svg xmlns="http://www.w3.org/2000/svg" viewBox="0 0 1000 450"
         width="1000" height="450" version="1.1" id="canvas"
          class="canvas">
          <circle cx="75" cy="225" r="50" fill="blue" id="circle">
          </circle>
          </svg>
        </div>
      </div>
    </div>


  </body>

</html>
```

The final example also uses transitions, this time animating the `fill` property from blue to red. This property is one of the earlier presentation properties defined as being available in CSS, so it's got better support in browsers than a property such as `cx` at this present time.

The CSS definition is very simple. There's a `fill` property set on the `#circle` definition, alongside a `transition` that watches for changes to `fill` and transitions the change over a 2-second duration.

In `#circle:hover` we change the `fill` to blue. Running it in a browser and hovering over the circle will animate the color of the circle element, without using any JavaScript and without figuring out how to animate from one named color to another:

```
<!doctype html>
<html lang="en">
<head>
  <meta charset="utf-8">
  <title>Mastering SVG- SVG Data Visualization</title>
  <link rel="stylesheet"
  href="https://maxcdn.bootstrapcdn.com/bootstrap/4.0.0/css/bootstrap.m
  in.css" integrity="sha384-
  Gn5384xqQ1aoWXA+058RXPxPg6fy4IWvTNh0E263XmFcJlSAwiGgFAW/dAiS6JXm"
    crossorigin="anonymous">
  <style type="text/css">
    #circle {
      fill: red;
      transition: fill 3s;
    }
    #circle:hover {
      fill: blue;
    }
  </style>
</head>
<body>
  <div class="container-fluid">
    <div class="row">
      <div class="col-12">
        <svg xmlns="http://www.w3.org/2000/svg" viewBox="0 0 450 450"
         width="450" height="450" version="1.1" id="canvas"
           class="canvas">
          <circle cx="225" cy="225" r="225" fill="blue" id="circle">
        </circle>
        </svg>
      </div>
    </div>
  </div>
</body>
</html>
```

All of these examples are intentionally basic and as mentioned, browser support for them is weak (none work in versions of IE older than Edge, for example); but they remain powerful. If your browser matrix support leans toward the latest and greatest browsers, then you can have a lot of fun with CSS and SVG.

Animating SVG with SMIL

Another interesting and powerful option for animating SVG has a similarly frustrating support matrix to CSS. SMIL isn't supported at all in Microsoft browsers and was even deprecated briefly by Chrome.

This is a shame, as there are some nice things about SMIL. It's a clear, declarative way to animate elements. It's not as powerful as JavaScript or as commonly used as a general-purpose technology like CSS, but it's still pretty great.

Take a look at an example.

In it, we have our now familiar markup: a simple `circle` on an otherwise blank SVG element. This time there's one small twist. There is an `animate` element as a child of the `circle` element. The `animate` element is where the animation is defined. It has several attributes that we need to look at:

- The `xlink:href` attribute points to the `#circle` element that will be animated. The fact that the `animate` element is a child of the `circle` element automatically associates the animation with it. Using the `xlink:href` attribute ensures that the connection is precisely defined.
- `attributeName` defines the attribute that will be animated. In this case it's the `cx` attribute.
- The `from` and `to` attributes indicate the beginning and endpoint of the animation. In this case we'll be moving from `"75"` to `"900"`.
- `dur` indicates the duration of the animation. In this case, it's defined as `"3s"`, for three seconds.
- The `begin` attribute indicates when the animation should begin. This lets you delay the animation as needed. In our case we start the animation immediately with `"0s"`.
- The `fill` attribute, confusingly named the same as the common `fill` attribute, indicates whether or not the animated values should remain on the element after the animation concludes. This value, `"freeze"`, indicates that the element should remain frozen at the state it reaches at the end of the animation.

There seems no good reason why `fill` is overloaded to do two separate, basically unrelated, tasks in the context of SVG. It's unfortunate.

Running this in the browser creates a similar animation to the one we've seen in several instances in this chapter; the ball starts on the left and over the course of three seconds moves over to the right:

```
<!doctype html>
<html lang="en">

<head>
 <meta charset="utf-8">
 <title>Mastering SVG- SVG Animation with SMIL</title>
 <link rel="stylesheet"
  href="https://maxcdn.bootstrapcdn.com/bootstrap/4.0.0/css/bootstrap.m
    in.css" integrity="sha384-
    Gn5384xqQ1aoWXA+058RXPxPg6fy4IWvTNh0E263XmFcJlSAwiGgFAW/dAiS6JXm"
    crossorigin="anonymous">
</head>

<body>

 <div class="container-fluid">
 <div class="row">
 <div class="col-12">
 <svg xmlns="http://www.w3.org/2000/svg" viewBox="0 0 1000 450"
    width="1000" height="450" version="1.1" id="canvas" class="canvas">
    <circle cx="75" cy="225" r="50" fill="blue" id="circle">
 <animate
 xlink:href="#circle"
 attributeName="cx"
 from="75"
 to="900"
 dur="3s"
 begin="0s"
 fill="freeze" />
 </circle>
 </svg>
 </div>
 </div>
 </div>
</body>

</html>
```

Now that we've looked at manual methods for data visualization and animation in SVG, let's look at some tools that will help with animating elements.

Animating SVG with Vivus

Vivus is a library that does one thing and does it really well (`https://maxwellito.github.io/vivus/`). Vivus allows you to "draw" the stroke of an SVG element across a period of time.

The following series of screenshots show how that will look. It's a nice effect.

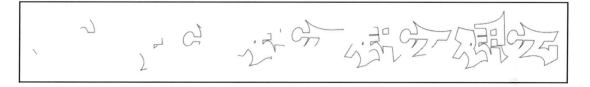

As a note, the same illustration is used in three samples in this chapter. The code samples printed in the book truncate the d attribute of each path element in order to shorten the code sample to a manageable length. If you'd like to see the full sample, please refer to the code on GitHub (`https://github.com/roblarsen/mastering-svg-code`).

As long as the `stroke` is set with a value and the `fill` is set to none, simply including the Vivus JavaScript file (in this case we do so by running `npm install` in the Vivus folder and then linking to the JavaScript file located in the `node_modules` folder) and then creating a new Vivus instance are all it takes.

Creating a new Vivus instance is very easy. Using the `new` keyword you can instantiate a new Vivus object with two arguments. The first is the `id` of the SVG element. The second is the configuration object. In this case, we're passing in just one option, the `duration` argument, setting the duration of the animation to three seconds (3,000 milliseconds).

The following code sample shows just how easy it is to work with Vivus:

```
<!doctype html>
<html lang="en">

<head>
  <meta charset="utf-8">
  <title>Mastering SVG- SVG Animation with Vivus</title>
  <style>
```

```
   .stroke{
     stroke-linejoin: round;
   }
   </style>
 </head>

 <body>

  <div class="container-fluid">
  <div class="row">
  <div class="col-12">
  <svg id="loader" xmlns="http://www.w3.org/2000/svg" viewBox="0 0
     250.23 131.83"><title>Logo</title><path fill="none" stroke="#000"
      d="M160.9,26.9l-.37.25c6.81,8.24,10.62,17.49"/>
 <path fill="none" stroke="#000"
  d="M28.14,92.59c1.43,1.56,2.81,3,4,4.45,3.56,4.31,6.05"/>
 <path fill="none" stroke="#000" d="M80.3,57.58c.27,4.74.54,9.34.81,14l-
  19.33,1v8.1a4.56,4.56,"/>
 <path fill="none" stroke="#000"
  d="M160.9,26.9a5.89,5.89,0,0,1,1.08.74c11.41,"/>
 <path fill="none" stroke="#000" d="M28.14,92.59c-3.72,5.21-7.28,"/>
 <path fill="none" stroke="#000"
  d="M80.3,57.58,59.18,59.36V56.54h21C79.42,"/>
 <path fill="none" stroke="#000"
  d="M43.87,73.26a5.31,5.31,0,0,1-.24,5.8c-1.51-.76-1.58-.91-1-2.4Z"/><path
 fill="none" stroke="#000" d="M103.13,55.28,90"/></svg>
  </div>
  </div>
  </div>
 <script src="node_modules/vivus/dist/vivus.js"></script>
 <script>
  new Vivus('loader', {duration: 3000});
 </script>
 </body>

 </html>
```

There are other configuration options available to Vivus, you can find them here: https://github.com/maxwellito/vivus#option-list. We won't go through them all, but we will illustrate one more, one that will be very useful, that of running a callback function once the animation is completed.

Everything about it is the same as the previous Vivus example, except we define a simple callback function, called `callback`, that goes through all instances of elements with the class `stroke` and changes their stroke to a different color.

The end result looks like the following screenshot. The text will be red once the animation completes and the callback function is executed:

The callback function is passed in as an optional third argument to the Vivus constructor. It then executes when the animation is completed.

The following code sample shows how that works:

```
<!doctype html>
<html lang="en">

<head>
  <meta charset="utf-8">
  <title>Mastering SVG- SVG Animation with Vivus</title>
  <style>
  .stroke{
    stroke-linejoin: round;
  }
  </style>
</head>

<body>
  <div class="container-fluid">
    <div class="row">
      <div class="col-12">
          <svg id="loader" xmlns="http://www.w3.org/2000/svg"
            viewBox="0 0 250.23 131.83"><title>Logo</title><path
              fill="none" stroke="#000"
              d="M160.9,26.91-.37.25c6.81,8.24,10.62,17.49"/>
<path fill="none" stroke="#000"
d="M28.14,92.59c1.43,1.56,2.81,3,4,4.45,3.56,4.31,6.05"/>
<path fill="none" stroke="#000"
d="M80.3,57.58c.27,4.74.54,9.34.81,14l-19.33,1v8.1a4.56,4.56,"/>
<path fill="none" stroke="#000"
d="M160.9,26.9a5.89,5.89,0,0,1,1.08.74c11.41,"/>
<path fill="none" stroke="#000" d="M28.14,92.59c-3.72,5.21-7.28,"/>
<path fill="none" stroke="#000"
d="M80.3,57.58,59.18,59.36V56.54h21C79.42,"/>
```

```
<path fill="none" stroke="#000" d="M43.87,73.26a5.31,5.31,0,0,1-
.24,5.8c-1.51-.76-1.58-.91-1-2.4Z"/><path fill="none" stroke="#000"
d="M103.13,55.28,90"/></svg>
    </div>
  </div>
</div>
<script src="node_modules/vivus/dist/vivus.js"></script>
<script>
  function callback(){
    for (const element of document.getElementsByClassName("stroke")){
      element.style.stroke = "#cc0033";
    };
  }
  new Vivus('loader', {duration: 500}, callback);
</script>
</body>

</html>
```

Now that we've looked at an animation library that does one thing, let's take a look at a more full-featured animation library, **GreenSock Animation Platform (GSAP)**.

Animating SVG with GSAP

GSAP is a set of powerful JavaScript tools for animation on the web. It works very well with SVG.

GSAP is a powerful set of tools and exploring all it has to offer in depth would spread across multiple chapters. *And that's just the free version.* There's also a premium version which includes even more features and functionality.

The good news is that, even though it's incredibly powerful, the GSAP API is straightforward, so once you find your desired feature and get a look at the strong documentation (`https://greensock.com/docs`), you're going to be able to do a lot very quickly.

Let's take a look at two separate examples to give you an intro to the sort of things that GSAP can do and how it does them.

This first example replicates the same animation we've done several times so far in this chapter. We're moving a ball from one side of the SVG element to the other. This one actually uses some familiar code from the initial JavaScript example to calculate the finishing position.

The markup is the same as we've seen several times so far. It's a `circle` element with an `id` of `circle` alone in an SVG element.

To get started using GSAP, we need to include their JavaScript in our demo. In this case, we're including the TweenMax script. Running `npm install` in the project folder will install GSAP and then we can include it from the project's `node_modules` folder.

 There are two different Tween* modules that GSAP provides: `TweenLite` and `TweenMax`.

They are described as follows:

> *TweenLite is an extremely fast, lightweight, and flexible animation tool that serves as the foundation of the GSAP. A TweenLite instance handles tweening one or more properties of any object (or array of objects) over time.*
> *TweenMax extends TweenLite, adding many useful (but non-essential) features like repeat(), repeatDelay(), yoyo(), and more. It also includes many extra plugins by default, making it extremely full-featured.*

We'll use TweenMax for this demo. If you're going to start to experiment with GSAP, TweenMax is going to offer you the largest footprint of tools to work with right off the bat. It's slightly slower but it's more powerful, and while you're experimenting with it, it's going to be more fun to have everything at your fingertips.

Now that we have the JavaScript file loaded, let's work with it.

The JavaScript should look familiar, at least to start with. We set several familiar consts: `doc` as an alias for the `document`, `canvas` as a reference to the SVG element, `circle` as a local reference to the circle we're going to animate, `viewBox` as a local reference for the `viewBox` of the SVG element, `width` for the `viewBox.width`, and `newX` for the calculated finish position of the circle element.

The new GSAP-specific code follows as we call `TweenMax.to`. `TweenMax.to` is a method that animates an HTML element to a certain state. The arguments are as follows:

- `"#circle"` is the CSS selector to use to match the element we're going to animate.
- `1` is the number of times the animation will run.
- Finally, there is a configuration object to define the animation. In our example we're passing in the `newX` variable as the new value of the `cx` element.

And that's all it takes; GSAP handles the rest, smoothly animating the circle from one end of the screen to the other:

```html
<!doctype html>
<html lang="en">

<head>
  <meta charset="utf-8">
  <title>Mastering SVG- SVG Animation with GSAP</title>

</head>

<body>

  <div class="container-fluid">
    <div class="row">
      <div class="col-12">
        <svg xmlns="http://www.w3.org/2000/svg" viewBox="0 0 1000 450"
        width="1000" height="450" version="1.1" id="canvas"
        class="canvas">
          <circle cx="75" cy="225" r="50" fill="blue" id="circle">
        </circle>
        </svg>
      </div>
    </div>
  </div>

<script src="node_modules/gsap/src/minified/TweenMax.min.js"></script>
<script>
const doc = document;
const canvas = doc.getElementById("canvas");
const circle = doc.getElementById('circle');
const viewBox = canvas.viewBox.baseVal;
const width = viewBox.width;
const newX = width - (circle.r.baseVal.value * 3);
TweenMax.to("#circle", 1, {attr:{cx:newX}, ease:Linear.easeNone});
</script>
</body>

</html>
```

This next example has the same setup, but changes the arguments that are passed into TweenMax.to and adds another chained method call to change the duration of the animation. In this example we pass in four separate attributes to animate the element against, cx, cy, r, and fill. This example illustrates one of the real powers of GSAP. You don't have to figure out anything about the timing of those multiple property animations, what the individual intervals look like, or how to sync them and parse them out so that they run smoothly. You just give GSAP an end state and watch it do its magic.

Additionally, we're adding a new method, chained to the end of the call to TweenMax.to. Calling TweenMax.duration changes the duration of the animation. Here we're passing in 5 to extend the animation to last a full five seconds. This chained interface allows you to work with animations in a manner similar to working with jQuery and many other JavaScript libraries. It's a powerful, friendly, interface:

```
<!doctype html>
<html lang="en">

<head>
  <meta charset="utf-8">
  <title>Mastering SVG- SVG Animation with GSAP</title>

</head>

<body>

  <div class="container-fluid">
    <div class="row">
      <div class="col-12">
        <svg xmlns="http://www.w3.org/2000/svg" viewBox="0 0 1000 450"
          width="1000" height="450" version="1.1" id="canvas"
          class="canvas">
          <circle cx="75" cy="225" r="50" fill="blue" id="circle">
          </circle>
          </svg>
        </div>
      </div>
    </div>

<script src="node_modules/gsap/src/minified/TweenMax.min.js"></script>
<script>
const doc = document;
const canvas = doc.getElementById("canvas");
const circle = doc.getElementById('circle');
const viewBox = canvas.viewBox.baseVal;
const width = viewBox.width;
const height= viewBox.height;
```

```
TweenMax.to("#circle", 1, {attr:{cx:width,cy:0,r:height,fill:"red"},
ease:Linear.easeNone}).duration(5);
</script>
</body>

</html>
```

Running the previous code in a browser produces the following output:

Summary

In this chapter, you learned about visualizations and animations with SVG. This included working with pure JavaScript, SMIL, CSS, and two libraries for animation: GSAP and Vivus.

In this chapter, we looked at:

- Creating a custom data visualization with JavaScript, SVG, and CSS. You took a data set, manipulated it with JavaScript, and used the results to create a nice looking visualization that illustrates a set of data in an easy-to-read way.
- Creating a custom SVG animation with JavaScript. This included calculating increments to animate over 60 frames-per-second and using `requestAnimationFrame` as a method to ensure that you're providing the smoothest possible experience.
- Animating SVG with CSS. You learned that the powerful options for animating SVG come with uncertain browser support.
- Animating SVG with SMIL, which also comes with uncertain browser support.
- Animating SVG with the Vivus library, which makes implementing a "drawing" animation in SVG as easy as including the library and adding a single line of JavaScript.
- Finally, you got a glimpse at the powerful GSAP library, which offers incredibly powerful options for the animation of SVG and other elements.

Now that we've introduced a couple of libraries into the mix, it will be a smooth transition into a whole chapter on helper libraries for SVG, Snap.svg, and SVG.js. These are important tools and will be invaluable if you're looking to do advanced, custom work with SVG.

Helper Libraries Snap.svg and SVG.js

9

We've learned a lot about SVG so far in this book. If you've made it this far, you're ready to do some serious SVG development, and for that there are three ways to go:

- Continue doing what we've, mostly, done so far in this book-learn about the way the core technologies interact and integrate SVG into your sites or applications, as you would in any markup. Manipulate it with JavaScript and CSS and you're ready to tackle basically anything. This is a valid approach and is the one I often take in my own work.
- Use task-specific frameworks and libraries. We've started to look at this a little bit with GSAP and Vivus for animation. We'll continue to look at this in `Chapter 10`, *Working with D3.js*, when we look at D3, a powerful visualization framework.
- Use general purpose SVG libraries that will help you with a variety of SVG-related tasks. SVG was brought into the mainstream of web development on the back of one such library, Raphael, and there are current libraries available for you to use in your own work. This option is the focus of this chapter.

As previously mentioned, SVG took many years to gain traction owing to limited browser support. A general-purpose SVG library called Raphael.js (`http://dmitrybaranovskiy.github.io/raphael/`) helped to bridge that support gap by offering a very clever **Vector Markup Language** (**VML**), `https://docs.microsoft.com/en-us/windows/desktop/vml/web-workshop---specs---standards----introduction-to-vector-markup-language--vml-`, polyfill for an older version of Internet Explorer. It also offered a friendly API for dealing with SVG in the browser, which helped people unfamiliar with SVG to get started quickly and easily.

This chapter deals with two of the most popular successors to Raphael.js:

- `Snap.svg`: a direct successor to Raphael, being a library authored by the author of Raphael.js, Dmitry Baranovskiy (`http://snapsvg.io/`)
- `svg.js`: another small, lightweight library that offers plenty of powerful options for manipulating SVG (`http://svgjs.com/`)

The rest of the chapter will look at the basics of each library and will then go through some familiar examples, reworked to utilize the power of these general purpose SVG tools.

We'll start with Snap.svg.

Working with Snap.svg

Snap.svg is an SVG utility library from Adobe authored by Dmitry Baranovskiy. It is relatively full-featured, has a friendly, easy-to-explore API and is open source. Development on this library has slowed recently, but it's still a useful tool and one you should be aware of if you're exploring a general purpose SVG library.

Let's get started.

Getting started with Snap.svg

Snap.svg is available on `npm`, so by far the easiest way to get started with `Snap.svg` is to install it using `npm`:

```
npm install snapsvg
```

It's also available for download directly from the website, `http://snapsvg.io/`, and is also available to download or clone from GitHub, `https://github.com/adobe-webplatform/Snap.svg`.

Once you've done that, it's as easy as including the `snap.svg-min.js` from `node_modules` or the downloaded folder, and you're ready to start using Snap.

In this first example, we load Snap into the document and then go through some Snap basics loading up the Snap API and manipulating some SVG.

Initially, in this first example, we get a reference to a containing div, using the ID #target. Then we create an instance of Snap, using the new keyword and storing it in a variable, S. There are two arguments passed in, 800 and 600. These represent the width and height of the SVG element.

While we will use the variable S to represent the Snap.svg API in this chapter, you can name the variable anything you like as long as you assign the return value of the Snap.svg constructor to it. There's nothing magical about S, other than the fact that it's the conventional variable name that the authors of Snap use for their examples.

Next we use the Snap utility method S.appendTo to add our new SVG element into the document, using our #target element as the container.

Now that the SVG element is on the page, we add two new SVG elements into the document to show the basic pattern for adding and manipulating SVG elements with Snap. We add a circle and a rectangle. The circle is added with S.circle, passing in three attributes, the center x, the center y, and the radius. Once the circle is added, we call the chained method attr, passing in a fill and a stroke.

Next we call S.rect to create a rectangle, passing in x, y, width, and height arguments and, again, using attr to add a fill and stroke.

This jQuery-like pattern of chaining method calls to manipulate SVG elements is the core of your interaction with Snap. If you've got experience with that style of development, you'll pick up Snap very quickly. The API is clear and logical, so it's easy to experiment with:

```
<!doctype html>
<html lang="en">

<head>
 <meta charset="utf-8">
 <title>Mastering SVG- Basic Snap.svg demo</title>
 <link rel="stylesheet"
  href="https://maxcdn.bootstrapcdn.com/bootstrap/4.0.0/css/bootstrap.m
  in.css" integrity="sha384-
  Gn5384xqQ1aoWXA+058RXPxPg6fy4IWvTNh0E263XmFcJlSAwiGgFAW/dAiS6JXm"
  crossorigin="anonymous">
</head>

<body>

 <div class="container-fluid">
 <div class="row">
 <div class="col-12" id="target">
```

```
    </div>
    </div>
    </div>

    <script src="node_modules/snapsvg/dist/snap.svg-min.js"></script>
    <script>
    const target = document.getElementById("target");
    const S = new Snap(800,600);
    S.appendTo(target);
    S.circle(250,250,100)
    .attr({
    "fill":"blue",
    "stroke":"green"
    });
    S.rect(550,250,100,100)
    .attr({
    "fill":"green",
    "stroke":"blue"
    });
    </script>
    </body>

    </html>
```

Running the preceding in a browser produces the following output:

Taking that basic pattern, we can now start to recreate some of the demos we did previously, using Snap. Seeing how we transition from core technologies to libraries can be instructive and can give you a feel for the library and whether or not it feels like something you want to use.

Animation with Snap

Since animation with SVG is such an important feature of the modern web, Snap offers several animation utilities. It also offers the ability to manipulate existing SVG elements and not just elements generated by Snap itself (which is something SVG.js can't do). This demo takes advantage of both of those features.

The setup is similar to what we saw in earlier examples of this animation demo. We start the demo by obtaining three element references, `doc` for the `document`, `canvas` for the parent SVG, and `circle` for the `circle` element. Next, we get a reference to the `viewBox` and associated `width`, in order to make some calculations about the finishing point of the circle. This new finishing point is stored as `newX`.

Next comes the Snap specific features of this example. First, we load up a reference to the `circle` element with Snap's API. We do this by passing the variable `circle`, a DOM reference to the `circle` element, into Snap. If you've worked a lot with jQuery, this might be a familiar pattern for you.

Once that is done we can use the Snap `animate` method to animate the circle across the screen. `animate`, in this instance, takes four arguments:

1. The first is an object indicating the end state of the animation. In this case we're animating the `cx` property to the calculated `newX` value.
2. Then we pass in the duration of the animation, three seconds in milliseconds.
3. After that we pass in the animation easing. Once again we're using bounce easing. This is available as part of Snap's `mina` object, which provides built-in easing options as well as some other utilities for working with animations.
4. Finally, we pass in a `callback` function to run after the animation is completed. This function changes the fill color to red:

```
<!doctype html>
<html lang="en">

<head>
  <meta charset="utf-8">
  <title>Mastering SVG- SVG Animation with Snap.svg</title>
  <link rel="stylesheet"
href="https://maxcdn.bootstrapcdn.com/bootstrap/4.0.0/css/boot
  strap.min.css" integrity="sha384-
Gn5384xqQ1aoWXA+058RXPxPg6fy4IWvTNh0E263XmFcJlSAwiGgFAW/dAiS6J
  Xm"
    crossorigin="anonymous">
</head>

<body>

  <div class="container-fluid">
    <div class="row">
      <div class="col-12">
        <svg xmlns="http://www.w3.org/2000/svg" viewBox="0 0
1000
```

```
                    450" width="1000" height="450" version="1.1"
        id="canvas"
                class="canvas">
                  <circle cx="75" cy="225" r="50" fill="blue"
                   id="circle"></circle>
              </svg>
            </div>
          </div>
        </div>


        <script src="node_modules/snapsvg/dist/snap.svg-
        min.js"></script>
          <script>
            const doc = document;
            const canvas = doc.getElementById("canvas");
            const circle = doc.getElementById("circle");
            const viewBox = canvas.viewBox.baseVal;
            const width = viewBox.width;
            const newX = width - (circle.r.baseVal.value * 3);
            const S = new Snap(circle);

            S.animate({ "cx": newX }, 3000, mina.bounce, () => {
              S.attr({ "fill": "red" })
            });
          </script>
        </body>

      </html>
```

In addition to the animation utilities seen in this example, Snap also includes other utilities for working with SVG. The next section will illustrate some of those utilities.

Snap.svg utilities

This example will illustrate a couple of useful Snap utilities available for working with SVG. The whole purpose of working with a general-purpose library like Snap is to use utility methods such as the following. This example shows just two such utilities, but this should be enough to show you the sort of things that are available.

The beginning of the example is standard Snap.svg development. You start by getting a reference to the #target element. We create a Snap variable, S, and then append it to the #target element.

Once it's in the document, we can use the first of two utilities. It's a single line assignment to the variable bbox, which returns the bounding box of an SVG element, in this case, a circle.

 A bounding box is the smallest possible rectangle that can contain a shape (or group of shapes).

Let's look at what happens in this assignment. First we create a new circle at (255, 255) with a 110 pixel radius. Then we add a fill and stroke so that we can see it on the SVG element. Then we call the getBbox method, which is stored as bbox.

When we console.log out the bbox variable, we see the following values:

```
▼ Object ▤                                                          9-2-snap-utilities.html:27
    cx: 255
    cy: 255
    h: 220
    height: 220
  ▶ path: (5) [Array(3), Array(3), Array(3), Array(3), Array(1), toString: f]
    r0: 155.67957709738948
    r1: 110
    r2: 110.16410815334564
    vb: "144.83589184665436 145 220.32821630669127 220"
    w: 220.32821630669127
    width: 220.32821630669127
    x: 144.83589184665436
    x2: 365.16410815334564
    y: 145
    y2: 365
  ▶ __proto__: Object
```

As you can see, the return value contains a lot more information than just the simple coordinates of the smallest possible rectangle that can contain the element. It has that information (the x, y, height, and width), but it also has several other properties that might be useful if you're manipulating the element in relation to another element in an animation, visualization, or dynamic drawing.

The following list shows the values of the bounding box and what they represent:

- cx the *x* value of the center of the box
- cy the *y* value of the center of the box
- h the height of the box
- height the height of the box
- path the path command for the box
- r0 the radius of a circle that fully encloses the box
- r1 the radius of the smallest circle that can be enclosed by the box

- r2 the radius of the largest circle that can be enclosed
- vb the box as a `viewBox` command
- w the width of the box
- `width` the width of the box
- x2 the *x* value of the right side of the box
- x the *x* value of the left side of the box
- y2 the *y* value of the bottom edge of the box
- y the *y* value of the top edge of the box

That's a very useful, but possibly unexceptional utility method. As you'll see in the SVG.js section, a bounding box is an important and common concept when working with SVG.

The next example utility is a little more interesting. Let's take a look at how it works.

To do so, we first create a `path` that represents a stylized letter R. You saw this R and the associated `path` previously as part of one of our animation examples. Once the letter R is inserted into the document, we add a `fill` and `stroke` to it, and then apply a transformation to it in order to center it on the `circle` we previously created. The end result is shown in the following screenshot:

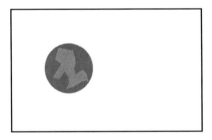

Once the path is inserted, we call `console.log` again, with another utility method, `path.getTotalLength()` passed in as an argument. `path.getTotalLength()` does what it says on the tin — it returns the total length of the referenced path element.

If you were, for example, animating along the path over a defined length of time, getting the length of the path would be a vital metric. As the following screenshot shows, this utility provides that powerful metric with very little fuss:

```
358.99090576171875                    9-2-snap-utilities.html:31

>
```

The entirety of the code just described is as follows:

```html
<!doctype html>
<html lang="en">

<head>
  <meta charset="utf-8">
  <title>Mastering SVG- Snap.svg utilities</title>
  <link rel="stylesheet"
   href="https://maxcdn.bootstrapcdn.com/bootstrap/4.0.0/css/bootstrap.
    min.css" integrity="sha384-
    Gn5384xqQ1aoWXA+058RXPxPg6fy4IWvTNh0E263XmFcJlSAwiGgFAW/dAiS6JXm"
    crossorigin="anonymous">
</head>

<body>

  <div class="container-fluid">
    <div class="row">
      <div class="col-12" id="target">
      </div>
    </div>
  </div>


  <script src="node_modules/snapsvg/dist/snap.svg-min.js"></script>
  <script>
    const target = document.getElementById("target");
    const S = new Snap(800,600);
    S.appendTo(target);
    const bbox = S.circle(255,255,110)
                    .attr({
                        "fill":"blue",
                        "stroke":"green"
                    }).getBBox();
    console.log("bounding box",bbox);

    const path =
    S.path("M28.14,92.59c1.43,1.56,2.81,3,4,4.45,3.56,4.31,6.05,9.14,6.3
    9,14.82.37,6.35-2,11.81-5.82,16.7-.61.76-1.27,1.48-
    2,2.35,3.15-.86,6.09-1.74,9.07-2.48,2.82-.7,5.66-1.4,8.54-
    1.82a6.54,6.54,0,0,0,2.84-1.15c4.26-2.9,8.5-5.84,12.87-
    8.56a30.61,30.61,0,0,1,10.12-
```

```
        4.23c3.16-.64,6.11-.57,7.81,3a73.85,73.85,0,0,0-.4-7.64c-.51-4.55-
        1.4-9-3.7-13-2.84-5-7-6.39-12.32-4.22a32.44,32.44,0,0,0-
        9.07,6.17c-.38.34-.77.65-1.51,1.26-.88-4.66-1.72-9-5.08-12.1.76-
        1.26,1.5-2.32,2.05-3.46a22.71,22.71,0,0,0,1.38-
        3.57,31.72,31.72,0,0,0-16.47c-1-4.39-2.26-8.73-3.33-13.11-.37-
        1.53-.53-3.12-.77-4.58-12-.08-23.06-3.78-34.44-
       6.66L6.21,65.08l14.68,9.47L.83,105.88c5.07.89,9.91,1.7,14.74,2.6a1.5
      ,1.5,0,0,0,1.76-.72C20.86,102.76,24.42,97.8,28.14,92.59Z")
        .attr({"fill":"gray","stroke":"burgundy"})
        .transform("s2 t110,85");

        console.log("total length", path.getTotalLength());

    </script>
  </body>

  </html>
```

Now that we've taken a look at some Snap utilities, let's look at Snap's events system, which allows you to work with SVG elements in an interactive way while still staying tightly within the confines of the Snap API.

Snap.svg events

While you may already have a handle on managing events manually using `Element.addEventListener` or are already using something like jQuery to handle your events, it's worth noting that Snap offers some event utilities of its own. This allows you to cut down on external dependencies if you're doing very focused work with SVG. It also allows you to skip over any of the quirks that a library like jQuery offers when working with SVG elements.

The following example is a familiar one modified to show how Snap.svg events work. In this example, we're once again adding `click` event handlers to a blank SVG canvas and inserting random sized circles into the SVG element at the point of the click. Using Snap to implement this demo is very similar to what you saw previously, but it has some conveniences that are worth noting, and it illustrates the straightforward way that Snap handles events.

The example starts off by getting access to the `#target` element, setting `height` and `width` variables, and then creating an instance of Snap appended to the `#target` element and stored in the standard Snap variable, `S`.

Once we have Snap loaded, we chain a series of method calls to add a circle using the S.circle method, set the fill using the attr method, and then add a click event handler to the element using Snap's click event utility.

The callback function called when the user clicks on the SVG element is almost the same as the vanilla JS Version, although it does use the Snap method S.circle to insert a circle element using the familiar randomized parameters fill, radius, newX, and newY:

```html
<!doctype html>
<html lang="en">

<head>
  <meta charset="utf-8">
  <title>Mastering SVG- SVG Events with Snap.svg</title>

</head>

<body>

  <div class="container-fluid">
    <div class="row">
      <div class="col-12" id="target">
      </div>
    </div>
  </div>


  <script src="node_modules/snapsvg/dist/snap.svg-min.js"></script>
  <script>
    const target = document.getElementById("target");
    const height = 600;
    const width = 800;
    const S = new Snap(width,height);
    S.appendTo(target);
    S.circle(250,250,100).attr({"fill":"blue"}).click(()=>{
      const newX = Math.random() * width;
      const newY = Math.random() * height;
      const r = Math.random() * height/2;
      const red = Math.random() * 255;
      const blue = Math.random() * 255;
      const green = Math.random() * 255;
      S.circle(newX,newY,r).attr({
        "fill":`rgba(${red},${blue},${green},${Math.random()})`
      });
    });
```

```
    </script>
  </body>

  </html>
```

If you're used to working with jQuery or other libraries that follow a similar pattern, then you should be able to pick up working with Snap's event utilities quickly.

Custom data visualization with Snap.svg

The final example using `Snap.svg` shows how it can be used to do custom data visualizations. This will show many features of `Snap.svg` in action and will provide a final, full look at the library.

This example will once again generate a visualization showing the positive/negative delta of home runs hit per year versus the average home runs hit per year by David Ortiz of the Boston Red Sox per year over his Red Sox career.

Since we've already seen this visualization, in this section we'll only focus on the areas where `Snap.svg` is being used and not on every line of the script. If you need a refresher on the hows and whys of data visualization itself and how the metrics are calculated, please look back at `Chapter 8`, *SVG Animation and Visualizations*, for a full explanation of the entire script.

The first file you'll see is the HTML file, which is similar to the original version of this visualization. The only real difference is including the `Snap.svg` source file from `node_modules`:

```
    <div class="container-fluid">
      <div class="row">
        <div class="col-12">
          <svg xmlns="http://www.w3.org/2000/svg" viewBox="0 0 1000 450"
            width="1000" height="450" version="1.1" id="canvas"
            class="canvas">
          </svg>
        </div>
      </div>
    </div>

    <script src="node_modules/snapsvg/dist/snap.svg-min.js"></script>
    <script src="scripts.js"></script>
```

Looking at the source of `scripts.js`, the `viz()` function is structurally the same, but has some Snap-related differences that you'll want to notice.

 The `data` variable is exactly the same and is truncated here to make the `viz()` function slightly easier to read. See `Chapter 8`, *SVG Animation and Visualizations*, or the source code to see the full data set.

Following the `data` variable, some of the interesting stuff starts with the `S` variable. As you saw previously, `S` is an instance of `Snap.svg` and that's going to be the interface through which we do a lot of our work. Following that, there aren't any changes between this version and the original version of this, until we use a reference to the Snap reference to the SVG element's DOM node, `S.node`, to access the SVG element's `viewBox`.

Following that, the biggest difference you'll notice is the ability to use the Snap convenience methods, `S.rect`, `S.line`, and `S.text` (all paired with `S.attr`) to add our lines, boxes, and text elements to the screen. We also use `S.addClass` to add a CSS class to one of our lines.

Because all of these methods exist in `Snap.svg`, the biggest difference between this example and our JavaScript-only example is the absence of our own, hand-rolled convenience methods. Since Snap provides so many convenient features, we don't need to provide them ourselves. Which is great in and of itself, and, of course, Snap includes many more convenience methods than `S.rect`, `S.line`, `S.text`, and `S.attr`:

```
function viz() {
  /*
    ES6
  */
  const data = [
    /* truncated for brevity - see Chapter 8 for the full data set*/
    {
      "year": 2016,
      "hrs": 38
    }
  ];

  const doc = document;
  const canvas = doc.getElementById("canvas");
  const S = new Snap(canvas);
  function maxDiffer(arr) {
    let maxDiff = arr[1] - arr[0];
    for (let i = 0; i < arr.length; i++) {
      for (let j = i + 1; j < arr.length; j++) {
        if (arr[j] - arr[i] > maxDiff) {
```

```
          maxDiff = arr[j] - arr[i];
        }
      }
    }
    return maxDiff;
  }
  document.addEventListener("DOMContentLoaded", () => {
    const viewBox = S.node.viewBox.baseVal;
    const width = viewBox.width;
    const height = viewBox.height;
    const x = viewBox.x;
    const y = viewBox.y;
    const padding = width / 200;
    const vizWidth = width - padding;
    const years = data.length;
    const total = data.reduce((total, item) => {
      return total + item.hrs;
    }, 0);
    const avg = total / years;
    const verticalMidPoint = (y + height) / 2;
    const diffs = data.map((item) => {
      return item.hrs - avg;
    });
    const maxDiff = maxDiffer(diffs);
    const yIntervals = verticalMidPoint / maxDiff;
    const xInterval = (vizWidth / years);
    for (const i in diffs) {
      const newX = xInterval * i;
      const newY = diffs[i] * yIntervals;
      if (diffs[i] < 0) {
        S.rect(
          newX + padding,
          verticalMidPoint,
          xInterval - padding,
          Math.abs(newY)
        ).attr({
          "fill": "#C8102E",
          "stroke": "#ffffff"
        });

        S.text(
          newX + padding,
          verticalMidPoint + Math.abs(newY) + (padding * 3),
          `${data[i].hrs} in ${data[i].year}`
        );
      }
      else if (diffs[i] > 0) {
        S.rect(
```

```
            newX + padding,
            verticalMidPoint - newY,
            xInterval - padding,
            newY,
        ).attr({
            "fill": "#4A777A",
            "stroke": "#ffffff"
        });

        S.text(
            newX + padding,
            verticalMidPoint - newY - (padding * 2)
            , `${data[i].hrs} in ${data[i].year}`
        );
    }
    S.line(
        x,
        verticalMidPoint,
        width,
        verticalMidPoint
    ).attr({
        "stroke": "#ffffff"
    });
    S.text(
        x + padding,
        height - (padding * 3)
        `Based on an average of ${avg} home runs over ${years} years`
    ).addClass("large");
    }
});

}

viz();
```

Now that we've taken a good look at `Snap.svg` and hopefully given you a feel for what it is like to work with, let's take a look at another `helper` library, the appropriately named SVG.js.

Working with SVG.js

SVG.js was created by Wout Fierens and is currently maintained by Ulrich-Matthias Schäfer, Jon Ronnenberg, and Rémi Tétreault. It's designed to be lightweight and fast, and to be a friendly interface for working with SVG. It's more actively maintained than `Snap.svg`, so it's got that going for it. As of the time of writing, the most recent code was added to the project within the past two weeks.

Getting started with SVG.js

Like `Snap.svg`, SVG.js is available on `npm`, so the easiest way to get started with SVG.js is to install it using `npm`:

```
npm install svg.js
```

Make sure you install `svg.js` with `npm` and not `svg.js`. Both work and both point to the correct project. `svg.js` is, however, out of date because the official package is `svg.js`.

It's also available for download directly from the website `http://svgjs.com/installation/#download`. It is also available to download or clone from GitHub, `http://svgjs.com/` and is available on `cdnjs`.

Once you've done that, it's as easy as including the `svg.min.js` from `node_modules` or the downloaded folder, and you're ready to start using SVG.js.

This first example repeats the earlier blue circle/green square demo. The convention with SVG.js, as shown in their demos, is to use a variable, `draw`, to hold the loaded instance of SVG.js that you work with.

To create an instance of SVG.js, you pass in a reference to a target HTML element and SVG.js inserts a loaded SVG element into the targeted element, ready for you to work with. You then chain a method, `SVG.size`, which will set the size of the newly created SVG element.

While we will use the variable `draw` to represent the SVG.js API in this chapter, you can name the variable anything you like. As long as you assign the return value of the SVG.js constructor to it, any variable name will work. There's nothing specifically magical about `draw`, other than the fact that it's the conventional variable name that the authors of SVG.js use for their examples.

The same is `true` of `Snap.svg` and the variable `S`. These are just conventions.

 SVG.js isn't designed to work with an existing SVG element, so you have to slightly change your approach if you're used to getting a reference to an existing SVG element and then manipulating it.

Once we have a reference to `draw` and our SVG element is added to the page, we can start to manipulate the SVG element, adding our square and circle.

Looking at the example of the circle, we call the clearly named method `draw.circle` to create a circle. `draw.circle` accepts *one* argument, the *radius* of the circle.

Interestingly, all of the other attributes are manipulated with the familiar (from jQuery and Snap) `attr` method. I think this is a peculiar choice since a circle with just a radius isn't very useful. The same goes for `draw.rect`, which requires the height and width of the rectangle as arguments and then does everything else as attributes with `attr`.

This syntax works just fine. But it is interesting that the attributes are spread across two methods:

```html
<!doctype html>
<html lang="en">

<head>
  <meta charset="utf-8">
  <title>Mastering SVG- Basic SVG.js demo</title>
  <link rel="stylesheet"
   href="https://maxcdn.bootstrapcdn.com/bootstrap/4.0.0/css/bootstrap.
    min.css" integrity="sha384-
    Gn5384xqQ1aoWXA+058RXPxPg6fy4IWvTNh0E263XmFcJlSAwiGgFAW/dAiS6JXm"
    crossorigin="anonymous">
</head>

<body>

  <div class="container-fluid">
    <div class="row">
      <div class="col-12" id="target">
      </div>
    </div>
  </div>


  <script src="node_modules/svg.js/dist/svg.min.js"></script>
  <script>
```

```
const draw = SVG('target').size(800,600);
draw.circle(200)
    .attr({
      "fill":"blue",
      "stroke":"green",
      "x":250,
      "y":250
    });
draw.rect(100,100)
    .attr({
      "fill":"green",
      "stroke":"blue",
      "x":550,
      "y":250
    });
</script>
</body>

</html>
```

Animation with SVG.js

Now that we've seen the basic example of inserting elements into the page, let's continue the same pattern we followed with Snap.svg and look at how to create an animation with SVG.js.

We need one more dependency to get animations running properly in SVG.js, svg.easing.js. This is a library of easing functions that work with SVG animations:

npm install svg.easing.js

Include that after you include the main SVG.js file and you're ready to go.

Getting started with this example, we create several variables to use throughout the animation, width, height, cx, cy, and radius. You saw these previously and they map to properties of SVG elements.

Then we create our SVG.js instance, using the height and width values as arguments, and store it in the draw variable. After that we create the circle element we will animate, by calling draw.circle with the radius variable as the sole argument. We then call attr with a blue fill value and the cx and cy variables as values for the cx and cy attributes respectively. This creates the blue circle in the correct spot on the SVG element.

Then we calculate the `newX` variable. We then animate the circle to that new value with the SVG.js method `circle.animate`. The `animate` method takes three arguments, `3000`, the length of the animation, `SVG.easing.bounce`, the easing function to use (from `svg.easing.js`), and `1000`, the animation delay.

Next up there is a chained manipulation method, `center`, which, in this example, indicates the type of animation to perform. `center`, by itself, moves an element's center to the new `(x, y)` coordinates passed into it. Chaining it with `animate` means that you will smoothly animate between the two states. In our example, `center` takes the `newX` and original `cy` variables as arguments, which gives us our new horizontal placement while retaining our original vertical placement.

Finally, to illustrate an animation `callback` method, we use the method `after`, which allows us to run a function after the animation has completed. Here we simply change the color of the circle with the `attr` method:

```html
<!doctype html>
<html lang="en">

<head>
  <meta charset="utf-8">
  <title>Mastering SVG- SVG Animation with SVG.js</title>
  <link rel="stylesheet"
   href="https://maxcdn.bootstrapcdn.com/bootstrap/4.0.0/css/bootstrap.
    min.css" integrity="sha384-
    Gn5384xqQ1aoWXA+058RXPxPg6fy4IWvTNh0E263XmFcJlSAwiGgFAW/dAiS6JXm"
    crossorigin="anonymous">
</head>

<body>

  <div class="container-fluid">
    <div class="row">
      <div class="col-12" id="canvas">

      </div>
    </div>
  </div>


  <script src="node_modules/svg.js/dist/svg.min.js"></script>
  <script src="node_modules/svg.easing.js/dist/svg.easing.min.js"></script>
  <script>
    const width = 1000;
    const height = 450;
    const radius = 50;
```

```
        const cx = 75;
        const cy = 225;
        const draw = SVG('canvas').size(width,height);
        const circle = draw.circle(radius * 2)
                          .attr({
                              "fill":"blue",
                              "cx":cx,
                              "cy":cy
                          });
        const newX = width - (radius * 3);
        circle.animate(3000, SVG.easing.bounce, 1000)
          .center(newX,cy)
          .after(function(situation) {
            this.attr({
              "fill": 'red'
            });
          });
      </script>
    </body>
    </html>
```

As we've seen in these two examples, there are some quirks in the SVG.js API. Since the quirks are consistent, like setting properties in two chained methods, you can very quickly get used to them.

SVG.js utilities

Like `Snap.svg`, SVG.js has a suite of utility functions to help you work with SVG. Some of them are really great. This example shows how many of them work.

To kick off this example we create a loaded SVG.js variable, draw, and pass in 800, 600 for the `height` and `width`.

Starting off immediately with some utilities, we call `draw.viewbox()` to get the `viewBox` of the SVG element. If you remember the visualization example done with `Snap.svg`, you'll recall that we had to navigate multiple properties to access the `viewBox` in Snap. There was no convenience method at all, just a property of the DOM Node that represented the SVG element.

Here we have a convenience method that returns it directly:

```
view box: ▼ create {x: 0, y: 0, width: 800, height: 600, zoom: 1} ⬚
              height: 600
              width: 800
              x: 0
              y: 0
              zoom: 1
          ▶ __proto__: Object
```

Next we load up a variable, `rect` with a `100` by `100` rectangle at (`100`, `100`) `console.log` out `rect.bbox()`, which returns the bounding box of the rectangle. As you can see in the following screenshot, it has fewer properties than the `Snap.svg` example of a bounding box, but it remains useful with all of the standard properties you would need to interact cleanly with this element:

```
bounding box: ▼ create {w: 100, h: 100, x2: 200, y2: 200, cx: 150, …} ⬚
                  cx: 150
                  cy: 150
                  h: 100
                  height: 100
                  w: 100
                  width: 100
                  x: 100
                  x2: 200
                  y: 100
                  y2: 200
              ▶ __proto__: create
```

One very useful utility related to the standard bounding box is illustrated next.

First, we transform the rectangle using SVG.js' `transform` method, rotating it by 125 degrees. `transform` is a `getter` / `setter` that will return the current transformation value when called without arguments and will set the value when called with arguments.

Once we've transformed the `rect` rectangle, we `console.log` out the return value of `rect.rbox()`, which returns a bounding box that represents a visual representation of the element which includes all transformations. This will save you a lot of coding if you're working with transformed elements:

```
rbox:                                                                          9-7-svg-js-utilities.html:28
▼ create {w: 139.27285766601562, h: 139.27285766601562, x2: 227.63640594482422, y2: 227.6364288330078, cx: 157.9999771118164, …}
    cx: 157.9999771118164
    cy: 158
    h: 139.27285766601562
    height: 139.27285766601562
    w: 139.27285766601562
    width: 139.27285766601562
    x: 88.3635482788086
    x2: 227.63640594482422
    y: 88.36357116699219
    y2: 227.6364288330078
```

The next method, `data`, works just like the jQuery data method. Called as a setter, `rect.data({"data":"storing arbitrary data"}),,` data sets arbitrary data on an object, stored under a user-supplied label. Called as a `getter`, with the label passed in as an argument, `rect.data("data")`, it returns the value of the labeled data:

```
data method: storing arbitrary data
```

The next utility method allows you to adjust the stack of SVG elements. Unlike absolutely positioned HTML elements, which have an explicit stacking order (z-index), SVG elements are layered based on their appearance in the DOM. Elements that are later in the DOM appear to sit on top of elements that appear earlier in the DOM.

The next code block shows how you can adjust this stacking order with SVG.js utilities.

First, we create two squares, a green square and then a blue square. When they appear on the screen initially, they look as shown in the following screenshot:

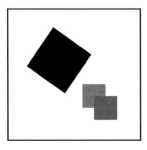

Then, inside a one second timeout, we call the `back()` method, which sends the element to the back of the stack. After that, the squares look as follows:

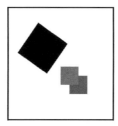

Now that we have two squares on the screen, it's time to look at one final, super useful, bounding box related utility. If you call `first.bbox().merge` and pass in `second.bbox()` as the argument, you get a combined bounding box. This is incredibly useful if you're working with multiple elements that are not part of a structured SVG group:

```
merged bounding box ▼ create {w: 75, h: 75, x2: 275, y2: 275, cx: 237.5, …} ⓘ
                      cx: 237.5
                      cy: 237.5
                      h: 75
                      height: 75
                      w: 75
                      width: 75
                      x: 200
                      x2: 275
                      y: 200
                      y2: 275
```

Here is the entire code sample:

```
<!doctype html>
<html lang="en">

<head>
  <meta charset="utf-8">
  <title>Mastering SVG- SVG.js utilities</title>
  <link rel="stylesheet"
    href="https://maxcdn.bootstrapcdn.com/bootstrap/4.0.0/css/bootstrap.
    min.css" integrity="sha384-
    Gn5384xqQ1aoWXA+058RXPxPg6fy4IWvTNh0E263XmFcJlSAwiGgFAW/dAiS6JXm"
    crossorigin="anonymous">
</head>
```

```
<body>

  <div class="container-fluid">
    <div class="row">
      <div class="col-12" id="canvas">
      </div>
    </div>
  </div>


  <script src="node_modules/svg.js/dist/svg.min.js"></script>
  <script>
    const draw = SVG('canvas').size(800,600);
    console.log("view box:",draw.viewbox());
    const rect = draw.rect(100,100)
                    .attr({
                        "x":100,
                        "y":100
                    });
    console.log("bounding box:", rect.bbox());
    rect.transform({ rotation: 125 });
    console.log("rbox:",rect.rbox());
    rect.data({"data":"storing arbitrary data"});
    console.log("data method:", rect.data("data"));

    const first = draw.rect(50,50)
                    .attr({
                        "x": 200,
                        "y": 200,
                        "fill": "green"
                    });
    const second = draw.rect(50,50)
                    .attr({
                        "x": 225,
                        "y": 225,
                        "fill": "blue"
                    });
    setTimeout(()=> {
      second.back();
    },2000);
    console.log("merged bounding box", first.bbox().merge(second.bbox()));

  </script>
</body>

</html>
```

SVG.js events

SVG.js also has event handling utilities. The following example will illustrate the very familiar event handling pattern provided by SVG.js.

Once again, we're illustrating event handling by binding `click` events to a function that inserts random-sized circles with random fills on the canvas. This will also illustrate one nice usage of the SVG.js `front()` method.

The example starts off by creating the `draw` variable, setting its height and width and then creating a `circle` variable with an SVG.js enhanced `circle` element.

After that, we bind a `click` event to the circle, which creates the randomly-sized/filled circle element using the event utility `circle.click`. It's straightforward. Like the `Snap.svg` example or examples from earlier versions of jQuery, you pass in the `callback` method as an argument to `click` and that's all it takes to bind your events properly.

Inside the `callback`, we use `draw.circle` to create our circles with the random values generated every time the function runs.

The one nice bonus of using SVG.js here is that you can always ensure that the clickable circle is at the top of the stack by calling `circle.front()` after every circle is added. Otherwise, it could eventually be buried by other elements appearing on top of it because they were inserted later on in the DOM:

```
<!doctype html>
<html lang="en">

<head>
  <meta charset="utf-8">
  <title>Mastering SVG- SVG.js Events

  </title>
</head>

<body>

  <div class="container-fluid">
    <div class="row">
      <div class="col-12" id="target">
      </div>
    </div>
  </div>
```

```
<script src="node_modules/svg.js/dist/svg.min.js"></script>
<script>
  const height = 600;
  const width = 800;
  const draw = SVG('target').size(width,height);
  const circle = draw.circle(100)
                   .attr({
                     "fill":"blue",
                     "cx":250,
                     "cy":250
                   });

  circle.click((e)=> {
    const newX = Math.random() * width;
    const newY = Math.random() * height;
    const r = Math.random() * height/2;
    const red = Math.random() * 255;
    const blue = Math.random() * 255;
    const green = Math.random() * 255;
    draw.circle(r)
      .attr({
        "cx": newX,
        "cy": newY,
        "fill":`rgba(${red},${blue},${green},${Math.random()})`
      });
    circle.front();
  });

</script>
</body>

</html>
```

Custom data visualization with SVG.js

The final example in this chapter is another example of doing a custom data visualization. We're going to once again revisit the visualization representing David Ortiz's home runs over his career as a member of the Boston Red Sox.

Since we've seen this multiple times, we can simply focus on the ways that SVG.js can help us do this work.

The first file you'll see is the HTML file. The only differences between this and the vanilla JS Version are the inclusion of the SVG.js source file from `node_modules` and the absence of a base SVG element:

```html
<div class="container-fluid">
  <div class="row">
    <div class="col-12" id="target">
    </div>
  </div>
</div>
<script src="node_modules/svg.js/dist/svg.min.js"></script>
<script src="scripts.js"></script>
</body>
```

The `viz()` function is similar to what we saw with the `Snap.svg` Version. Once again we've clipped the data object for readability.

Following that there's the familiar pattern for working with SVG.js. We set `width` and `height` variables and then create the `draw` SVG.js instance using the `width` and `height` variables as the arguments.

The first place where SVG.js comes into play is the easy-to-use `viewBox()` method in the `DOMContentLoaded callback` function, which returns the SVG element's `viewBox`. We use this variable to calculate multiple variables used in the visualization. After more than 20 lines of creating familiar variables (see `Chapter 8`, *SVG Animation and Visualizations*, for a refresher on what each of these does), we draw some boxes, we draw some lines, and we add some text.

Let's look at an example of how SVG.js can help with each of these.

Drawing boxes allows us to expose some nice convenience methods that SVG.js offers as a replacement to setting properties in `attr`. `draw.rect` is called the same as before, passing in the calculated width and height for each box. Then, we chain three more method calls to it: `attr` is used to set the `x` and `y` and then, as an illustration of their availability, we also use two convenience methods, `fill` and `stroke`, to set the `fill` and `stroke` directly. It's quite possible to simply set everything as an argument to `attr`, but if you prefer to chain method calls in this way, it's a nice option for you to be able to call `fill` and `stroke` to set those properties.

Drawing text introduces a new method, `draw.plain`. There is a `draw.text` method, but `draw.text` is designed to work with larger blocks of text and therefore introduces `tspan` elements into the mix to help control flow and line breaks. That's actually very clever and is a useful option for many situations where you're working with long blocks of text in SVG since everything to do with flow and line breaks has to be handled manually. In those situations, having multiple elements to work with is great.

`draw.plain`, however, is perfect for our needs here as we're only interested in individual text elements. To use it, we call the `draw.plain`, pass in our concatenated string as an argument, and then set the `(x,y)` coordinates using our good friend `attr`.

Drawing lines requires four initial arguments, the starting `(x,y)` and the finishing `(x,y)`. Once we provide those values as calculated by the rest of the `viz()` function, we can do things like add a stroke, via `draw.attr` (as in this example) or `draw.stroke` (if you prefer), or add a class using the convenience method `draw.addClass`:

```
function viz() {
  /*
    ES6
  */
  const data = [
/* truncated for brevity - see Chapter 8 for the full data set */
    {
      "year": 2016,
      "hrs": 38
    }
  ];
  const width = 1000;
  const height = 450;
  const draw = SVG("target").size(width, height);
  function maxDiffer(arr) {
    let maxDiff = arr[1] - arr[0];
    for (let i = 0; i < arr.length; i++) {
      for (let j = i + 1; j < arr.length; j++) {
        if (arr[j] - arr[i] > maxDiff) {
          maxDiff = arr[j] - arr[i];
        }
      }
    }
    return maxDiff;
  }
  document.addEventListener("DOMContentLoaded", () => {
    const viewBox = draw.viewbox();
    const width = viewBox.width;
    const height = viewBox.height;
    const x = viewBox.x;
```

```
const y = viewBox.y;
const padding = width / 200;
const vizWidth = width - padding;
const years = data.length;
const total = data.reduce((total, item) => {
  return total + item.hrs;
}, 0);
const avg = total / years;
const verticalMidPoint = (y + height) / 2;
const diffs = data.map((item) => {
  return item.hrs - avg;
});
const maxDiff = maxDiffer(diffs);
const yIntervals = verticalMidPoint / maxDiff;
const xInterval = (vizWidth / years);
for (const i in diffs) {
  const newX = xInterval * i;
  const newY = diffs[i] * yIntervals;
  if (diffs[i] < 0) {
    draw.rect(
      xInterval - padding,
      Math.abs(newY)
    )
    .attr({
      "x": newX + padding,
      "y": verticalMidPoint,
    })
    .fill("#C8102E")
    .stroke("#ffffff");

    draw.plain(`${data[i].hrs} in ${data[i].year}`)
    .attr({
      "x": newX + padding,
      "y": verticalMidPoint + Math.abs(newY) + (padding * 3)
    });
  }
  else if (diffs[i] > 0) {
    draw.rect(
      xInterval - padding,
      newY,
    )
    .attr({
      "x": newX + padding,
      "y": verticalMidPoint - newY
    })
    .fill("#4A777A")
    .stroke("#ffffff");
```

```
        draw.plain(`${data[i].hrs} in ${data[i].year}`)
          .attr({
            "x": newX + padding,
            "y": verticalMidPoint - newY - (padding * 2)
          });
      }
    }
    draw.line(
      x,
      verticalMidPoint,
      width,
      verticalMidPoint
    )
    .attr({
      "stroke": "#ffffff"
    });

    draw.plain(`Based on an average of ${avg} home runs over ${years}
years`)
      .attr({
        "x": x + padding,
        "y": height - (padding * 3)
      })
      .addClass("large");
  });

}

viz();
```

Summary

This chapter has provided you with a rapid-fire introduction to two separate libraries for working with SVG, Snap.svg and SVG.js. Doing the same, familiar tasks you previously tackled in vanilla JS in the two libraries has allowed you to see the differences between doing these SVG manipulations with vanilla JS and doing them with a library. You've also been able to compare the two libraries themselves across similar tasks.

Overall, you've learned a number of different topics with these two libraries, including how to get started, how to animate elements, how to handle events, and how to do custom data visualizations.

Now that we've learned about general purpose libraries, we're going to take a look at one final SVG library with a very specific purpose, D3.js. D3 is used for heavy duty data visualizations and is one of the most powerful tools out there for working with SVG.

10
Working with D3.js

aahis chapter will introduce you to **Data-Drive Documents (D3)**, a powerful visualization library and one of the most popular open source projects in the world. Interestingly, while it's most important for its data manipulation features, D3 is simply one of the most powerful libraries for working with SVG, full stop. Even in the context of being a `helper` library of the sort we discussed in the previous chapter, it has many very useful features for working with SVG documents, including many that replicate the sorts of things that `Snap.svg` and SVG.js offer and many more beyond that.

D3 doesn't stop there, however. It goes well beyond that SVG authoring and utility feature set and goes on to offer a rich suite of tools to do data manipulation and subsequent generation of data visualizations. What's more, D3 uses the same web standards under the hood that you've been working with throughout the book and marries it with a robust API to offer up a true playground for working with SVG and data.

Born out of an earlier visualization library called Protovis (`http://mbostock.github.io/protovis/`), D3 has been around since the early 2010s and remains under the watchful eye of the project's original developer, Mike Bostock. The project is under active development, and offers up copious documentation and a wonderful selection of examples to learn from.

It's also, once you get the hang of it, a lot of fun. This is the last new technology introduced in the book that's used for working with SVG directly, so it's nice to be ending this phase of the book on a high note.

Let's have some fun.

In this chapter, we'll learn about several topics, including:

- How to install D3 and how to do basic SVG manipulations with the library
- How to do a bar chart with D3 using scales and functions that help define the x and y axes of a chart
- How to use the `d3-fetch` utility to get and parse JSON and CSV data
- How to use the `enter` and `exit` selections to manipulate the SVG DOM based on the changes to a dataset
- How to implement a donut chart in D3 using the `arc` and `pie` functions from D3
- How to implement a chord diagram; a complicated visualization with multiple components

Getting started with D3

The D3 API can take some getting used to. The examples in this chapter will strive to illustrate some of the basic concepts as well as dive deeper as we move forward to show some of the best that D3 has to offer.

Before we can do any of that, you need to get D3 into your page. To do so, you can use npm to install it into your project folder:

```
npm install d3
```

Once you've got it installed, you can link to the minified D3 source from your document using a script tag:

```
<script src="node_modules/d3/dist/d3.min.js"></script>
```

If you'd prefer not to use npm, it's also available to be linked to from d3js.org directly:

```
<script src="https://d3js.org/d3.v5.js"></script>
```

Additionally, if you want a local copy, you can clone the project from GitHub (https://github.com/d3/d3)), or download the project from d3js.org and then organize your files in any way you like.

Once you've got the project installed, you're ready to start to explore the D3 API.

The following example shows how to implement a simple bar chart using D3. You've seen some of the concepts used to generate a bar chart already in this book, but the difference here is that D3 will do it for you. D3 knows all about visualizations so it will generate the required metrics for you.

This visualization will compare the top ten individual comic book sales of all time. The data (`https://itsalljustcomics.com/all-time-record-comic-book-sales/`) it will illustrate is as follows:

Title/Issue #/Grade	Date of sale	Sale price
Action Comics 1 9.0	2014/08/24	$3,207,852.00
Action Comics 1 9.0	2011/11/30	$2,161,000.00
Action Comics 1 8.5	2018/06/13	$2,052,000.00
Action Comics 1 8.5	2010/03/29	$1,500,000.00
Amazing Fantasy 15 9.6	2011/03/09	$1,100,000.00
Detective Comics 27 8.0	2010/02/25	$1,075,000.00
Action Comics 1 Kansas City 8.0	2010/02/22	$1,000,000.00
Action Comics 1 5.5	2016/08/04	$956,000.00
All Star Comics 8 9.4	2017/08/27	$936,223.00
Action Comics 1 5.0	2018/03/20	$815,000.00

The end result of the visualization will look like the following screenshot:

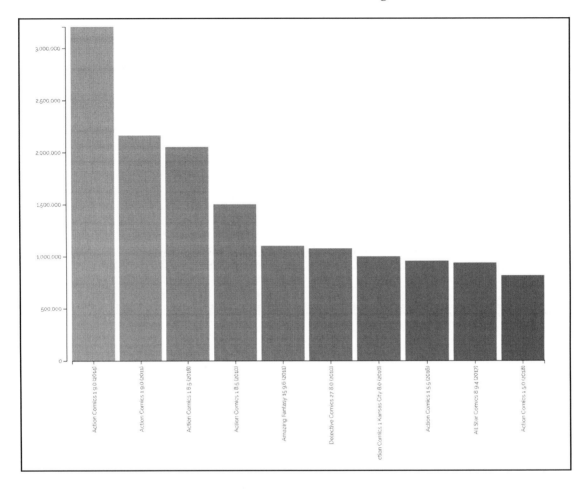

 All JavaScript code in this chapter is written to take advantage of ES6 features, such as arrow functions, const, and let.

The markup, which follows, is very simple. We once again include Bootstrap for simple layout tasks and `Raleway`, our font of choice in this book. Then we set some base CSS styles for text elements and set up a simple container to hold the visualization. After that, we include three files: `d3.min.js`, the main D3 file, `d3-fetch.min.js`, a Fetch utility from D3 (https://developer.mozilla.org/en-US/docs/Web/API/Fetch_API), and our visualization file, `bar.js`:

```
<!doctype html>
<html lang="en">

<head>
 <meta charset="utf-8">
 <title>Mastering SVG- D3 Bar Chart</title>
 <link rel="stylesheet"
   href="https://maxcdn.bootstrapcdn.com/bootstrap/4.0.0/css/bootstrap.
    min.css" integrity="sha384-
    Gn5384xqQ1aoWXA+058RXPxPg6fy4IWvTNh0E263XmFcJlSAwiGgFAW/dAiS6JXm"
    crossorigin="anonymous">
 <link href="https://fonts.googleapis.com/css?family=Raleway"
   rel="stylesheet">
 <style type="text/css">
  text {
    font-family: Raleway;
    font-size: 1em;
   }
 </style>
</head>

<body>
 <div class="container">
  <div class="row">
   <div class="col-12" id="target">

   </div>
  </div>
 </div>
 <script src="node_modules/d3/dist/d3.min.js"></script>
 <script src="node_modules/d3-fetch/dist/d3-fetch.min.js"></script>
 <script src="_assets/js/bar.js"></script>
</body>
</html>
```

Since the JavaScript here is complicated and introduces many new concepts, I'm going to go through each block separately. Look at the full file in the downloaded source code if you'd like to see the entire file in one go.

Looking at bar.js, it consists of one function that draws the entire visualization on screen. The start of the function sets several constants that are used throughout the visualization: width, height, chartHeight (used to set the size of the chart itself versus the size of the overall SVG), and a margin const used to ensure that there's enough margin to hold the entirety of the visualization in the SVG element:

```
function bar() {
  const width = 960,
```

```
      height = 800,
      chartHeight = 600,
      margin = 30;
```

Following that, we start to work directly with D3. D3 allows you to access and manipulate existing SVG elements and also, as in the case of the D3 demos in this book, generate a D3-enhanced SVG element and append it to the DOM.

In this case, we're using D3's query selector utility, d3.select, to select the #target element and then append a new SVG element into it. We then use the increasingly familiarly named function attr to set the height and width of the SVG element. Once the SVG element is in the document, we append a new g element and immediately translate it by the margin on the *x* and *y* axes.

Chained D3 methods behave like jQuery or other libraries that use this pattern so the variable svg is a D3-enabled reference to the final element in the chain, the newly added g. Anything that interacts with that variable will start from within the context of that g element:

```
let svg = d3.select("#target").append("svg")
    .attr("width", width)
    .attr("height", height)
    .append("g")
    .attr("transform", `translate(${margin},${margin})`);
```

Next, we use some methods to set the scale for the *x* and *y* axes and then actually generate both the *x* and *y* axes. This is where D3 really shines. Doing this work isn't impossible. It's often simple math. It's just that no one wants to write these functions all the time and D3 makes it easy with an entire suite of scale functions (https://github.com/d3/d3-scale).

The x variable holds the return value of a scaleBand method call. scaleBand allows you to break up a numeric scale into component *bands*, which we will use to create the horizontal spacing of our bar chart. The initial call is chained to two subsequent calls, each of which inform the band about our specific visualization. The range method call sets the *x* scale to range from 10 pixels up to a calculated upper bound (the width minus two horizontal margins). paddingInner sets the inner padding of the bands. This property allows us to create some space between the columns.

The y variable is created as a linear scale. Linear scales are continuous, regular scales between two values. The values for this particular scale are set with a call to range with chartHeight and 0 as the range values.

Following that, we use the newly created x and y scales to call two convenience methods, axisLeft and axisBottom. These methods render human-readable reference marks for scales. The xAxis is created and then the just-created x scale is passed in to wire up xAxis with the values from the x scale. The y axis is generated in exactly the same way:

```
let x = d3.scaleBand()
    .range([10, (width - margin.left - margin.right)])
    .paddingInner(0.1);
let y = d3.scaleLinear()
    .range([chartHeight, 0]);
let xAxis = d3.axisBottom()
    .scale(x);
let yAxis = d3.axisLeft()
    .scale(y);
```

We then use another scale method, scaleOrdinal, to create a map between our discrete data values and a corresponding set of colors:

```
let color = d3.scaleOrdinal()
    .range([
      "#1fb003",
      "#1CA212",
      "#199522",
      "#178732",
      "#147A41",
      "#126C51",
      "#0F5F61",
      "#0C5170",
      "#0A4480",
      "#073690"
    ]);
```

The rest of the method uses a utility from d3-fetch and d3.json to access our data file and then, as callback to the fetch request, process the data and generate our visualization.

The callback methods begin with two calls to domain for both the x and y axes.

For an ordinal scale, the xAxis and domain accept an array and sets the domain for the scale to the specific set of values in the array. Here, we map the returned data to create a collection of the title properties as the values to use in the xAxis.

For a linear scale, calling `domain` limits the continuous scale to the specific set of values. In this case, we're setting the scale to 0 at the minimum and the return value of d3.max, which returns the largest value in an array, as the maximum.

Following that we start manipulating SVG elements to create the actual visualization.

The first set of chained methods appends a new SVG group element, g, and adds a pair of classes to it, x and `axis`, and then translates it to a point at (0, chartHeight). This places this group at the bottom of the chart, which is precisely where you want the legend for the *x*-axis to be.

Then we use the d3.call function to call xAxis and generate our *x*-axis. d3.call is a utility method that allows you to call a function on a selection and then return the modified selection. This allows you to encapsulate some functionality in a reusable function in a way that enables chaining. Here, we call xAxis, the configured axisBottom method we created earlier, in order to create the *x*-axis – complete with all the elements that make up the *x*-axis. Without doing anything else, the *x*-axis now looks like the following:

As you can see, for some values that layout might be okay, but for our purposes, it's not functional. Because of the length of our titles, we need to tweak our labels to be legible. We'll rotate them 90 degrees.

To do so, we chain a few more methods onto our current chain. First we select all text elements that are child nodes of the current selection. These are all the text elements we just created with xAxis. Once we have that selection, we apply a transformation of -90 degrees to the text elements. This reorients the text to be vertical. Following that, we adjust the dx and dy properties to line the text up neatly.

Next up, we append a new g element.

Using these groups is not strictly necessary, but they help to organize the generated code for debugging and allow you to more easily create selections that are easy to manipulate. This is what groups are for.

This new g element will hold the *y*-axis. The *y*-axis is created in a similar way to the *x*-axis – although it's a simpler process, since there's no need to manipulate the text elements. A horizontal text layout is fine for the *y*-axis. In this call, we add classes to the g element, y and axis, and then call yAxis, which generates all of the elements that make up the *y*-axis.

The final method chain in this callback function illustrates a common pattern when working in D3. The first call is to d3.selectAll. selectAll will access *all* the elements that match the provided selector. This returned value is called the *selection* in D3. The selection can either be a list of DOM elements or, in this case, an array of placeholder elements matching the items in the data. So, empty, in this context is okay, as we will go through the process of manipulating the selection and adding our elements to it based on the received data.

We'll illustrate enter and the associated method, exit, in more depth in the next section, but in short, if your selection has fewer elements than the number of points in the dataset, then those extra data points are stored in what's referred to as the *enter selection*. Calling enter allows us to enter into and manipulate this enter selection. In our case, we're adding a number of rect elements to the SVG element.

Each of those rect elements is manipulated in the following ways:

- Its fill is set referencing a member of the color scale.
- The x property is created based on the members of the x scale.
- The width is calculated using x-bandwidth, which is a method that takes the member of the x scale and calculates a width based on that scale, including any defined padding.
- The y property is created based on the y scale previously created
- The height is calculated by subtracting this data point's y scale value from the chartHeight. This, in effects, hangs the box from the y value down to the bottom of the chart.

All of these properties combine to create the heart of the visualization:

```
d3.json("data/top-ten.json").then((data) => {
  x.domain(data.map((d) => {
    return d.title;
  }));
  y.domain([0, d3.max(data, (d) => {
    return d.price;
  })]);
  svg.append("g")
    .attr("class", "x axis")
    .attr("transform", `translate(0, ${chartHeight})`)
```

```
        .call(xAxis)
        .selectAll("text")
        .style("text-anchor", "end")
        .attr("transform", "rotate(-90)")
        .attr("dx", -10)
        .attr("dy", -5);
    svg.append("g")
        .attr("class", "y axis")
        .call(yAxis);
    svg.selectAll("rect")
        .data(data)
        .enter().append("rect")
        .style("fill", (d) => {
          return color(d.price);
        })
        .attr("x", (d) => {
          return x(d.title); })
        .attr("width", () => {
          return x.bandwidth();
        })
        .attr("y", (d) => {
          return y(d.price);
        })
        .attr("height", (d) => {
          return chartHeight - y(d.price);
        });
    });
  }
  bar();
```

The final line of the file simply calls `bar()` to create the visualization.

D3's enter and exit

As I mentioned in the last section, I want to take a quick, simplified look at `enter` and the associated method, `exit`. These methods are important for dealing with dynamic datasets. With these methods, you can take an arbitrary selection, blend it with data and then manipulate it with D3's tools to craft visualizations.

In this section, you'll see three examples. The first shows an example of using `enter` that illustrates calling the method against a completely empty selection. The second illustrates calling `enter` on a selection with existing elements. The third illustrates how `exit` works.

In this first example, we select the `#target` element and then call `selectAll` with `p` as the argument. Since there are no paragraphs in that `#target` element, this is an empty selection. Calling `data` on it binds that empty selection to our data. Calling `enter` on that bound selection allows us to manipulate our selection based on each data point.

If you were to log out the return value of `d3.select("#target").selectAll("p").data(data).enter()` at this point, it would look like the following screenshot, showing an array of five elements with the original data stored as an internal __data__ property:

```
                                                                                    10-1.5-enter-demo:22
▼ ut {_groups: Array(1), _parents: Array(1)} 
  ▼ _groups: Array(1)
    ▼ 0: Array(5)
      ▼ 0: U
          namespaceURI: "http://www.w3.org/1999/xhtml"
        ▶ ownerDocument: document
          data  : "a"
          _next: null
        ▶ _parent: div#target.col-12
        ▶ __proto__: Object
      ▶ 1: U {ownerDocument: document, namespaceURI: "http://www.w3.org/1999/xhtml", _next: null, _parent: div#target.col-12, __data__: "b"}
      ▶ 2: U {ownerDocument: document, namespaceURI: "http://www.w3.org/1999/xhtml", _next: null, _parent: div#target.col-12, __data__: "c"}
      ▶ 3: U {ownerDocument: document, namespaceURI: "http://www.w3.org/1999/xhtml", _next: null, _parent: div#target.col-12, __data__: "d"}
      ▶ 4: U {ownerDocument: document, namespaceURI: "http://www.w3.org/1999/xhtml", _next: null, _parent: div#target.col-12, __data__: "e"}
        length: 5
      ▶ __proto__: Array(0)
      length: 1
    ▶ __proto__: Array(0)
  ▶ _parents: [div#target.col-12]
  ▶ __proto__: Object
```

Next we simply `append` a paragraph to the document for each data point and use the `text` method to insert a text node representing the data into the document:

```html
<!doctype html>
<html lang="en">

<head>
  <meta charset="utf-8">
  <title>Mastering SVG- D3 Enter</title>
</head>

<body>
  <div class="container">
    <div class="row">
      <div class="col-12" id="target">

      </div>
    </div>
  </div>
  <script src="node_modules/d3/dist/d3.min.js"></script>
  <script src="node_modules/d3-fetch/dist/d3-fetch.min.js"></script>
```

```
<script>
  function enter() {
    const data = ["a", "b", "c", "d", "e"];
    d3.select("#target")
      .selectAll("p")
      .data(data)
      .enter().append("p")
      .text((d) => d);
  }
  enter();

</script>
</body>

</html>
```

Running the code in the browser results in the following output:

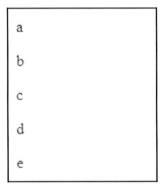

The next example is similar, except for the fact that it has an existing paragraph element in the `#target  div`. Since there's an existing p element, calling `d3.select("#target").selectAll("p").data(data).enter()` on the selection results in the following output. As you can see, the _groups array has the same five members, but the first entry, the one that corresponds to the existing member in `selection` is empty. That's because it's not part of the enter selection (as it corresponds to an *existing* element):

```
▼ ut {_groups: Array(1), _parents: Array(1)} ⓘ
  ▼ _groups: Array(1)
    ▶ 0: (5) [empty, U, U, U, U]
       length: 1
    ▶ __proto__: Array(0)
  ▶ _parents: [div#target.col-12]
  ▶ __proto__: Object
▶ |
```

Everything else about this example is the same as the previous example of using `enter`:

```
<!doctype html>
<html lang="en">

<head>
  <meta charset="utf-8">
  <title>Mastering SVG- D3 Enter with existing content</title>
</head>

<body>
  <div class="container">
    <div class="row">
      <div class="col-12" id="target">
        <p>This is an existing paragraph</p>

      </div>
    </div>
  </div>
  <script src="node_modules/d3/dist/d3.min.js"></script>
  <script src="node_modules/d3-fetch/dist/d3-fetch.min.js"></script>
  <script>
    function enter() {
      const data = ["a", "b", "c", "d", "e"];
      d3.select("#target")
        .selectAll("p")
        .data(data)
        .enter()
        .append("p")
        .text((d) => d);
    }
    enter();
```

```
    </script>
  </body>

  </html>
```

Since we're only updating the enter selection in this example, running the preceding code in the browser produces the following output:

```
This is an existing paragraph

b

c

d

e
```

To update the *entire* selection, you simply need to manipulate the original selection before you update the enter selection:

```
const data = ["a", "b", "c", "d", "e"];
d3.select("#target")
  .selectAll("p")
  .data(data)
  .text((d) => d)
  .enter()
  .append("p")
  .text((d) => d);
```

The `exit` selection allows you to clean up elements that no longer have data associated with them. The following example shows how this works.

The `render` function initially goes through some patterns we've already seen. The function calls `selectAll` on p elements that are children of `#target div`, loads it up with data, enters the enter selection, and appends a series of paragraph elements with the correct data.

Next we repeat the process and instead of calling `enter`, we call `exit` and then immediately call `remove`. The `exit` selection returns any elements in the selection that don't correspond to a data point. `remove` removes those elements from the document. The first time this runs, no elements are removed because the data has just been loaded. All elements in the selection are populated with the proper data.

The interesting thing happens in `setTimeout`. In that `callback` function, if there are still members of the data array, `data.pop()` is called. `pop` removes the last element from the array and then `render` is called, recursively after 1 second. When the function runs again and we get to the exit selection, where we call `exit.remove`, there *is* a mismatch between the data and the selection. The first time this is called recursively, there are five paragraphs, but only four data points. Because the fifth paragraph doesn't have a data point associated with it, it's removed from the document.

This process repeats until there are no data points or paragraphs left and the recursive calls stop:

```html
<!doctype html>
<html lang="en">

<head>
  <meta charset="utf-8">
  <title>Mastering SVG- D3 Exit</title>
</head>

<body>
  <div class="container">
    <div class="row">
      <div class="col-12" id="target">

      </div>
    </div>
  </div>
  <script src="node_modules/d3/dist/d3.min.js"></script>
  <script>
      const data = ["a", "b", "c", "d", "e"];
      function render(){
        d3.select("#target")
          .selectAll("p")
          .data(data)
          .enter()
          .append("p")
          .text((d) => d );
        d3.select("#target")
          .selectAll("p")
          .data(data)
          .exit()
          .remove();
        if (data.length) {
          setTimeout(()=>{
            data.pop();
            render();
          }
```

```
            ,1000);
        }
      }
    render();
  </script>
</body>

</html>
```

Hopefully, these simplified examples, dealing with the simplest possible element, a humble paragraph, are enough to illustrate the way that this very powerful pattern can help to work with datasets.

Now that we've taken a look at these two methods, let's return to some more of the fun stuff, with a new, slightly more complicated visualization.

Implementing a donut chart with D3

This next sample illustrates another basic data visualization: in this case, a donut chart. Slightly more complicated than a pie chart, this visualization illustrates some new features of D3. When complete, the visualization will look like the following screenshot.

It represents the distribution of individual comic books (referenced by title and issue number) among the top 50 comic book sales of all time (public sales, at the time of writing). There are a few comics that dominate lists like that and this chart will show which ones dominate the most:

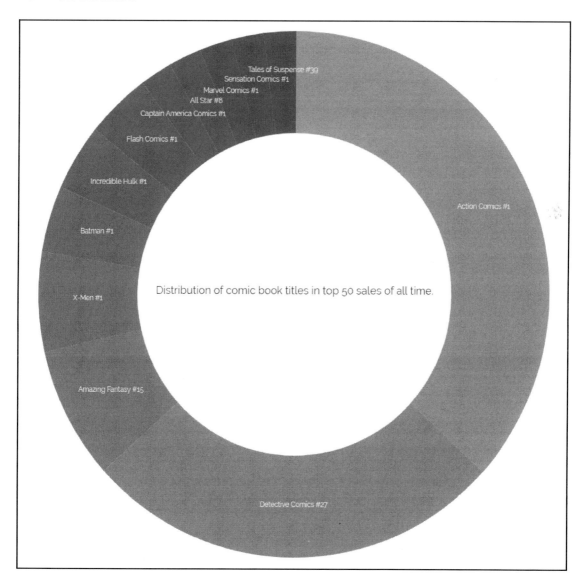

The data looks like the following CSV:

```
title,numbers
"Action Comics #1",18
"All Star #8", 1
"Amazing Fantasy #15",4
"Batman #1",2
"Captain America Comics #1", 1
"Detective Comics #27",13
"Flash Comics #1", 2
"Incredible Hulk #1", 2
"Marvel Comics #1", 1
"Sensation Comics #1", 1
"Tales of Suspense #39", 1
"X-Men #1", 3
```

The HTML file is very simple. It includes, once again, `Raleway`, **Bootstrap**, `d3-fetch`, and D3 for dependencies. It includes the same markup we've been working within several examples in this book and then includes our `donut.js` file, which is where everything interesting happens:

```html
<!doctype html>
<html lang="en">

<head>
    <meta charset="utf-8">
    <title>Mastering SVG- D3 Chord Diagram</title>
    <link rel="stylesheet"
href="https://maxcdn.bootstrapcdn.com/bootstrap/4.0.0/css/bootstrap.min.css
" integrity="sha384-
Gn5384xqQ1aoWXA+058RXPxPg6fy4IWvTNh0E263XmFcJlSAwiGgFAW/dAiS6JXm"
        crossorigin="anonymous">
    <link href="https://fonts.googleapis.com/css?family=Raleway"
     rel="stylesheet">
    <style type="text/css">
        text {
            font-family: Raleway;
            font-size: .8em;
            text-anchor: middle;
            fill: #fff;
        }
        text.legend{
            font-size: 1.25em;
            fill: #000;
        }
    </style>
</head>
```

```
<body>
    <div class="container">
        <div class="row">
            <div class="col-12" id="target">

            </div>
        </div>
    </div>


    <script src="node_modules/d3/dist/d3.min.js"></script>
    <script src="node_modules/d3-fetch/dist/d3-fetch.min.js"></script>
    <script src="_assets/js/donut.js"></script>

</body>

</html>
```

Looking at donut.js, there's a lot going on, so we'll once again go through the file section by section. If you want to see the whole file, please look at the full source code.

The file starts with setting several constants for the height, width, and radius of the visualization. We then create a color scale that steps through 13 shades of blue and green:

```
const width = 1000,
  height = 1000,
  radius = Math.min(width, height) / 2;

const color = d3.scaleOrdinal()
  .domain(d3.range(13))
  .range([
    "#1fb003",
    "#1CA212",
    "#199522",
    "#178732",
    "#147A41",
    "#126C51",
    "#0F5F61",
    "#0C5170",
    "#0A4480",
    "#073690",
    "#05299F",
    "#021BAF",
    "#000EBF"
  ]);
```

The next two method calls are there just to set up for the later visualization. At this point, we don't have any data to work with, but we can still create some loaded D3 tools to work with the data when it arrives. The first constant, arc, will allow us to draw arcs with an outerRadius that reaches near to the edge of the SVG element and an innerRadius 200 pixels in from the outerRadius. That creates a 190 pixel ring.

Following that we call d3.ie, which is a method that takes data and returns arcs that represent the correct proportional slice of data for a pie or donut chart. We don't have data yet, but we set the method up to know to use the numbers property of the data object when it creates the arcs:

```
const arc = d3.arc()
  .outerRadius(radius - 10)
  .innerRadius(radius - 200);

const pie = d3.pie()
  .value((d) => {
    return d.numbers;
  });
```

Next we start to implement some SVG. The first call should be common to you by this point. We call d3.select to grab the #target element and then append an SVG element into the DOM. Then we use attr to set the height and width and then append a group, g, element to the SVG document. That g is then transformed to the center of the SVG element, translating it by half the width and half the height of the SVG element.

Following that we append a new text element to the g element that contains a small legend for the visualization:

```
let svg = d3.select("#target").append("svg")
  .attr("width", width)
  .attr("height", height)
  .append("g")
  .attr("transform", `translate(${width / 2},${height / 2})`);

svg.append("text")
  .text("Distribution of comic book titles in top 50 sales of all time.")
  .attr("class","legend");
```

Now that we've done all of this setup, it's time to crunch some data and draw the visualization. We're starting by using another method from d3-fetch, d3.csv, to fetch a CSV file that contains our data and work with it after D3 parses it.

Inside `callback`, there's the now familiar D3 pattern. First, there is a call to `svg.selectAll("arc")`, which at this point returns an empty selection. Then we call `data`, passing in `pie(data)`. `pie` takes the data in and returns the start and end angles that we'll use for our donut chart. Next we go into the enter selection and append `g` elements for every member of the selection. We haven't drawn anything yet, but we have groups set up for each of our data points and we have calculated start and end angles applied to the dataset.

The next section illustrates just how nice it can be to work with D3.

At this point, we've got the angles generated by the call to `pie`, attached to a number of empty `g` elements. In this next call, we append a `path` element, and, with a call to the previously created `arc` method, we populate the `d` attribute with the full `arc` required to draw the visualization. That's all it takes.

All that's left now, for the chart itself, is to populate the fill of the arc by returning a value from the color scale we created earlier. This is selected based on the index of the data. The data is sorted by its ranking among the comic book titles. This creates the nice gradient we see when we run this visualization. And if you stopped here, you would actually have a visualization. It wouldn't have any text associated with it, but you'd have a nice looking donut chart. Such is the power of D3.

That said, we should add some labels, so let's look at how that works. The initial pattern is one you should start to be familiar with. We call `selectAll(".label")`, load it up with data (manipulated by another call to `pie` to get the same start and end angles) and then we manipulate it in the enter selection. In the enter selection, we append a `text` element and then take several steps to place the text in a useful place across the entire visualization.

The first step is to translate the text element to be in the center of `arc` using the `arc.centroid` method. Again, this is a great example of how useful D3 can be. One small call will allow you to access the geometric center of a complicated shape. This works for most of the text elements. We're nearly done.

We just need to tweak the text in two specific cases. Without the next call, the text overlaps in unattractive ways in the last few elements of the visualization, as can be seen in the following screenshot:

To adjust the placement of those two overlapping elements, we need to figure out which ones they are. we know that they are the last two and that they would be near the end of the circle. The angles here are measured in radians (360 degrees is 2PI or around 6.28 radians). Using rough shorthand for one slice (0.125 radians represents roughly one slice in our visualization), we work backward from the full circle to test for the last two slices and adjust them slightly using the dy attribute. The first one is adjusted by .6em. The next, final, text element is adjusted by 1.5em. This means that every label is clear to read.

The final call actually appends the text to the element using a call to text with the data's title as an argument:

```
d3.csv("data/top-fifty-comics-data.csv").then((data) => {
  let g = svg.selectAll(".arc")
    .data(pie(data))
    .enter()
    .append("g");

  g.append("path")
    .attr("d", arc)
    .style("fill", (d) => {
      return color(d.index);
    });
```

```
svg.selectAll(".label")
  .data(pie(data))
  .enter()
  .append("text")
  .attr("class", "text")
  .attr("transform", (d) => {
    return `translate(${arc.centroid(d)})`;
  })
  .attr("dy", (d) => {
    if (d.startAngle > 6.0 && d.startAngle < 6.125) {
      return "-.6em";
    } else if (d.startAngle > 6.125) {
      return "-1.5em";
    }
  })
  .text((d) => {
    return d.data.title;
  });

});
```

Now that we've done two standard charts, it's time to do one that's a little bit more fun, a chord diagram. This final example will illustrate even more features of D3. It'll be fun.

Implementing a chord diagram in D3

This final visualization is more complicated on both the data and coding fronts. The visualization is based on data released several years ago as part of the Hubway Data Visualization Challenges (`http://hubwaydatachallenge.org/`). It's a large dataset that represents every trip, including departure and arrival stations, on Boston's Hubway bike-share program (now called Blue Bikes). This visualization shows the relationship between the top ten most popular stations, illustrating the number of trips that happened between stations in the top ten. This is interesting to see which of the major hubs are illustrating potential holes in the public transportation network (lots of people are taking trips between transit hubs like North Station and South Station) or are potentially being used by tourists to see the sights in Boston (many South Station trips return back to South Station).

The final visualization looks like this. Each `arc` represents a departure station and the ribbons between the two stations show the relative weight of trips between the two stations. The width of the bar when it leaves the `arc` represents the numbers of trips. The color of the `arc` is owned by the station in the pair that generated more trips between the two:

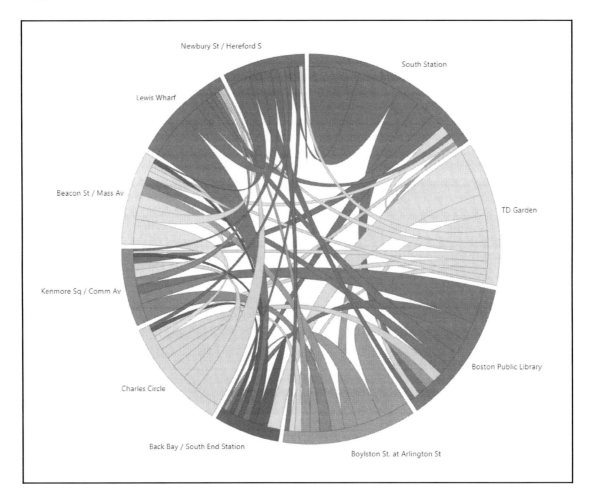

The HTML for this visualization, like the rest of these D3 examples is very simple. We have `Raleway` and Bootstrap in the head. Then there's a block of CSS at the top to add some text styles, as well as a small definition to add a stroke color to the small ticks that show the scale numbers along the outer edge of the circle.

Additionally, there's an H1 with a legend describing the visualization. Then we include just the main D3 file and our visualization file. Everything important happens in chord.js:

```
<!doctype html>
<html lang="en">

<head>
    <meta charset="utf-8">
    <title>Mastering SVG- D3 Chord Diagram</title>
    <link rel="stylesheet"
href="https://maxcdn.bootstrapcdn.com/bootstrap/4.0.0/css/bootstrap.min.css
" integrity="sha384-
Gn5384xqQ1aoWXA+058RXPxPg6fy4IWvTNh0E263XmFcJlSAwiGgFAW/dAiS6JXm"
        crossorigin="anonymous">
    <link href="https://fonts.googleapis.com/css?family=Raleway"
rel="stylesheet">
    <style type="text/css">
    h1 {
        font-family: Raleway;
    }
    text {
        font-family: Raleway;
        font-size: 1em;
    }
    text.tick {
        font-size: .8em;
        fill: #999;
    }
    .group-tick line {
        stroke: #999;
    }
    </style>
</head>

<body>
    <div class="container-fluid">
        <div class="row">
            <div class="col-12" id="target">
                <h1>Trip connections between the top 10 Hubway
                    departure stations. Data from the
                    <a href="http://hubwaydatachallenge.org/">Hubway
                    Data Visualization Challenge</a>
                </h1>

            </div>
        </div>
    </div>
```

```
<script src="node_modules/d3/dist/d3.min.js"></script>
<script src="_assets/js/chord.js"></script>

</body>

</html>
```

Let's start looking at `chord.js` by looking at the data. The top of the file has hardcoded data for the entire visualization. This is a distillation of a much larger dataset and in the original version of this visualization, there was a lot of code written to create this data in the specific format required for the visualization. The code to generate this data is available on GitHub along with the rest of the source code for the book.

A chord diagram requires a *square matrix*. This is an array of arrays where the total number of members in the array matches the total number of members in the child arrays and you can map between them. In our example, the parent array represents a *departure* station and the values of the child arrays represent the total trips to each *arrival* station. The indices of the child arrays match up to the indices of the parent array. A departure station can also be an arrival station.

The `names` const holds the names for each departure station, matched to the index of the departure station in the `matrix` array:

```
function drawChord() {
  const names = [
    "South Station",
    "TD Garden",
    "Boston Public Library",
    "Boylston St. at Arlington St",
    "Back Bay / South End Station",
    "Charles Circle",
    "Kenmore Sq / Comm Av",
    "Beacon St / Mass Av",
    "Lewis Wharf",
    "Newbury St / Hereford S"
  ];
  const matrix = [
  [2689, 508, 1170, 189, 1007, 187, 745, 248, 263, 2311],
  [1064, 121, 830, 323, 2473, 393, 453, 312, 533, 599],
  [506, 296, 813, 530, 988, 540, 1936, 578, 747, 268],
  [706, 311, 1568, 526, 1273, 371, 618, 694, 481, 227],
  [178, 701, 277, 176, 663, 227, 379, 284, 330, 111],
  [550, 270, 548, 445, 196, 769, 868, 317, 1477, 195],
  [344, 141, 468, 955, 172, 346, 502, 388, 415, 97],
  [333, 207, 455, 545, 196, 1322, 618, 254, 659, 62],
  [655, 120, 301, 90, 2368, 108, 226, 99, 229, 875],
```

```
    [270, 221, 625, 436, 239, 278, 548, 1158, 320, 90]
];
```

Now that we've got the data sorted out, let's start to take a look at how we generate the actual visualization. The first five blocks of code are all for setup. This is what you do with D3, in general, and this one is a little more complicated than others so there's more need to do the setup.

The first block involves just the creation of consts for various metrics that are required for the visualization. width and height are common to all of our D3 examples. radius is a calculated value that represents the full radius of a circle that would fit in a square created by the height and width. The padding const is used to calculate the outerRadius of the actual circle of the visualization. We then use outerRadius to calculate innerRadius.

Following that, we will start to work directly with D3. The first call is to d3.chord, the result of which is stored in a const, chord. chord is a loaded method that will generate a chord diagram with our settings. The first setting, padAngle, is a radians argument indicating the space between the arcs. With a complicated visualization like this, it's nice to have a little space between the arcs in order to bring some clarity to the separate sections. The second setting indicates whether or not we want to sort the sub-groups. In our case, we do want that, so we pass in d3.descending as the predefined sort.

The next variable, arc, loads up an instance of d3.arc with our calculated innerRadius and outerRadius, just like the donut chart. Once you start to think about these things as components you can fit together, possibilities open up.

Following that, we will create an instance of D3 ribbon with innerRadius as the only configuration setting, passed in as an argument to the radius method. This method is used with the chord method to create the core of the visualization, joining the two ends of the ribbons that connect, which, in our example, are the departure and arrival stations.

Finally, we create a color scale to map the stations to a rainbow set of colors:

```
const width = 1200,
    height = 1200,
    radius = Math.min(width, height) / 2,
    padding = 200,
    outerRadius = radius - padding,
    innerRadius = outerRadius - 25;

const chord = d3.chord()
    .padAngle(0.025)
    .sortSubgroups(d3.descending);
```

```
const arc = d3.arc()
  .innerRadius(innerRadius)
  .outerRadius(outerRadius);

const ribbon = d3.ribbon()
  .radius(innerRadius);

const color = d3.scaleOrdinal()
  .domain(d3.range(9))
  .range([
    "#e6194b",
    "#ffe119",
    "#0082c8",
    "#f58231",
    "#911eb4",
    "#46f0f0",
    "#f032e6",
    "#d2f53c",
    "#808000",
    "#008080"
  ]);
```

Now that we've set all of that up, it's time to work on getting the visualization on the screen. The first block should be very familiar at this point. In it we select the #target element, append an SVG element, and then set its width and height.

The next block should be mostly familiar as well. In it we add a g group to the SVG element, and then translate it to the center of the screen. The interesting bit here is a call to datum, which is a method very similar to data, except it propagates the data all the way down the tree. Here we pass in our instance of chord, along with our matrix, and the chord method returns the building blocks for our data visualization.

The final block in this section creates the groups that will hold our arc sections, paths, and group ticks. We enter the enter selection and append a child g element for the each item of matrix:

```
const svg = d3.select("#target")
  .append("svg")
  .attr("height", height)
  .attr("width", width);

const g = svg.append("g")
  .attr("transform", `translate(${width / 2},${height / 2})`)
  .datum(chord(matrix));

const group = g.append("g")
```

```
.attr("class", "groups")
.selectAll("g")
.data((chords) => chords.groups)
.enter()
.append("g");
```

At this point, we've done *all* of our setup. It's time, now, to actually draw some elements onto the screen.

The first sections added to the visualization are the `arcs`. This pattern will be familiar to you from the donut chart. This is exactly the same pattern; just here it's part of a larger visualization.

The `group` variable is *already part of an* **Enter selection** so both this and the next section, where we add the legends, are already operating on the full dataset.

First we append a `path` and we set the `d` attribute of the `path` with the result of our call to `arc`. This returns angles for the start and end of the slice. Then we give it a `fill` and a `stroke`. The `stroke` provides our first glimpse of another one of D3's utilities. D3.color (`https://github.com/d3/d3-color`) offers up several options to work with colors. Here, we're using `d3.color.darker` to return a slightly darker shade of the color chosen for the `arc` in question, in order to give it just enough contrast to show the edges. Finally, we add two event handlers that will allow a user to mouse over this station's arc and fade all other station's arcs and ribbons. This will allow them to examine this specific station's connections without any of the other stations getting in the way. We'll talk more about that feature later on.

Next we add the ribbons. This is a very similar pattern to the `arc`. We start with the core `g` group, and append a new group to it, adding a class of ribbons. Then we call `selectAll("path")` to get a selection, call `data` to it to apply the chord data, and then we go into the `enter` selection to build out the ribbons. For each member of the dataset, we append a new `path` and set the path's `d` attribute with a call to `ribbon`. The return value of `ribbon` creates a path that connects two angles on one side of the `arc` to two angles on the other side of the `arc`. After that, we set the `stroke` and `fill` in the exact same manner that we did with the arcs, so everything matches up:

```
group.append("path")
  .attr("d", arc)
  .style("fill", (d) => color(d.index))
  .style("stroke", (d) => d3.color(color(d.index)).darker())
  .on("mouseover", fade(.1))
  .on("mouseout", fade(1));
```

```
g.append("g")
  .attr("class", "ribbons")
  .selectAll("path")
  .data((chords) => chords)
  .enter()
  .append("path")
  .attr("d", ribbon)
  .style("fill", (d) => color(d.source.index))
      .style("stroke", (d) => {
    return d3.color(color(d.source.index)).darker();
  });
```

At this point, the visualization is drawn onto the screen. We can still make it better though, so let's do that.

The next section adds the small label for each station. As before, we're already in an enter selection, so we're already operating on the correct dataset. The first call in this chain is to each, which allows us to run a function on each member of the selection. The callback function passed in adds a new property to the dataset, angle. angle is calculated by adding together the start angle and finishing angle of the arc and dividing it by two, getting the middle of the arc. We'll use that angle to place the labels in the very next call.

The labels we did with the donut chart sat on top of the arc. That won't actually look all that great with the chord diagram that we have set up and the long text labels we have, so we want to move the labels off of the circle. We do that with some trigonometry.

The following diagram shows how this works. All of these text elements are in a group that is in the center of the SVG element. We're looking to move them to their new position, outside the circle in line with the middle of the arc they are labeling. To do that we take the d.angle property that we calculated and use that as the hypotenuse (longest side) of a right-angled triangle. Once we've got that angle, we can calculate the sine (the ratio of the length of the opposite side to the length of the hypotenuse) and the cosine (the ratio of the length of the adjacent side to the length of the hypotenuse). Once we have those ratios, we simply multiply them by the outerRadius (plus a few extra pixels to give it some room) to get the length of the adjacent and opposite sides of the triangle. We use those values as the x and y needed to translate the text elements to their new position.

This technique will come in handy, all the time:

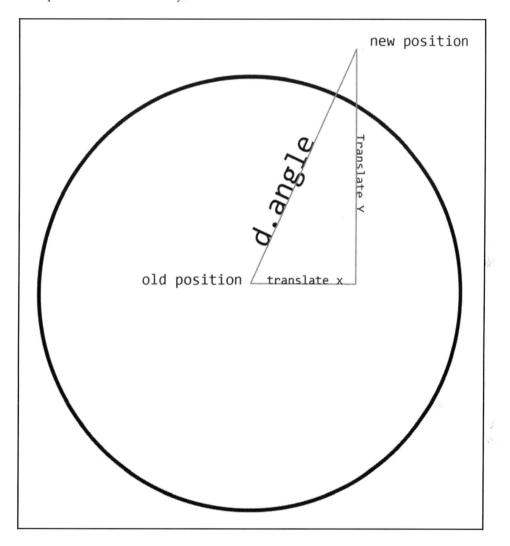

The next section adjusts the text-anchor property based on the position of the text element on the arc. If it's greater than halfway (there are two PI radians in a circle, so Math.PI is equivalent to halfway around the circle), then we need to set text-anchor to end in order to balance them with the labels on the right side of the circle. If we don't adjust the text-anchor in this way, text elements on the left side of the visualization will overlap with the arcs on that side.

Finally, we append the text itself:

```
group.append("text")
    .each((d) => d.angle = (d.startAngle + d.endAngle) / 2)
    .attr("text-anchor", (d) => {
      if (d.angle > Math.PI) {
        return "end";
      }
    })
    .attr("transform", (d) => {
      const y = Math.sin(d.angle) * (outerRadius + 10),
        x = Math.cos(d.angle) * (outerRadius + 20);
      return `translate(${y},${(-x)})`;
    })
    .text((d) => {
      return names[d.index];
    });
```

The final SVG elements we're going to do for this visualization is to add the group ticks and tick labels to the outer edge. These will allow us to indicate, in a friendly way, the scale of the visualization, in thousands.

We start off by creating a new const, groupTick, which sets up a new enter selection based on the data returned by a call to the groupTicks method. groupTick takes in the existing data from the chain and returns a newly manipulated set of data, representing a new tick for every 1,000 units. These new groupTick data entries have a new angle corresponding to the correct placement on the arc for the tick, and a reference to the original data's value. Once the groupTick data is returned, we enter the selection, append a new group and add a class, group-tick. Then we rotate the element to visually circle the outer edge and translate it to a point on outerRadius.

Once that's done, we add a six pixel long gray `line` at each tick. Remember, `groupTick` is still in an enter selection in this new chain so we can still operate on every data point even though we broke the previous chain.

Finally, we enter the selection again and `filter` the data, guarding against empty data and then testing whether or not the value is divisible by 5,000 with no remainder using the modulus (or remainder) operator (`https://developer.mozilla.org/en-US/docs/Web/JavaScript/Reference/Operators/Arithmetic_Operators#Remainder_()`). If it is divisible by 5,000, we need to add some text to indicate that we've hit 5,000 trips for this station. The steps to do this are as follows. Adjust the `x` property, to move it further off of `outerRadius`. Adjust the `dy` property to move the text element up just a little bit to line up better against the tick line.

Transform the `text` element if the angle is past the halfway point of the circle. Once again, we test against `Math.PI` and then, if it is past the halfway point, we `rotate` the text by 180 degrees and then translate it by negative 16 pixels, to fit it nicely along the edge of `outerRadius`. We also do the same test to see if the `text` element is past the halfway point of the circle and if it is we change the `text-anchor` property to pin the right edge of the text to the circle's edge. Finally, we add a class, `ticks`, to the `text` element and append the actual text, using `d3.formatPrefix`. `d3.formatPrefix` formats the number to be a friendlier representation of the value. `d3.formatPrefix` returns a function that formats numbers based on the supplied formatting argument.

In this case, we are looking to format the numbers with SI (system of units) prefixes (`https://en.wikipedia.org/wiki/Metric_prefix#List_of_SI_prefixes`), which will convert `5000` to `5k`:

```
const groupTick = group.selectAll(".group-tick")
  .data((d) => groupTicks(d, 1000))
  .enter()
  .append("g")
  .attr("class", "group-tick")
  .attr("transform", (d) => {
    return `rotate(${(d.angle * 180 / Math.PI - 90)})
translate(${outerRadius},0)`;
  });

groupTick.append("line")
  .attr("x2", 6);

groupTick
  .filter((d) => d.value && !(d.value % 5000))
  .append("text")
  .attr("x", 8)
```

```
        .attr("dy", ".35em")
        .attr("transform", (d) => {
          if (d.angle > Math.PI) {
            return "rotate(180) translate(-16)";
          }
        })
        .style("text-anchor", (d) => {
          if (d.angle > Math.PI) {
            return "end";
          }
        })
        .attr("class", "tick")
        .text((d) => d3.formatPrefix(",.0", 1000)(d.value));

    function groupTicks(d, step) {
      let k = (d.endAngle - d.startAngle) / d.value;
      return d3.range(0, d.value, step).map((value) => {
        return {
          value: value,
          angle: value * k + d.startAngle
        };
      });
    }
```

The final code is the `fade` method referenced earlier. This function selects all elements that match the CSS selector. `.ribbons path` filters out any that are associated with the current selection and sets their `opacity` to the provided `opacity` argument:

```
    function fade(opacity) {
      return function(g, i) {
        svg.selectAll(".ribbons path")
          .filter((d)=> {
            return d.source.index !== i && d.target.index !== i;
          })
          .transition()
          .style("opacity", opacity);
      };
    }
```

The effect looks like the following screenshot:

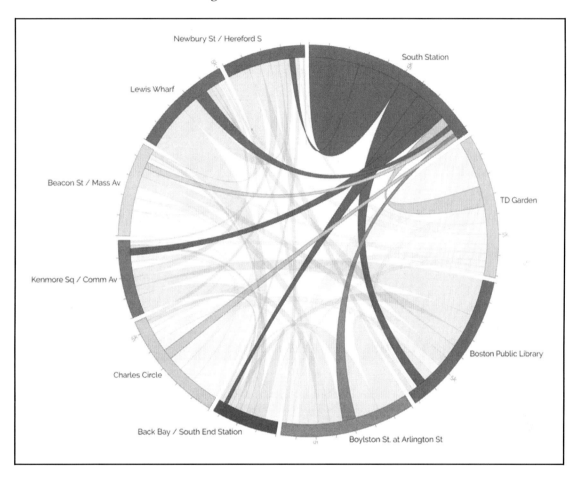

And with that, the chord diagram is complete. It's not the most complicated visualization you'll ever see with D3, but it's pretty good. Along with the donut chart and the bar chart, these three combine to illustrate many of the important features of D3.

Summary

This chapter has introduced you to the world of D3. As deep as this chapter has been, it only brushed the surface of what D3 has to offer. Hopefully, you'll take what you've learned here and you'll continue to experiment with it in the months and years to come. It's a rewarding tool to master.

We have just one, short chapter, remaining in this book where we'll talk about some ways to optimize SVG for serving over the web. It's a vital area to at least have some knowledge of, especially if you're doing a lot of SVG in your site or application.

Tools to Optimize Your SVG **11**

Now that you've learned all about SVG in this book — everything from the basics of pure SVG markup to the dynamic, JavaScript-based SVG work you've done over the past few chapters — you're ready to take advantage of everything that SVG offers.

One final aspect of SVG that we should look at is how to make sure the work you do is presented in the best possible way when you serve it to your users. SVG should be optimized for performance, both in terms of performance over the wire and in terms of complexity. Keeping your SVG files as lean as they can be and serving them efficiently is going to make for a much better experience for your users.

This chapter will serve as a high-level introduction to the many ways that you can optimize your SVG images. Some of what follows is pure, performance-related engineering. Others are pure SVG tooling.

In this chapter, you'll learn about the following:

- Compressing SVG on the server in three popular server platforms (IIS, Apache, and nginx)
- SVGO and its associated suite of tools
- svgcleaner, an alternative to SVGO that offers lossless optimizations

Serving compressed SVG

One of the most straightforward performance enhancements you can do when working with SVG is to compress `gzip` files when you serve them. While text files generally benefit from being gzipped when served to the browser, SVG is an especially important target because of the way that SVG images are used (often for the core interface) and because of the potential size of some of the files. You want your images to load fast, and SVG is no exception.

Depending on what your platform is, this may be as easy as adding a few lines of code or checking a box in a dialog box. The next few sections show you how to implement this action on three common web servers.

gzipping SVG on Apache

Where to place the following code depends on how your Apache instance is set up and what access you have to the server. Most people on shared hosting will be doing this in their .htaccess file. .htaccess is a special file in the server root that allows you to configure Apache behavior without having to have access your main configuration file (httpd.conf). Assuming your server allows you to access this functionality (some hosts do not allow you to turn on compression, since it uses more server resources), gzipping text content is as easy as adding the following to your .htaccess file. Example code is drawn from the H5BP Apache server configs project (https://github.com/h5bp/server-configs-apache/blob/master/dist/.htaccess#L795). There are three sections:

- The first fixes a problem where request headers are being mangled by proxy servers and assets are therefore not being served gzipped (this fixes more than just SVG)
- The second actually tells Apache to compress files of the listed MIME types (abbreviated here; there are normally dozens of different MIME types listed)
- The third ensures that SVG files compressed and saved in a compressed format, .svgz, are served properly:

```
#
##################################################################
#######
# # WEB PERFORMANCE #
#
##################################################################
#######

# -------------------------------------------------------------
---------
# | Compression |
# -------------------------------------------------------------
---------

<IfModule mod_deflate.c>

    # Force compression for mangled `Accept-Encoding` request
headers
    #
```

```
    #
https://developer.mozilla.org/en-US/docs/Web/HTTP/Headers/Accep
t-Encoding
    #
https://calendar.perfplanet.com/2010/pushing-beyond-gzipping/

    <IfModule mod_setenvif.c>
        <IfModule mod_headers.c>
            SetEnvIfNoCase ^(Accept-EncodXng|X-cept-
Encoding|X{15}|~{15}|-{15})$ ^((gzip|deflate)\s*,?\s*)+|[X~-
]{4,13}$ HAVE_Accept-Encoding
            RequestHeader append Accept-Encoding "gzip,deflate"
env=HAVE_Accept-Encoding
        </IfModule>
    </IfModule>


    # - - - - - - - - - - - - - - - - - - - - - - - - - - - - -
- - - -


    # Compress all output labeled with one of the following
media types.
    #
    #
https://httpd.apache.org/docs/current/mod/mod_filter.html#addou
tputfilterbytype

    <IfModule mod_filter.c>
        AddOutputFilterByType DEFLATE "application/atom+xml" \
                                      "application/javascript"
\
                                      "application/json" \
# Many other MIME types clipped for brevity
                                      "image/svg+xml" \
# Many other MIME types clipped for brevity
                                      "text/xml"

    </IfModule>


    # - - - - - - - - - - - - - - - - - - - - - - - - - - - - -
- - - -


    # Map the following filename extensions to the specified
    # encoding type in order to make Apache serve the file
types
    # with the appropriate `Content-Encoding` response header
    # (do note that this will NOT make Apache compress them!).
    #
    # If these files types would be served without an
```

```
appropriate
    # `Content-Enable` response header, client applications
(e.g.:
    # browsers) wouldn't know that they first need to
uncompressed
    # the response, and thus, wouldn't be able to understand
the
    # content.
    #
    #
https://developer.mozilla.org/en-US/docs/Web/HTTP/Headers/Conte
nt-Encoding
    #
https://httpd.apache.org/docs/current/mod/mod_mime.html#addenco
ding

    <IfModule mod_mime.c>
        AddEncoding gzip svgz
    </IfModule>

</IfModule>
```

SVG compression on nginx

Similar to Apache, turning on `gzip` compression for SVG is just a matter of a few lines of configuration. This code block, sourced from the HTML5 boilerplate nginx server configs project (`https://github.com/h5bp/server-configs-nginx/blob/master/nginx.conf#L89`), provides an example of how to do so. The code will turn `gzip` compression on, set the `gzip` compression level, stop compression for already small objects, set some values for proxies, and then add the SVG MIME type to the list of objects that should be compressed (again, abbreviated here; there are normally dozens of different MIME types listed):

```
# Enable gzip compression.
  # Default: off
  gzip on;

  # Compression level (1-9).
  # 5 is a perfect compromise between size and CPU usage, offering about
  # 75% reduction for most ASCII files (almost identical to level 9).
  # Default: 1
  gzip_comp_level 5;

  # Don't compress anything that's already small and unlikely to shrink
much
```

```
  # if at all (the default is 20 bytes, which is bad as that usually leads
to
  # larger files after gzipping).
  # Default: 20
  gzip_min_length 256;

  # Compress data even for clients that are connecting to us via proxies,
  # identified by the "Via" header (required for CloudFront).
  # Default: off
  gzip_proxied any;

  # Tell proxies to cache both the gzipped and regular version of a
resource
  # whenever the client's Accept-Encoding capabilities header varies;
  # Avoids the issue where a non-gzip capable client (which is extremely
rare
  # today) would display gibberish if their proxy gave them the gzipped
version.
  # Default: off
  gzip_vary on;

  # Compress all output labeled with one of the following MIME-types.
  # text/html is always compressed by gzip module.
  # Default: text/html
  gzip_types
    # Many other MIME types clipped for brevity
    image/svg+xml
    # Many other MIME types clipped for brevity
```

SVG compression on IIS

IIS doesn't compress SVG files by default. Depending on how your server is configured, the following change needs to be made in your applicationHost.config (C:\Windows\System32\inetsrv\config) or web.config file. You simply need to add the SVG MIME type to the staticTypes and dynamicTypes elements in the httpCompression module and you're ready to go:

```
<httpCompression directory="%SystemDrive%\inetpub\temp\IIS Temporary
Compressed Files">
    <scheme name="gzip" dll="%Windir%\system32\inetsrv\gzip.dll" />
        <staticTypes>
            <add mimeType="image/svg+xml" enabled="true" />
        </staticTypes>
        <dynamicTypes>
            <add mimeType="image/svg+xml" enabled="true" />
        </dynamicTypes>
```

```
</httpCompression>
```

Now that we've learned about serving SVG efficiently, it's time to look at some ways to optimize SVG before they get on the server.

SVGO

SVG Optimizer (`https://github.com/svg/svgo`) is a Node.js utility for optimizing SVG files. SVG files, especially those generated by editors, can have a lot of cruft associated with them. SVGO can clean up the metadata, comments, hidden elements, and so on, without changing the rendering of the SVG element itself.

To install it, assuming you have Node.js installed, run the following on the command line:

```
$ npm install -g svgo
```

Usage is as simple as this:

```
svgo svgo.svg
```

Running that on a small file generated by Inkscape, reduces the file size by over 50 percent:

```
$ svgo svgo.svg

svgo.svg:
Done in 109 ms!
3.825 KiB - 58.4% = 1.592 KiB
```

The difference is apparent if you look at the change in the `svgo.svg` source code, before and after optimization.

The following screenshot shows the metadata added by Inkscape during the authoring process:

```xml
<?xml version="1.0" encoding="UTF-8" standalone="no"?>
<svg
   xmlns:dc="http://purl.org/dc/elements/1.1/"
   xmlns:cc="http://creativecommons.org/ns#"
   xmlns:rdf="http://www.w3.org/1999/02/22-rdf-syntax-ns#"
   xmlns:svg="http://www.w3.org/2000/svg"
   xmlns="http://www.w3.org/2000/svg"
   xmlns:sodipodi="http://sodipodi.sourceforge.net/DTD/sodipodi-0.dtd"
   xmlns:inkscape="http://www.inkscape.org/namespaces/inkscape"
   version="1.1"
   id="Layer_1"
   x="0px"
   y="0px"
   viewBox="0 0 330.02805 436.1265"
   xml:space="preserve"
   sodipodi:docname="happy-inkscape.svg"
   inkscape:version="0.92.2 (5c3e80d, 2017-08-06)"
   width="330.02805"
   height="436.1265"><metadata
   id="metadata846"><rdf:RDF><cc:Work
       rdf:about=""><dc:format>image/svg+xml</dc:format><dc:type
       rdf:resource="http://purl.org/dc/dcmitype/StillImage"
       /><dc:title></dc:title></cc:Work></rdf:RDF></metadata><defs
   id="defs844" /><sodipodi:namedview
   pagecolor="#ffffff"
   bordercolor="#666666"
   borderopacity="1"
   objecttolerance="10"
   gridtolerance="10"
   guidetolerance="10"
   inkscape:pageopacity="0"
   inkscape:pageshadow="2"
   inkscape:window-width="1280"
   inkscape:window-height="962"
   id="namedview842"
   showgrid="false"
   inkscape:zoom="0.57393851"
   inkscape:cx="165.51339"
   inkscape:cy="221.56158"
```

This screenshot shows the cleaned-up file after optimization:

```
1   <svg xmlns="http://www.w3.org/2000/svg" width="330.028" height="436.127"><path
    d="M252.913 297.26517.7-.3 5.1-13.2-1.7 22.2 25.4-4.5 2.7-4.5h-10.9l3.4-15.9
    2.7 11.3 31.2-1.4-2.1-30.2s-6 1.4-6.1 5.9c-.1 7.2.8 17 .8 17l-3.5
    1v-23.6s7.9-16.2 7.9-21.8c1.7-.3-9.7-4-9.7-4s6.9-31 6.4-36.7c-.5-5.7
    2.9-18.2-14.7-46.5-7.9-12.7-44.8-62.1-45.6-61.8h-13.7l-5.2-34.6s-7-20.3-8.4-22.
    5c-1.5-2.2-12.1-29.5-34-19.6-19.1 8.7-9.1 32.1-9.1 32.1l26.3-17.9 3.5 4.6-17.8
    12.4 17 .1v7l-27.8.9 6.6 14.7s2-7.5 7.7-6.1c6.6 1.7 5.8 6.5 9 7.9 1.9.9 2.1-3.1
    2.9-9.3.4-2.8 5.8-2.9 7.7-1.6 1.8 1.3.3 1.3 2.1 2.5s-3.2-.6-3.2-.6-2.9-.6-3.1
    1.3c-.2 1.9.5 6.1-2.2 10.4-2.9 4.6-6.4 2.1-12.3-4.8-2.3-2.6-6.4 2.2-5.1 4.9 2
    4.2 9.1 8.6 9.1 8.6s6.6 5.6 17.2-2.8c4.9-3.9 3.5-20.7 3.5-20.7s2.6 1.1 2.5
    8.2c0 2.6-.1 4.3-.3 8.4-.5 10-3.1 10.5-3.1 10.5l.6 7.4-16.8.5s-15.1 22.4-16.1
    25.6c-1 3.2-31.5 34.6-31.5 34.6l-19-28.3 22.5-20.6-13.2-20.6-23.2 14.1 22.4
    5.1-3.6 3.9-35.3-7.5 34.8-21.8-4.4-5.6-19.4 12.4-12.7-10.3-26.7 16.9 10
    18.8-10.2 7.4 26.3 8.6-4.6-7.8 24.6 1.8-.8-9 7.4 1.2-.1 14-20.7.1 4.2
    5.9-24-2.9 12.7 16.9 14.4-11.2 38.2 38.2 38.3-44.8 10.3-12.2 2.6 18s-1.4
    33.5-2.5 38.9c-.5 2.3-9.7 29.4-9.7 29.4l-6.9 11.3-74.7-47.4-30.5
    84.4s-17.9-3.1-25.9-2.4c-12.6 1.1-44.1 6.4-46.6 12l71.9 26.3 31.9-100.2 63.9
    49-21.6 25.8s-27.9 25.3-29.1 26.6c-1.2 1.3-24.1 20.2-24.1 20.2l71.9 45.3-8
    46.5s-19.4 9.3-23.8 25.3c0 2.3 68.1-2.3 68.1-2.3l-5.7-66.8-77.1-49.7
    66.9-56.2s29.4-38.5 35.2-53.3c17.9-46.1 18.3-88.2 18.3-88.2s34.6 32.5 46.1
    69.7c8.6 21.7-13.8 51.6-13.8 51.6l-27.7 7.1-19.1 37.7 19 1.1z" fill="#fff"
    stroke="#000" stroke-width="2.835" stroke-miterlimit="10"/></svg>
```

It's a great tool, with many configuration options (https://github.com/svg/svgo#usage) and integrations with other tools (https://github.com/svg/svgo#other-ways-to-use-svgo).

SVGOMG

One of the integrations listed in the preceding link is with a web frontend for SVGO, called SVGOMG (`https://jakearchibald.github.io/svgomg/`). SVGOMG is a web frontend for SVGO. Having almost all of the options exposed in the UI allows you to dive deeper into the optimizations that SVGO offers without having to pore over all of the configuration options. Loading an SVG element into the interface presents you with the following view:

The loaded SVG is on the left, shown in the optimized view. You can toggle the **Show original** button to see if there is any degradation of the visible image because of the optimizations.

 Keep in mind that some of the optimizations that SVGO offers are potentially *lossy*. This means that the image itself might change in some visible way; the effective data of the image will be lost, because of the optimizations that are run.

Then, along the right side are many of the options available to you to tweak your images. There's a preview of the savings and then a download button that will allow you to download your handiwork.

While many people will automate this optimization as part of a build process, it's nice to know that you can have fine-grained control of this tool right on the web, with immediate feedback for your changes.

SVGO authoring plugins

In addition to the command-line tools available and the web-based interface, there are a couple of authoring plugins available for you to integrate SVGO right into your authoring workflow. SVG-NOW is a plugin for Adobe Illustrator (although it appears to have been abandoned; it hasn't been updated since 2014) and SVGO Compressor is an actively developed plugin to the popular application, Sketch. If you've got a design team, you can save yourself time and then surprises by integrating these optimizations earlier into the production process. Since they'll be in control of the export process, they'll know precisely what the output of SVGO optimization will be.

svgcleaner

svgcleaner is an alternative to SVGO that offers *lossless optimizations* (https://github.com/RazrFalcon/svgcleaner). In comparison with SVGO, which has the potential to break things, svgcleaner promises to never break an SVG file. Browse their charts (https://github.com/RazrFalcon/svgcleaner#charts) to see how they compare themselves to SVGO and scour (another alternative).

What's more, there's also a downloadable GUI (`https://github.com/RazrFalcon/svgcleaner-gui/releases`) that you can run on your desktop. The following screenshot shows it in action. All that's happened to get to this state is to load an SVG element and to hit the Play button, which runs the optimization:

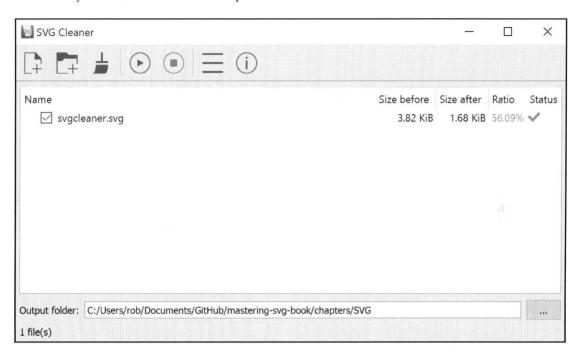

Since it's built-in Rust and isn't a native Node.js application, it doesn't play as nicely with the `npm`/`node` world, but it's still a great tool.

Summary

This has been the lightest chapter in the book, but you still learned some things that will help you with SVG optimization. Keeping these factors and these tools in mind will ensure the best possible outcome for your users and will make sure your hard work with SVG will be seen in the best possible light.

And with that, our journey through the world of SVG comes to an end. From the most basic SVG elements, through complicated JavaScript visualizations and CSS-based animations, you've experienced the full breadth of what SVG has to offer. Hopefully, you've enjoyed the journey and will continue to work with SVG in the future.

Other Books You May Enjoy

If you enjoyed this book, you may be interested in these other books by Packt:

Learn Three.js - Third Edition
Jos Dirksen

ISBN: 9781788833288

- Work with the different types of materials in Three.js and see how they interact with your 3D objects and the rest of the environment
- Implement the different camera controls provided by Three.js to effortlessly navigate around your 3D scene
- Work with vertices directly to create snow, rain, and galaxy-like effects
- Import and animate models from external formats, such as OBJ, STL, and COLLADA
- Create and run animations using morph targets and bones animations
- Explore advanced textures on materials to create realistic looking 3D objects by using bump maps, normal maps, specular maps, and light maps
- Interact directly with WebGL by creating custom vertex and fragment shaders

Hands-On UX Design for Developers
Elvis Canziba

ISBN: 9781788626699

- What UX is and what a UX designer does
- Explore the UX Process and science of making products user-friendly
- Create user interfaces and learn which tools to use
- Understand how your design works in the real world
- Create UI interaction, animation, wireframes, and prototypes
- Design a product with users in mind
- Develop a personal portfolio and be well-prepared to join the UX world

Leave a review - let other readers know what you think

Please share your thoughts on this book with others by leaving a review on the site that you bought it from. If you purchased the book from Amazon, please leave us an honest review on this book's Amazon page. This is vital so that other potential readers can see and use your unbiased opinion to make purchasing decisions, we can understand what our customers think about our products, and our authors can see your feedback on the title that they have worked with Packt to create. It will only take a few minutes of your time, but is valuable to other potential customers, our authors, and Packt. Thank you!

Index

Printed in Germany
by Amazon Distribution
GmbH, Leipzig

22468980R00179